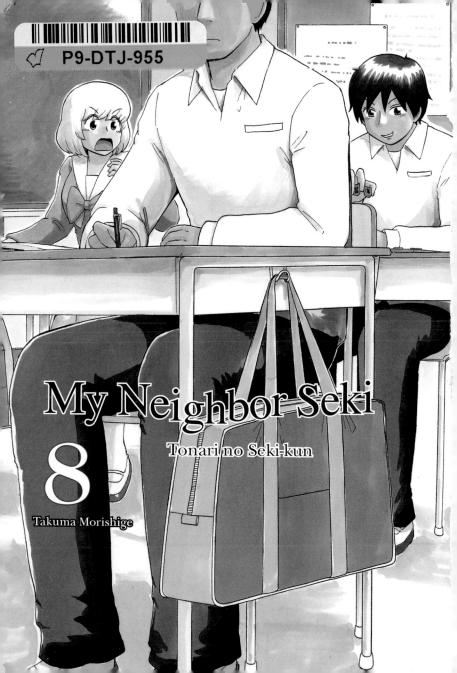

My Neighbor Seki

Tonari no Seki-kun

8

Takuma Morishige

Schedule

My Neighbor Seki

8

95th Period ③	96th Period ⑬	97th Period ㉕	98th Period ㉝
99th Period ㊳	100th Period ㊺	101st Period ㊻	102nd Period ㊺
103rd Period ㊕	104th Period ⑩	105th Period ⑲	106th Period ⑰
107th Period ⑭	Bonus ① ⑰	Bonus ② ⑲	

* THIS IS A WORK OF FICTION. NAMES, CHARACTERS, PLACES AND INCIDENTS ARE PRODUCTS OF THE AUTHOR'S IMAGINATION OR USED FICTITIOUSLY. ANY RESEMBLANCE TO ACTUAL EVENTS OR LOCALES OR PERSONS, LIVING OR DEAD, IS ENTIRELY COINCIDENTAL.

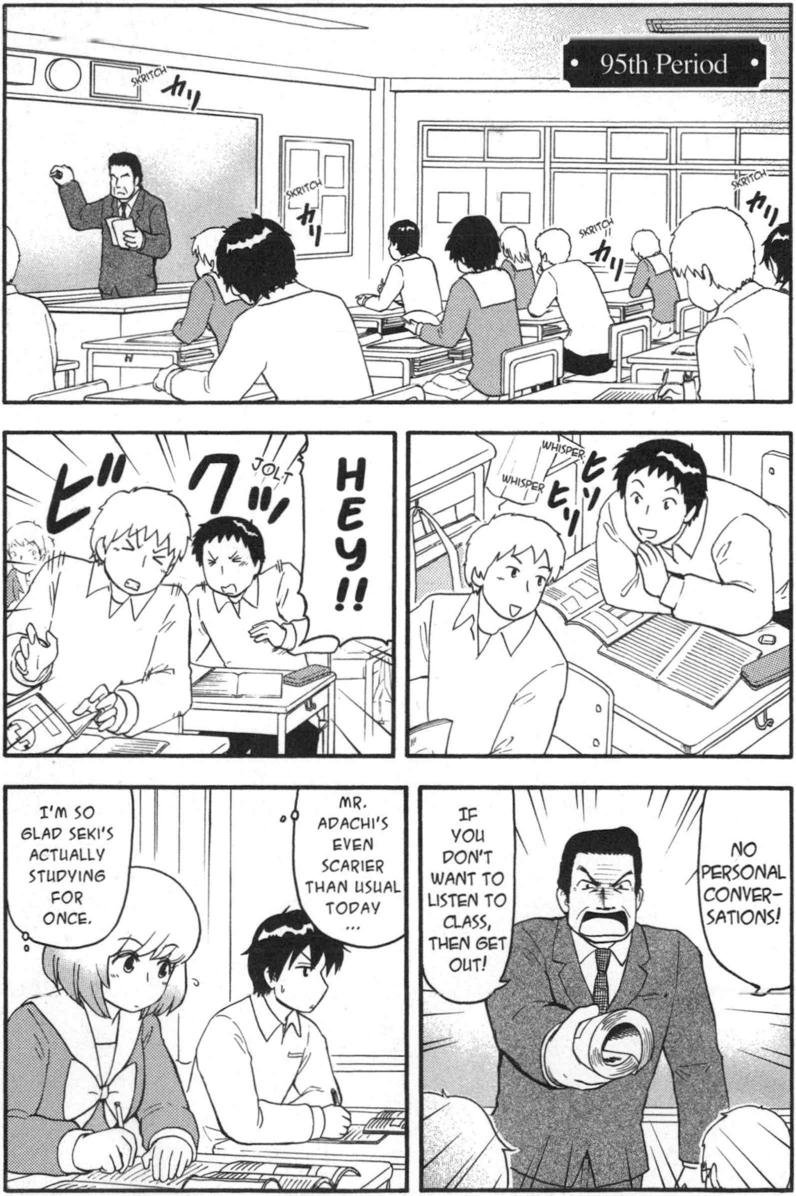
95th Period
SKRITCH
SKRITCH
SKRITCH
SKRITCH
WHISPER
WHISPER
JOLT
HEY!!
NO PERSONAL CONVERSATIONS!
IF YOU DON'T WANT TO LISTEN TO CLASS, THEN GET OUT!
MR. ADACHI'S EVEN SCARIER THAN USUAL TODAY...
I'M SO GLAD SEKI'S ACTUALLY STUDYING FOR ONCE.

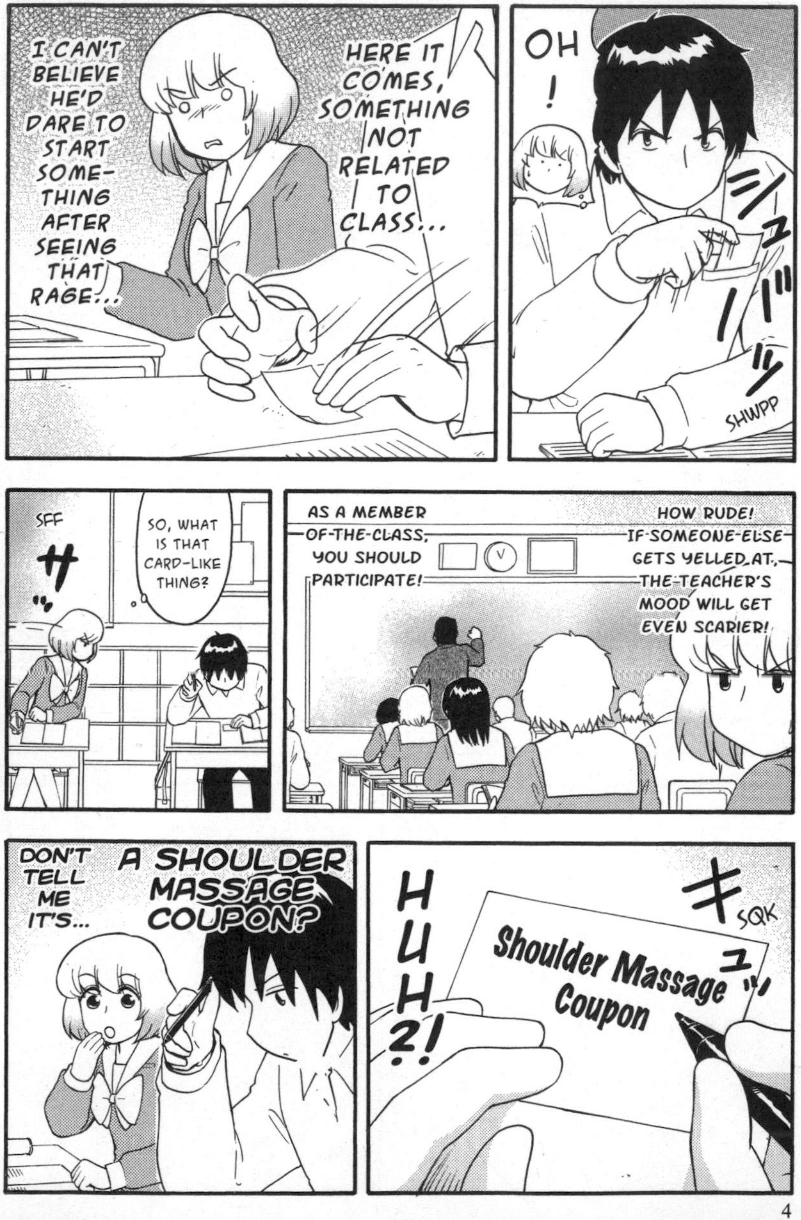

OH!
SHWPP
HERE IT COMES, SOMETHING NOT RELATED TO CLASS...
I CAN'T BELIEVE HE'D DARE TO START SOME-THING AFTER SEEING THAT RAGE...
HOW RUDE! IF SOMEONE ELSE GETS YELLED AT, THE TEACHER'S MOOD WILL GET EVEN SCARIER!
AS A MEMBER OF THE CLASS, YOU SHOULD PARTICIPATE!
SFF
SO, WHAT IS THAT CARD-LIKE THING?
HUH?!
SQK
Shoulder Massage Coupon
DON'T TELL ME IT'S...
A SHOULDER MASSAGE COUPON?

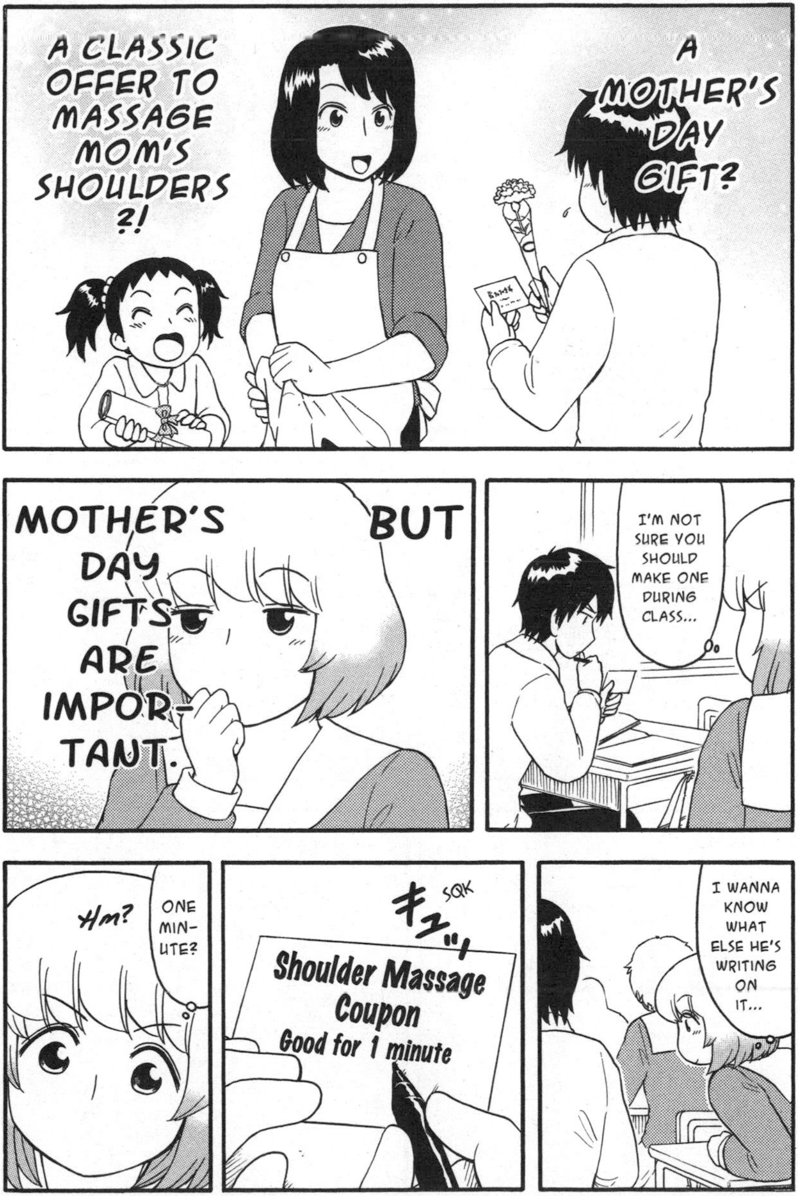
A MOTHER'S DAY GIFT?
A CLASSIC OFFER TO MASSAGE MOM'S SHOULDERS ?!
I'M NOT SURE YOU SHOULD MAKE ONE DURING CLASS...
BUT
MOTHER'S DAY GIFTS ARE IMPOR-TANT.
I WANNA KNOW WHAT ELSE HE'S WRITING ON IT...
キュッ
SQK
Shoulder Massage Coupon
Good for 1 minute
ONE MIN-UTE?
Hm?

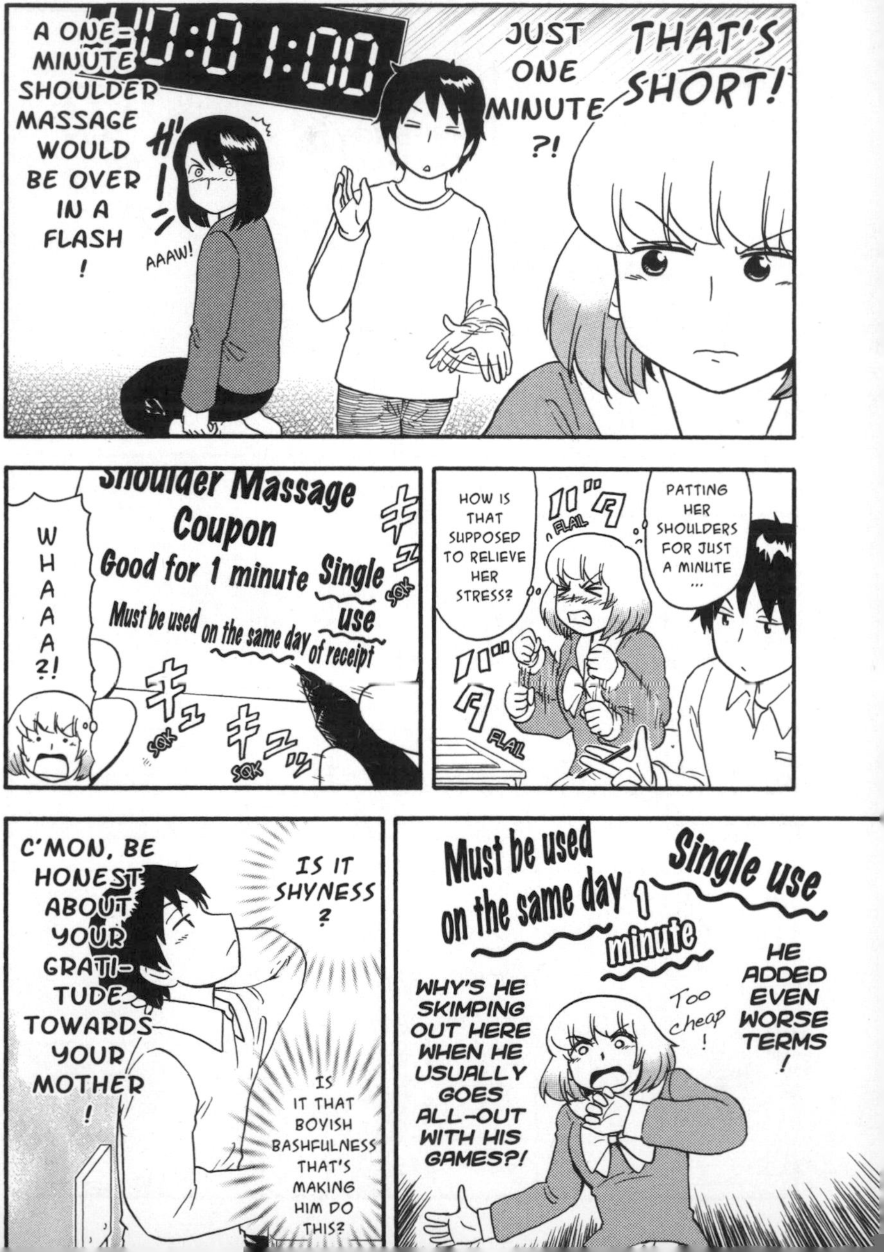
THAT'S SHORT!
JUST ONE MINUTE ?!
A ONE-MINUTE SHOULDER MASSAGE WOULD BE OVER IN A FLASH !
AAAW!
PATTING HER SHOULDERS FOR JUST A MINUTE ...
HOW IS THAT SUPPOSED TO RELIEVE HER STRESS?
FLAIL
FLAIL
Shoulder Massage Coupon
Good for 1 minute
Single use
Must be used on the same day of receipt
SQK
SQK
SQK
WHAAAA?!
Must be used on the same day
Single use
1 minute
HE ADDED EVEN WORSE TERMS !
Too cheap !
WHY'S HE SKIMPING OUT HERE WHEN HE USUALLY GOES ALL-OUT WITH HIS GAMES?!
IS IT SHYNESS ?
C'MON, BE HONEST ABOUT YOUR GRATITUDE TOWARDS YOUR MOTHER !
IS IT THAT BOYISH BASHFULNESS THAT'S MAKING HIM DO THIS?

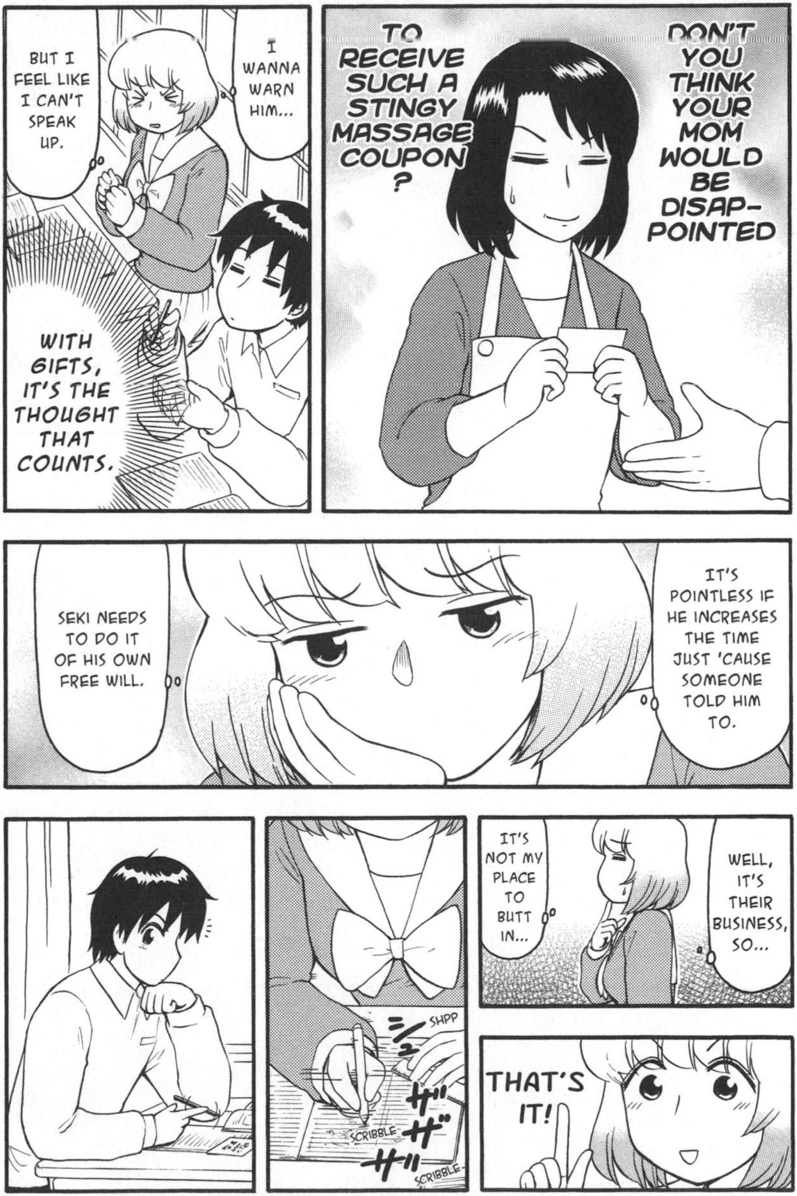
DON'T YOU THINK YOUR MOM WOULD BE DISAPPOINTED
TO RECEIVE SUCH A STINGY MASSAGE COUPON?
I WANNA WARN HIM...
BUT I FEEL LIKE I CAN'T SPEAK UP.
WITH GIFTS, IT'S THE THOUGHT THAT COUNTS.
IT'S POINTLESS IF HE INCREASES THE TIME JUST 'CAUSE SOMEONE TOLD HIM TO.
SEKI NEEDS TO DO IT OF HIS OWN FREE WILL.
WELL, IT'S THEIR BUSINESS, SO...
IT'S NOT MY PLACE TO BUTT IN...
THAT'S IT!
SHPP
SCRIBBLE
SCRIBBLE

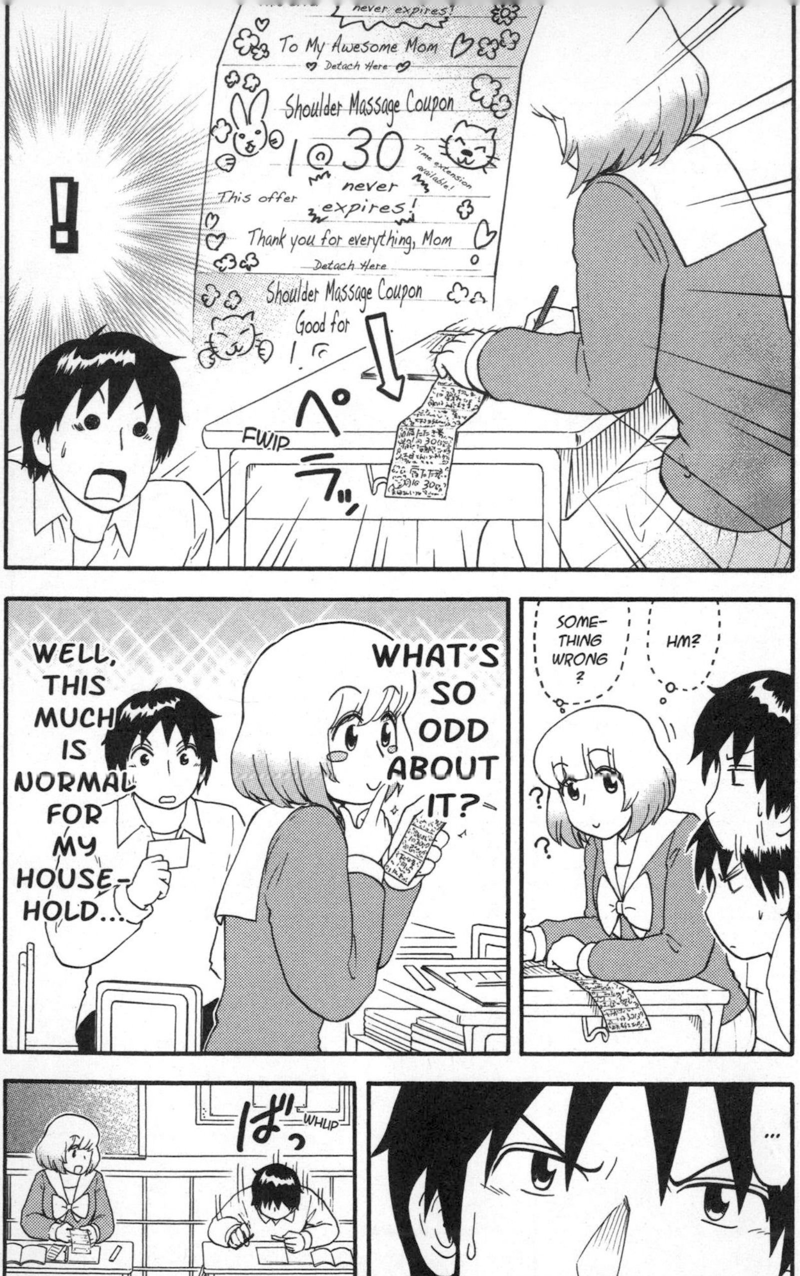
never expires!
To My Awesome Mom
Detach Here
Shoulder Massage Coupon
1@30
Time extension available!
This offer never expires!
Thank you for everything, Mom
Detach Here
Shoulder Massage Coupon
Good for
!
ペ
FWIP
ラッ
HM?
SOME-THING WRONG?
WHAT'S SO ODD ABOUT IT?
WELL, THIS MUCH IS NORMAL FOR MY HOUSE-HOLD...
...
ぱっ
WHIP

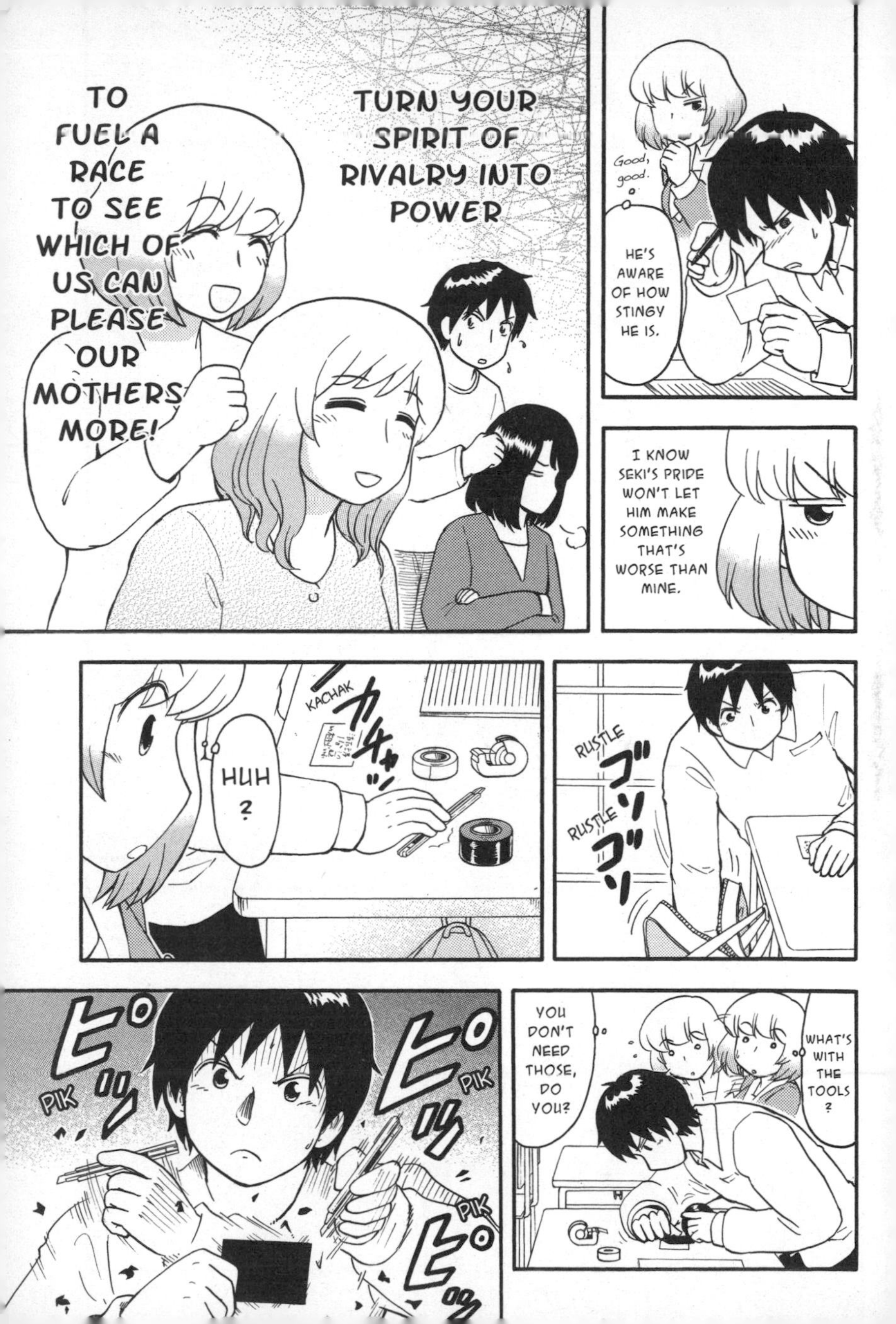
Good, good.
HE'S AWARE OF HOW STINGY HE IS.
I KNOW SEKI'S PRIDE WON'T LET HIM MAKE SOMETHING THAT'S WORSE THAN MINE.
TURN YOUR SPIRIT OF RIVALRY INTO POWER
TO FUEL A RACE TO SEE WHICH OF US CAN PLEASE OUR MOTHERS MORE!
RUSTLE
RUSTLE
KACHAK
HUH?
WHAT'S WITH THE TOOLS?
YOU DON'T NEED THOSE, DO YOU?
PIK
PIK
PIK

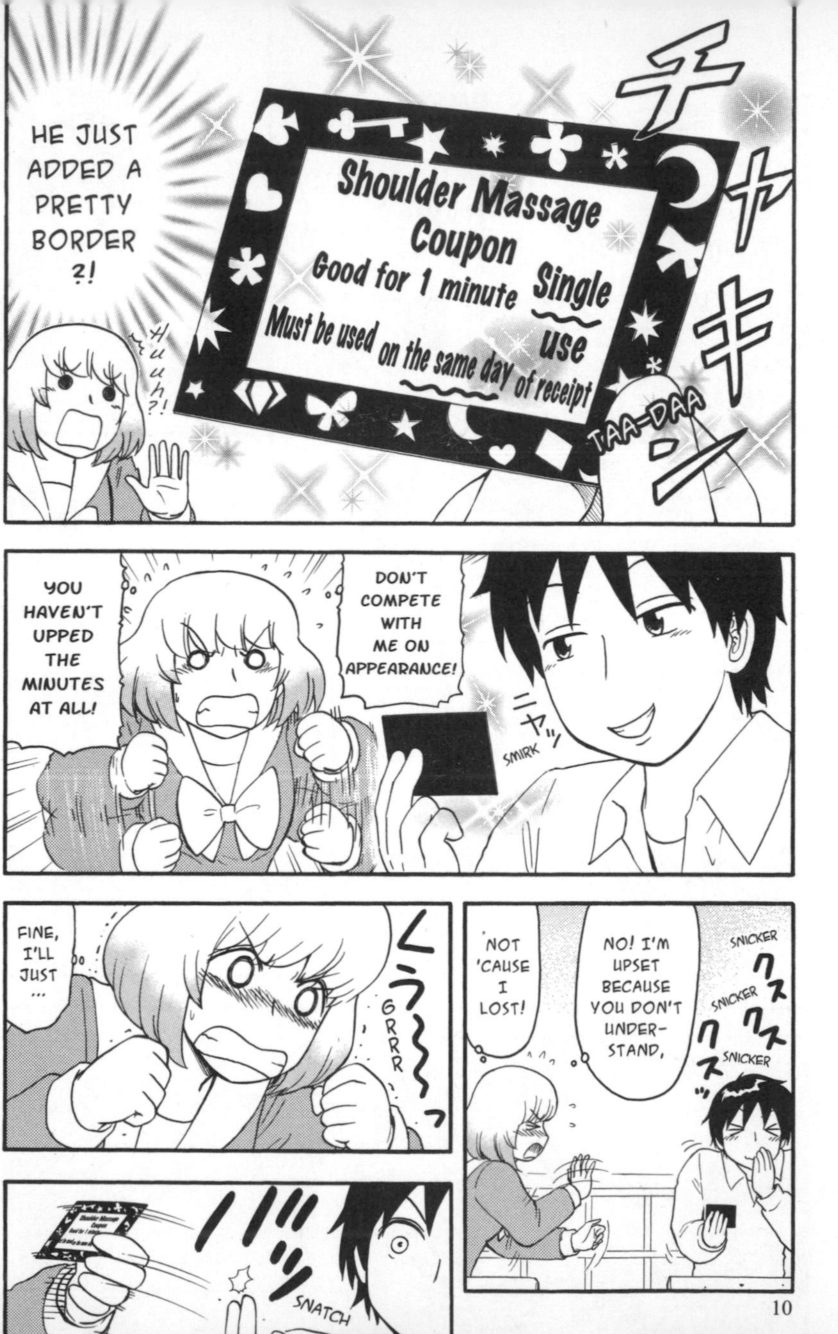

チャキーン
TAA-DAA
Shoulder Massage Coupon
Good for 1 minute
Single use
Must be used on the same day of receipt
HE JUST ADDED A PRETTY BORDER ?!
Huuuh?!
DON'T COMPETE WITH ME ON APPEARANCE!
YOU HAVEN'T UPPED THE MINUTES AT ALL!
ニヤッ
SMIRK
クスクスクスッ
SNICKER
SNICKER
SNICKER
NO! I'M UPSET BECAUSE YOU DON'T UNDER-STAND,
'NOT 'CAUSE I LOST!
くぅ~~っ
GRRR
FINE, I'LL JUST ...
バッ
SNATCH

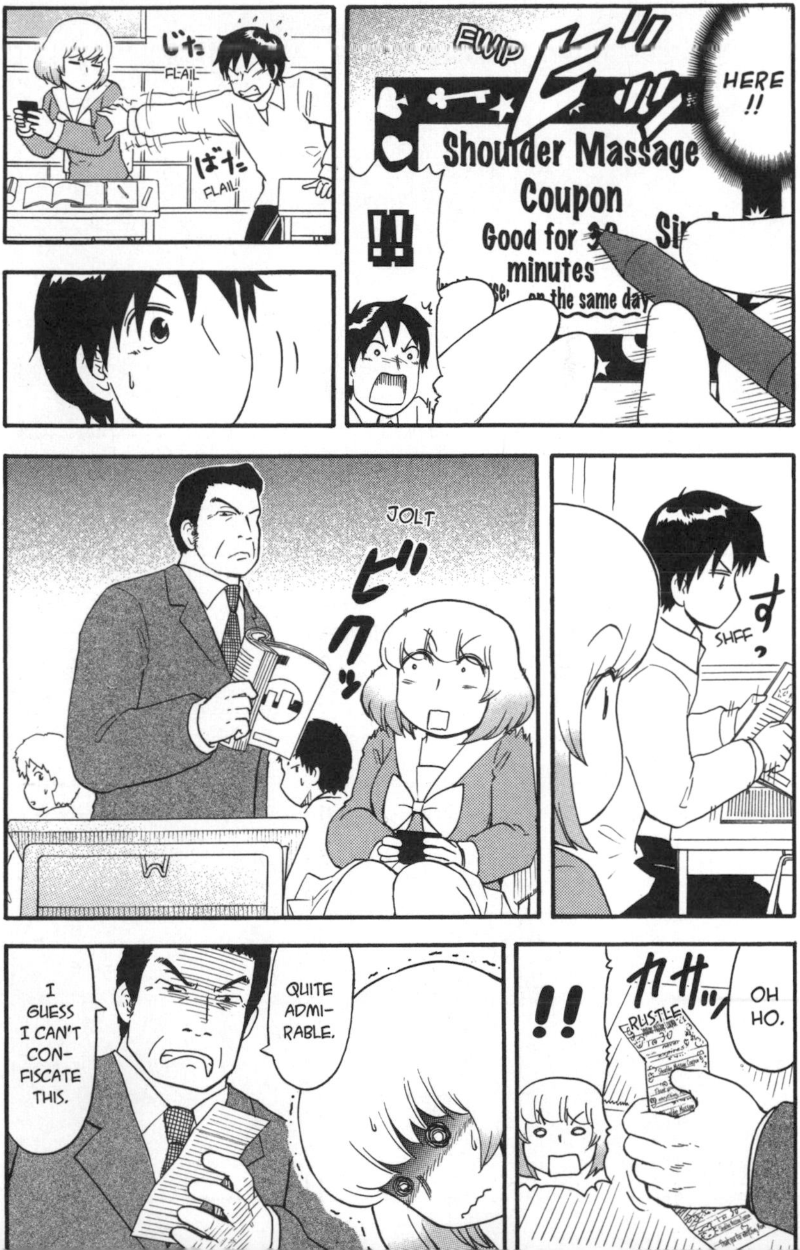
FWIP
ピュッ
HERE !!
Shoulder Massage
Coupon
Good for
minutes
on the same day
!!
じた
FLAIL
ばた
FLAIL
す
SHFF
JOLT
ビクッ
カサッ
RUSTLE
OH HO.
!!
QUITE ADMIRABLE.
I GUESS I CAN'T CONFISCATE THIS.

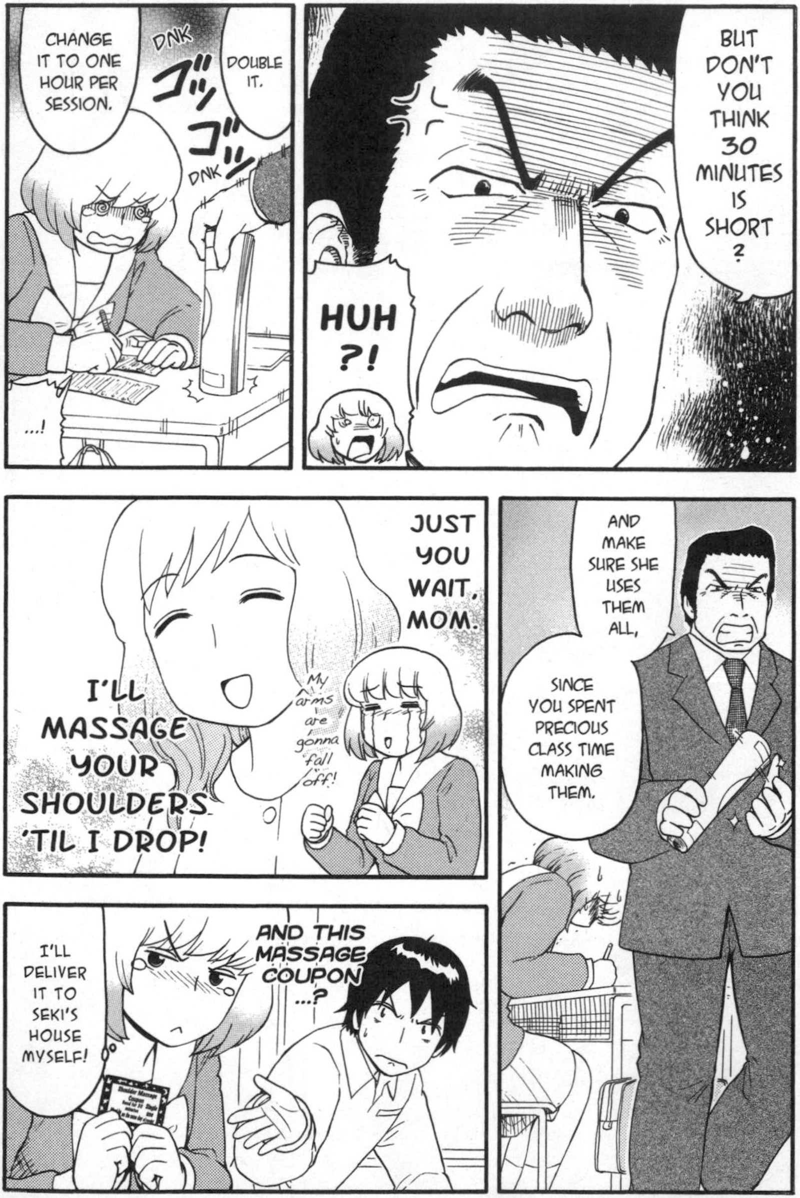
BUT DON'T YOU THINK 30 MINUTES IS SHORT?
HUH?!
DOUBLE IT.
DNK
ゴッ
ゴッ
DNK
CHANGE IT TO ONE HOUR PER SESSION.
...!
AND MAKE SURE SHE USES THEM ALL,
SINCE YOU SPENT PRECIOUS CLASS TIME MAKING THEM.
JUST YOU WAIT, MOM.
I'LL MASSAGE YOUR SHOULDERS 'TIL I DROP!
My arms are gonna fall off!
AND THIS MASSAGE COUPON...?
I'LL DELIVER IT TO SEKI'S HOUSE MYSELF!

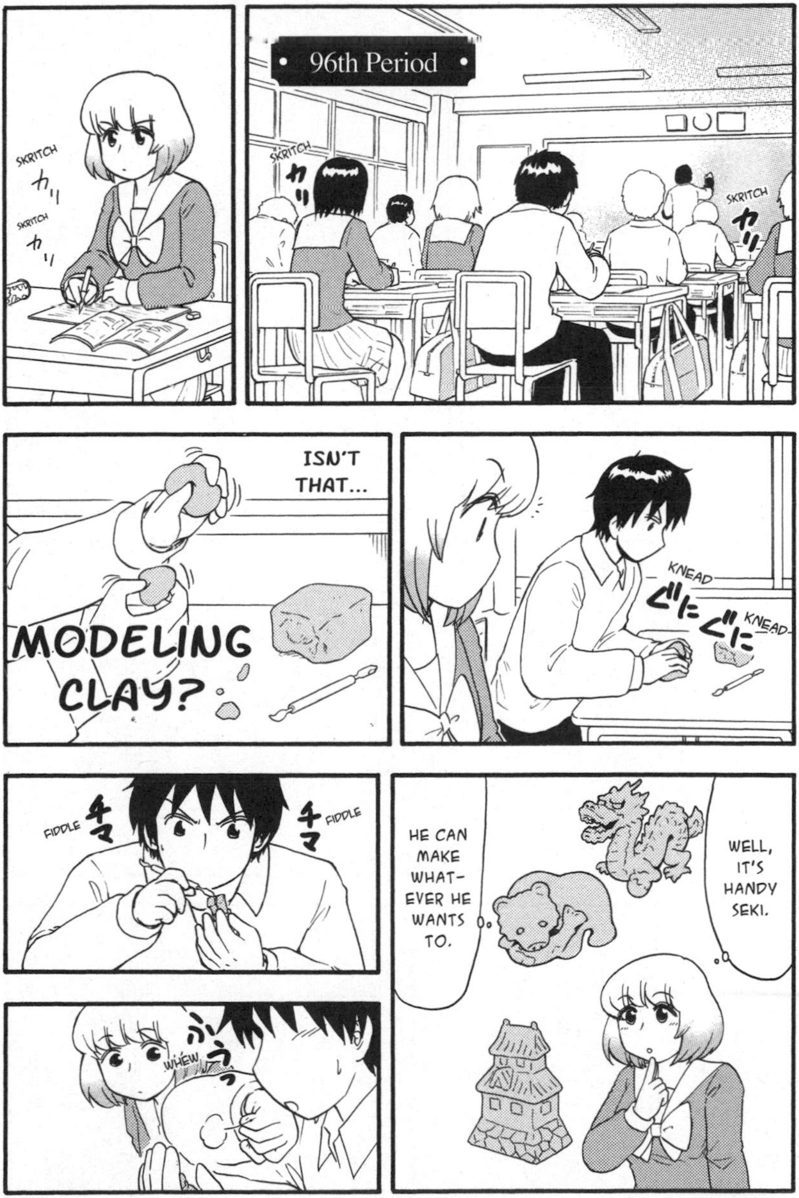
96th Period
SKRITCH カリ
SKRITCH カリ
SKRITCH カリ
SKRITCH カリ
SKRITCH カリ
KNEAD ぐに
KNEAD ぐに
ISN'T THAT...
MODELING CLAY?
WELL, IT'S HANDY SEKI.
HE CAN MAKE WHATEVER HE WANTS TO.
FIDDLE チマ
FIDDLE チマ
WHEW ふうっ

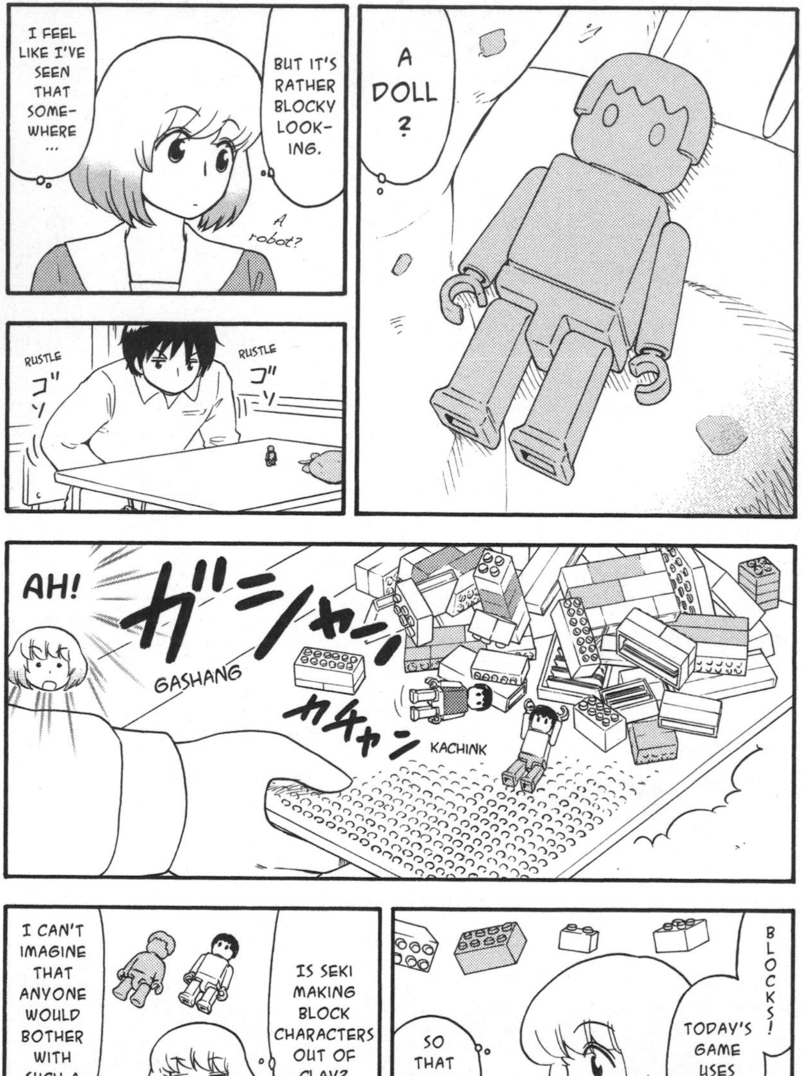

A DOLL?
BUT IT'S RATHER BLOCKY LOOKING.
I FEEL LIKE I'VE SEEN THAT SOME-WHERE...
A robot?
RUSTLE
ゴソ
RUSTLE
ゴソ
AH!
ガシャン
GASHANG
カチャン
KACHINK
BLOCKS!
TODAY'S GAME USES BLOCKS, RIGHT?
SO THAT FIGURE IS A BLOCK CHAR-ACTER.
Brings me back!
IS SEKI MAKING BLOCK CHARACTERS OUT OF CLAY?
I CAN'T IMAGINE THAT ANYONE WOULD BOTHER WITH SUCH A THING!

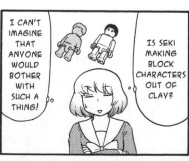

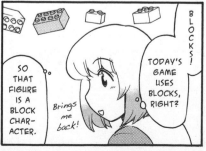

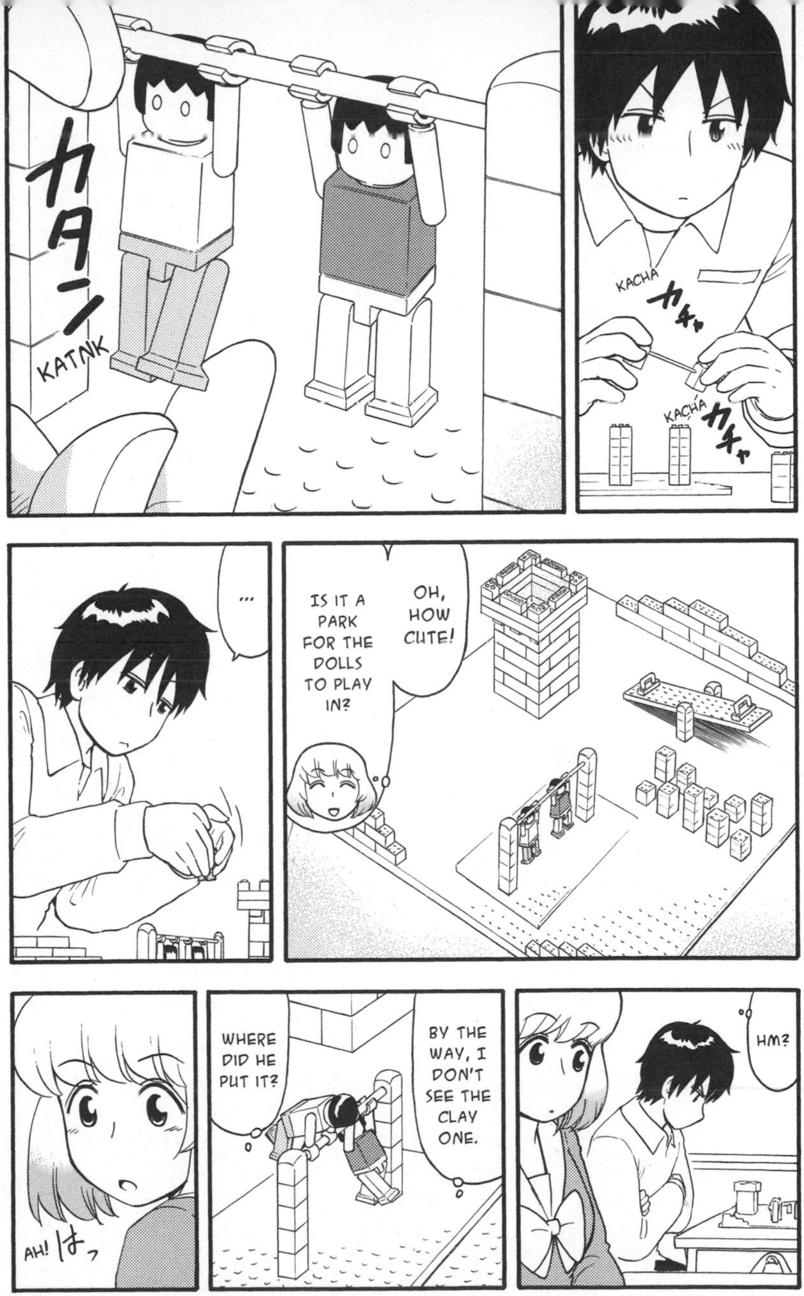
KACHA カチャ
KACHA カチャ
カタン
KATNK
OH, HOW CUTE!
IS IT A PARK FOR THE DOLLS TO PLAY IN?
...
HM?
BY THE WAY, I DON'T SEE THE CLAY ONE.
WHERE DID HE PUT IT?
AH! はっ

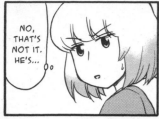

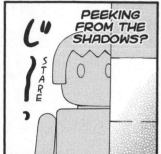

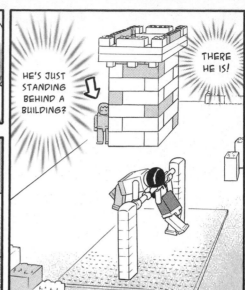

THERE HE IS!
HE'S JUST STANDING BEHIND A BUILDING?
NO, THAT'S NOT IT. HE'S...
PEEKING FROM THE SHADOWS?
じー
STARE
IS THIS A PLAYGROUND JUST FOR REAL BLOCK CHARACTERS?
THEN WHAT DID YOU MAKE THE CLAY ONE FOR?
WHY CAN'T THEY ALL PLAY TOGETHER?
OH, BUT ...
MAYBE THE CLAY ONE IS SOFT AND FRAGILE?

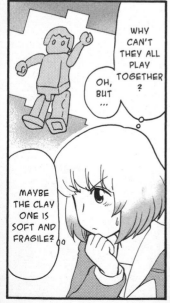

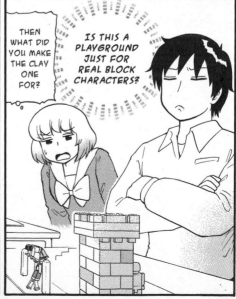

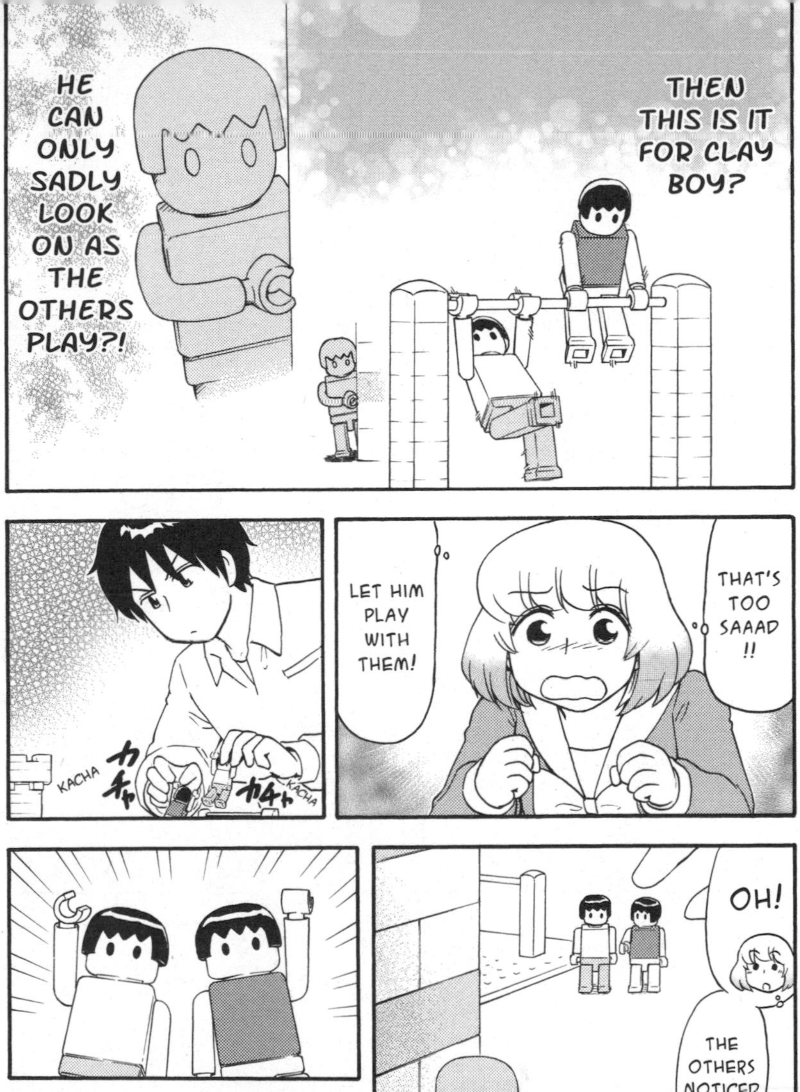
THEN THIS IS IT FOR CLAY BOY?
HE CAN ONLY SADLY LOOK ON AS THE OTHERS PLAY?!
THAT'S TOO SAAAD !!
LET HIM PLAY WITH THEM!
KACHA
KACHA
OH!
THE OTHERS NOTICED HIM?

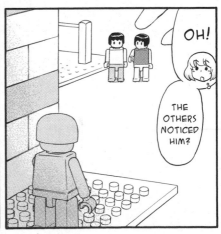

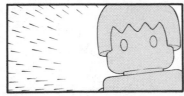

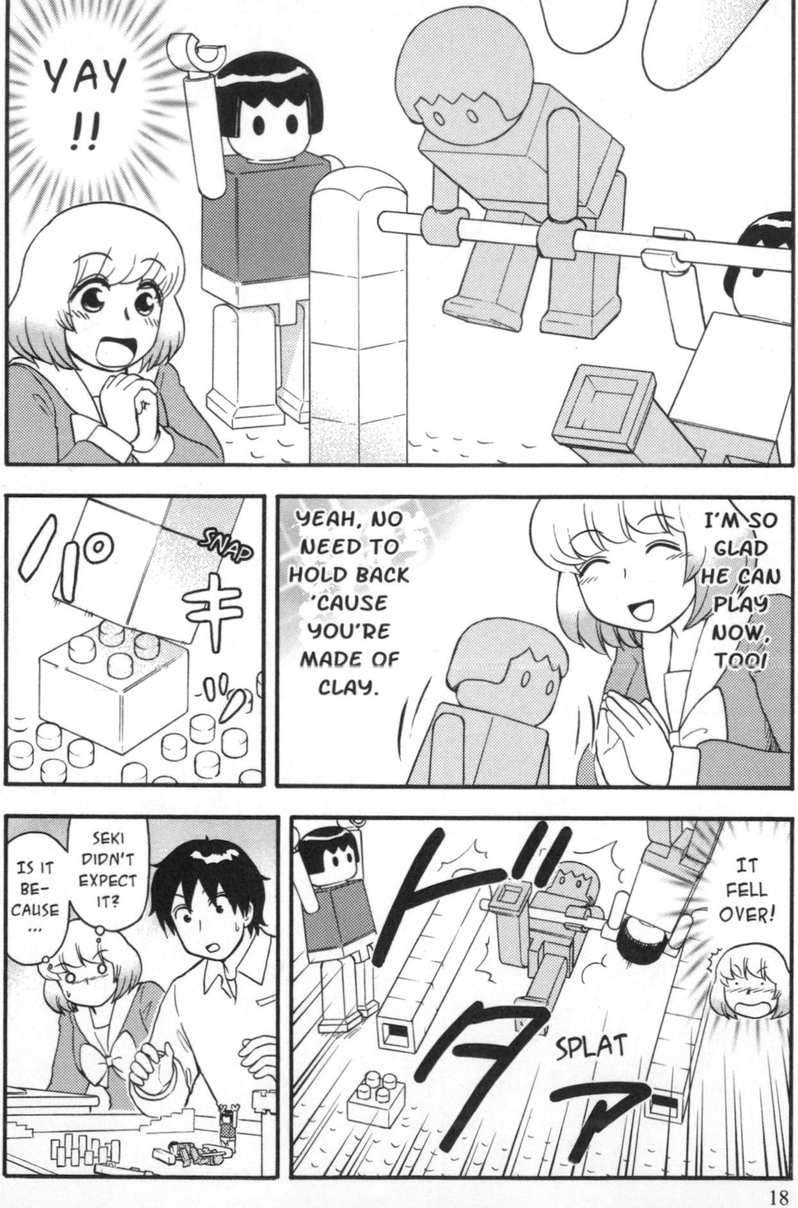
YAY !!
I'M SO GLAD HE CAN PLAY NOW, TOO!
YEAH, NO NEED TO HOLD BACK 'CAUSE YOU'RE MADE OF CLAY.
パキ
SNAP
IT FELL OVER!
ドタァー
SPLAT
SEKI DIDN'T EXPECT IT?
IS IT BE-CAUSE ...

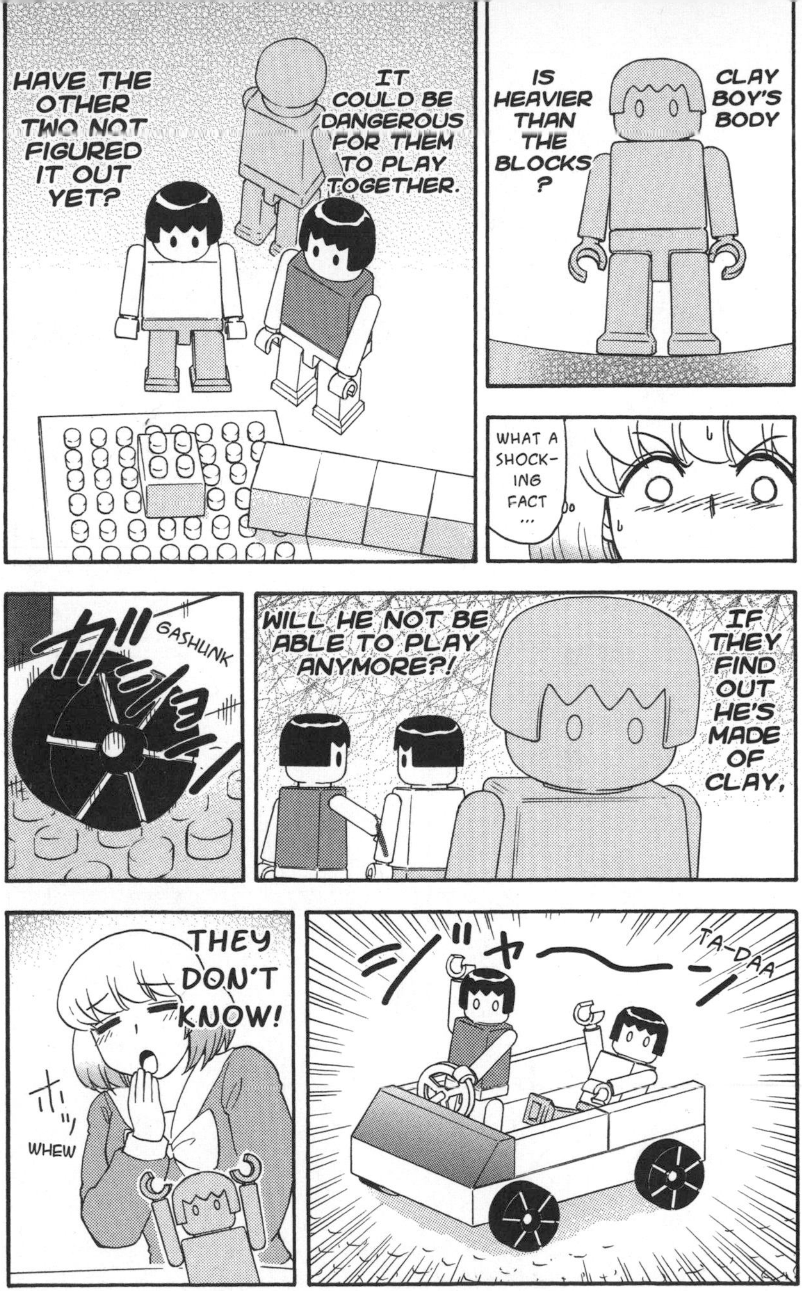
CLAY BOY'S BODY
IS HEAVIER THAN THE BLOCKS?
WHAT A SHOCKING FACT...
IT COULD BE DANGEROUS FOR THEM TO PLAY TOGETHER.
HAVE THE OTHER TWO NOT FIGURED IT OUT YET?
IF THEY FIND OUT HE'S MADE OF CLAY,
WILL HE NOT BE ABLE TO PLAY ANYMORE?!
GASHUNK
TA-DAA
THEY DON'T KNOW!
WHEW

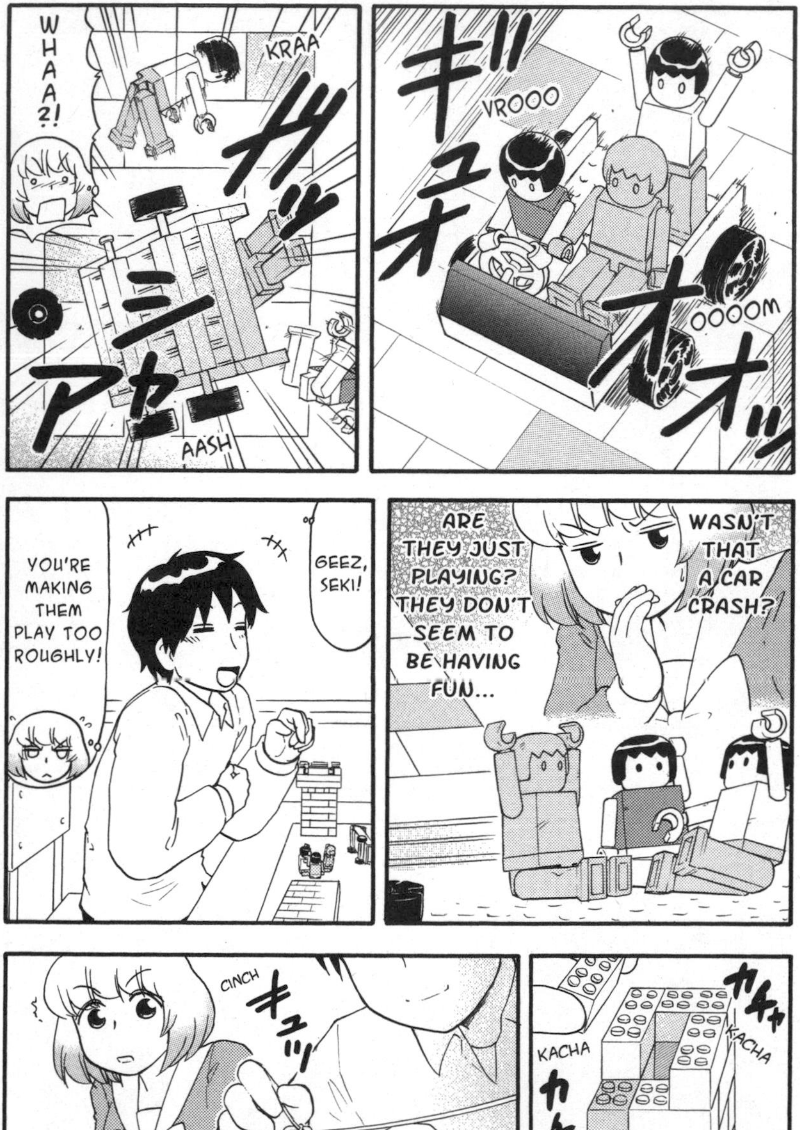
VROOO
OOOOM
WHAAA?!
KRAA
AASH
WASN'T THAT A CAR CRASH?
ARE THEY JUST PLAYING? THEY DON'T SEEM TO BE HAVING FUN...
GEEZ, SEKI!
YOU'RE MAKING THEM PLAY TOO ROUGHLY!
カチャ
KACHA
KACHA
カチャ
CINCH
キュッ

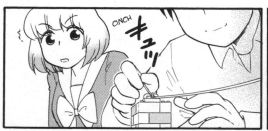

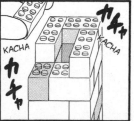

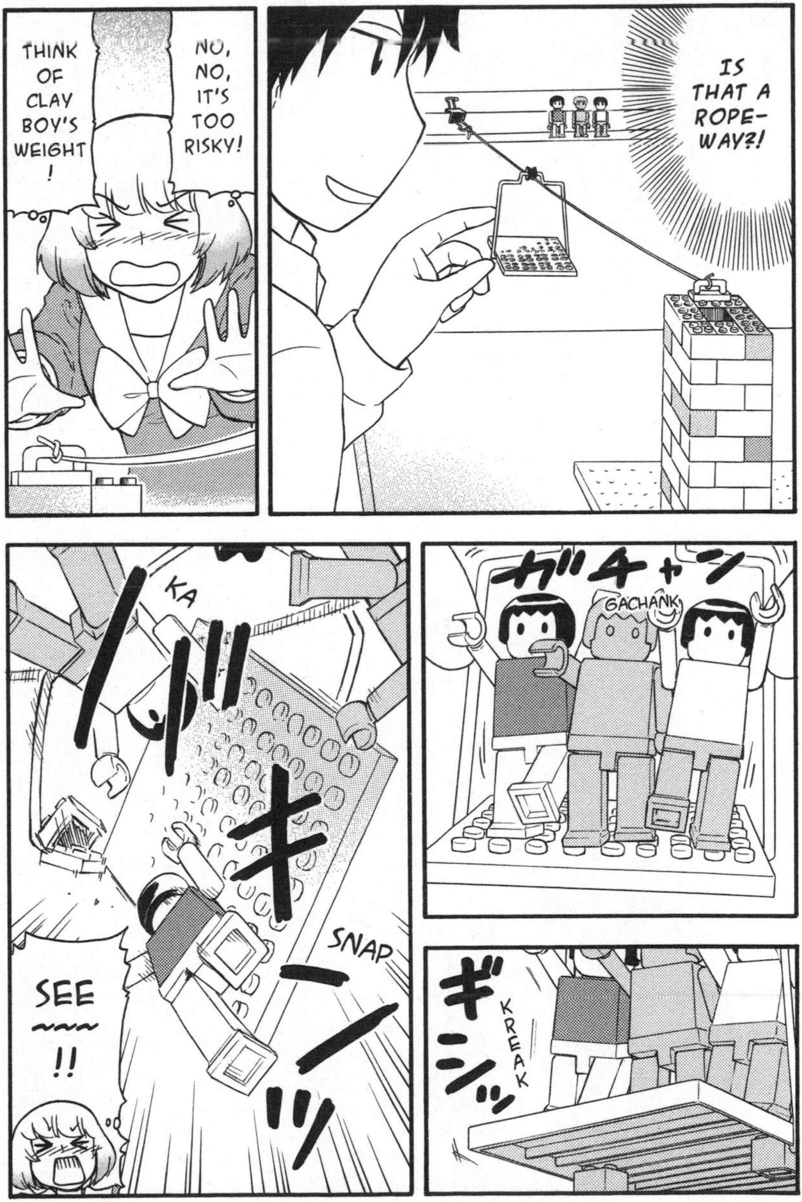
IS THAT A ROPE-WAY?!
NO, NO, IT'S TOO RISKY!
THINK OF CLAY BOY'S WEIGHT!
ガチャン
GACHANK
ギシッ
KREAK
KA
バキーッ
SNAP
SEE ~~~!!

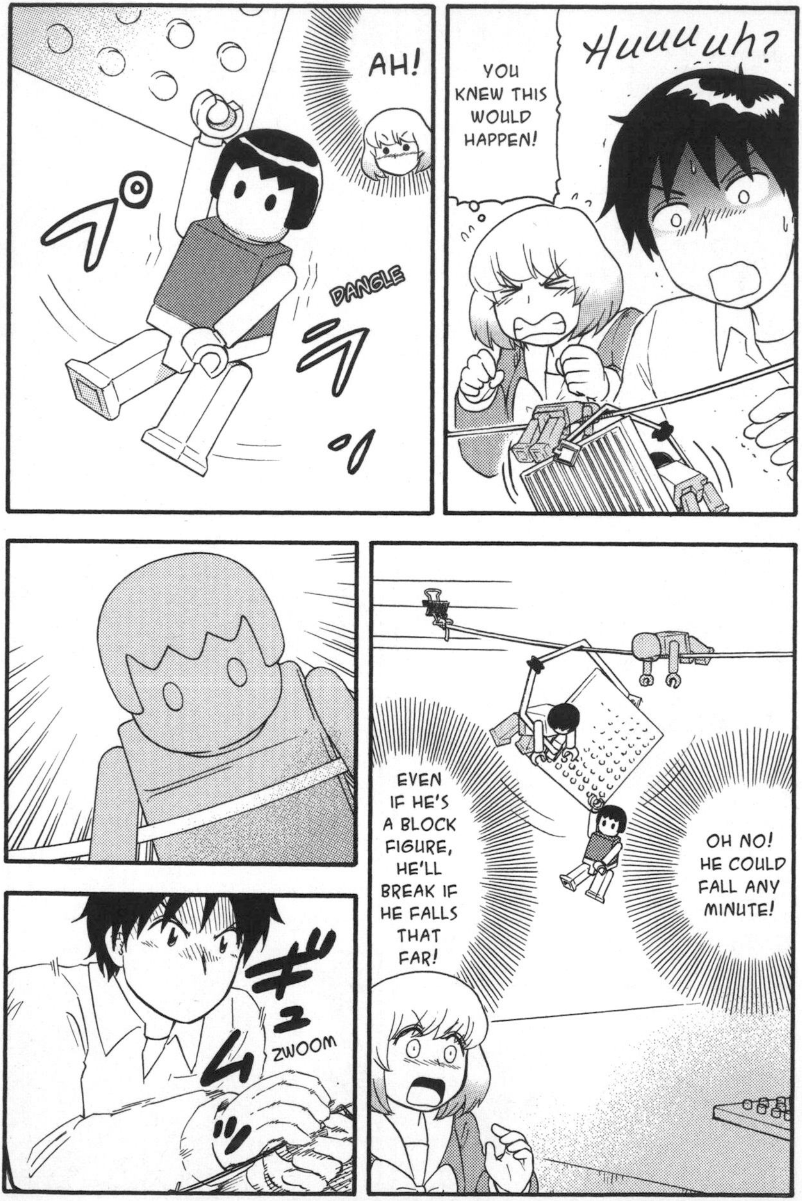
Huuuuh?
YOU KNEW THIS WOULD HAPPEN!
AH!
DANGLE
OH NO! HE COULD FALL ANY MINUTE!
EVEN IF HE'S A BLOCK FIGURE, HE'LL BREAK IF HE FALLS THAT FAR!
ZWOOM

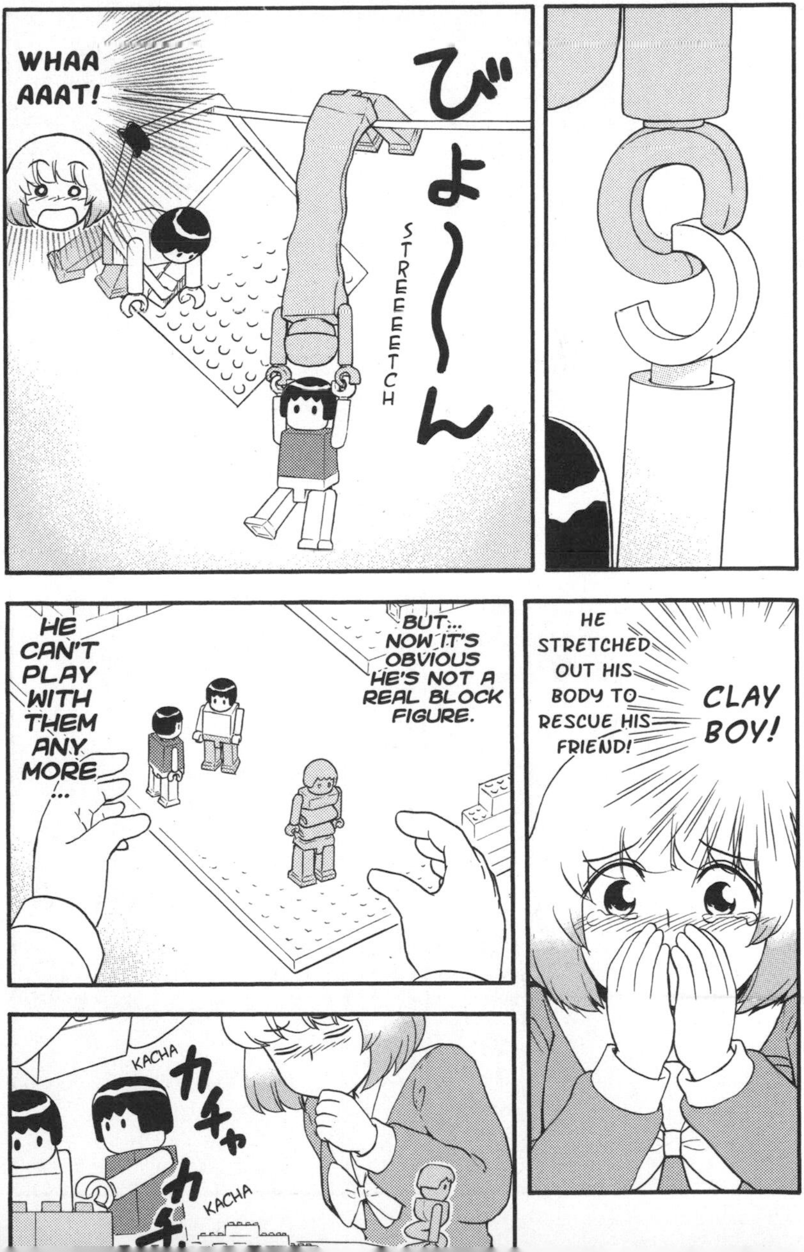

WHAA AAAT!
びょ〜〜ん
STREEEETCH
HE STRETCHED OUT HIS BODY TO RESCUE HIS FRIEND!
CLAY BOY!
BUT... NOW IT'S OBVIOUS HE'S NOT A REAL BLOCK FIGURE.
HE CAN'T PLAY WITH THEM ANY MORE...
KACHA
カチャ
KACHA
カチ

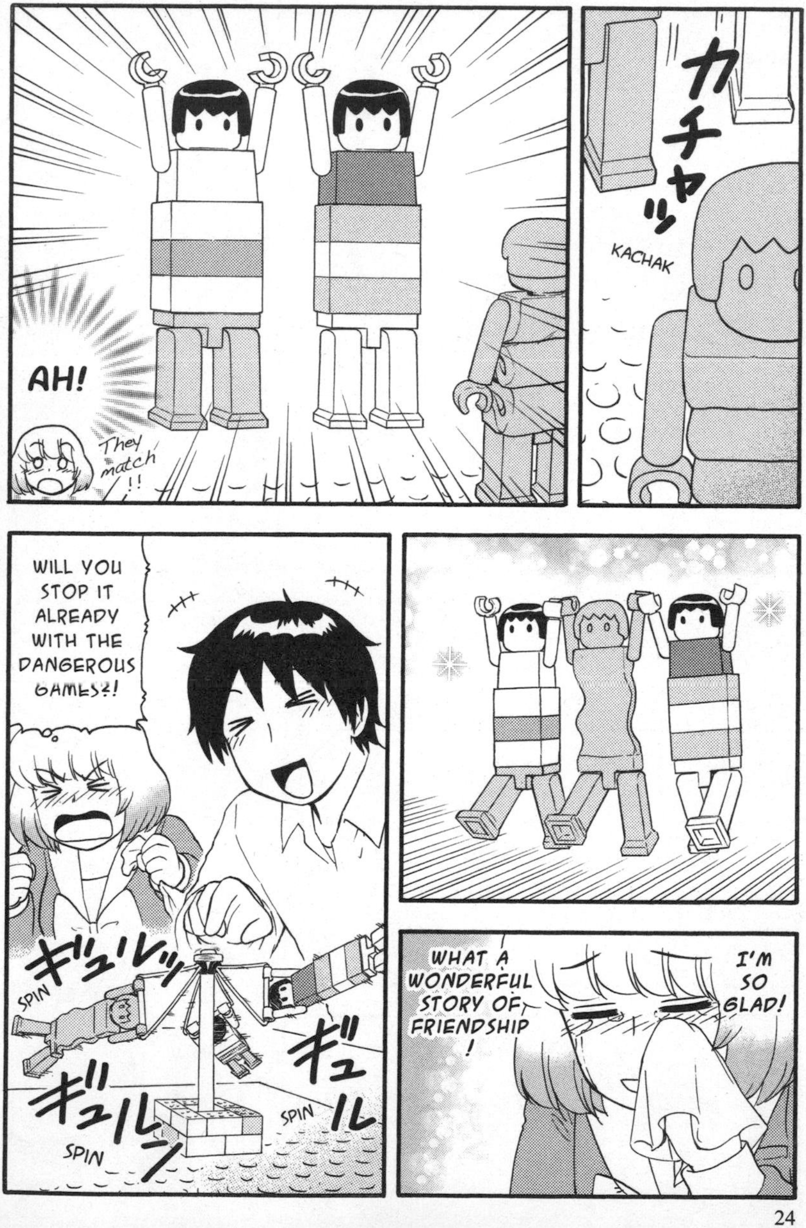
カチャッ
KACHAK
AH!
They match!!
WHAT A WONDERFUL STORY OF FRIENDSHIP!
I'M SO GLAD!
WILL YOU STOP IT ALREADY WITH THE DANGEROUS GAMES?!
ギュルッ
SPIN
ギュル
SPIN
ギュルン
SPIN

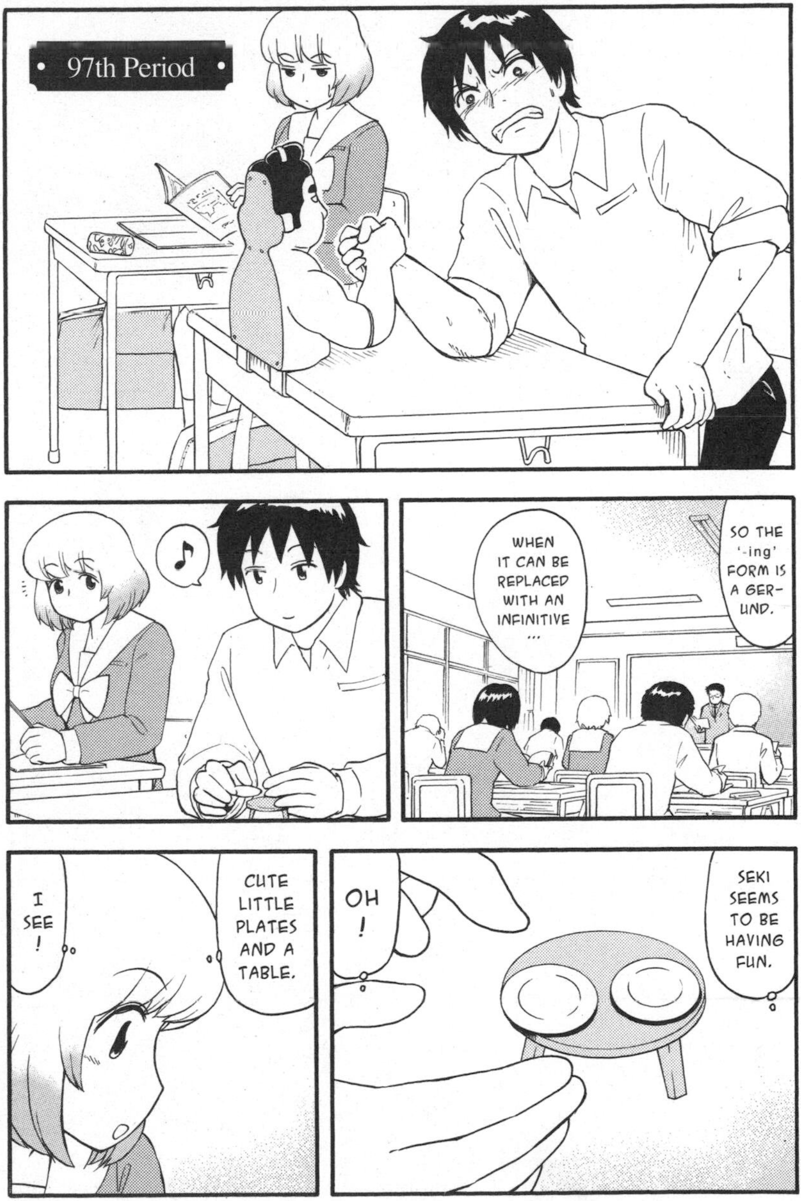
97th Period
SO THE '-ing' FORM IS A GERUND.
WHEN IT CAN BE REPLACED WITH AN INFINITIVE ...
SEKI SEEMS TO BE HAVING FUN.
OH!
CUTE LITTLE PLATES AND A TABLE.
I SEE!

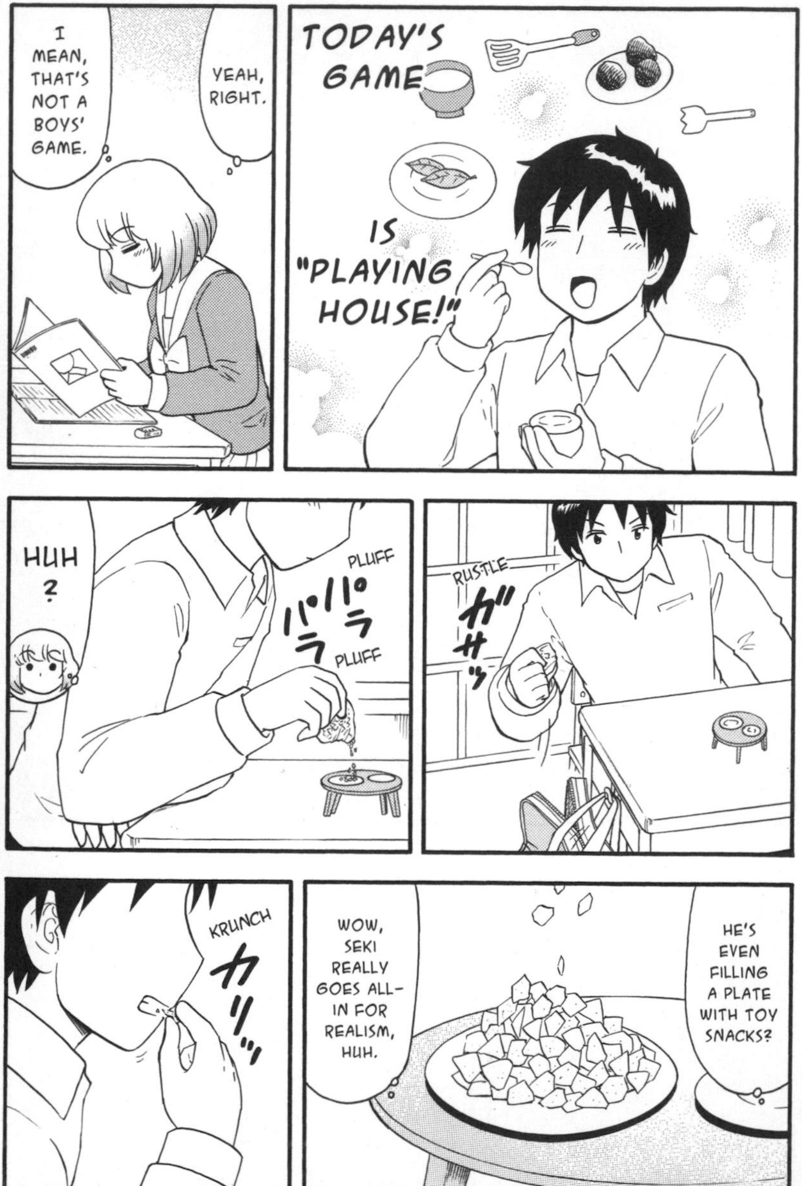
TODAY'S GAME IS "PLAYING HOUSE!"
YEAH, RIGHT.
I MEAN, THAT'S NOT A BOYS' GAME.
RUSTLE
ガサッ
PLUFF
パラ
PLUFF
パラ
HUH?
HE'S EVEN FILLING A PLATE WITH TOY SNACKS?
WOW, SEKI REALLY GOES ALL-IN FOR REALISM, HUH.
KRUNCH
カリッ

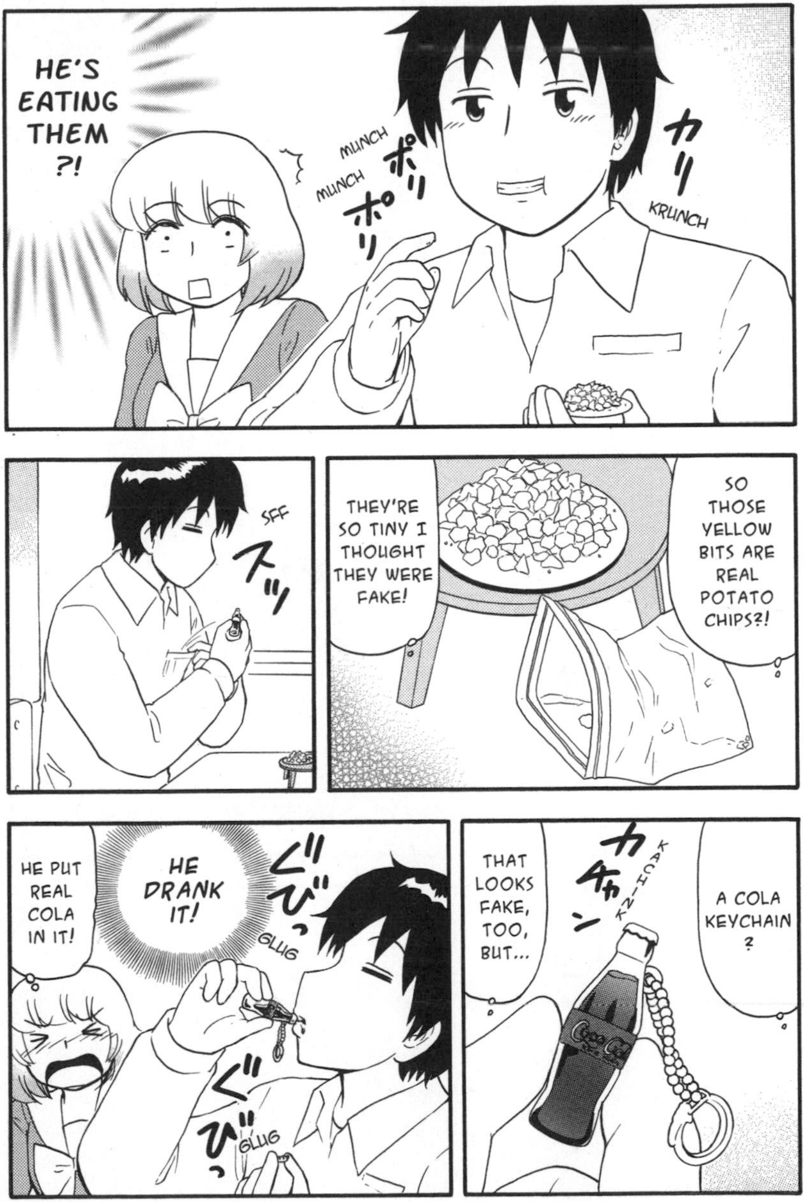
カリ
KRUNCH
ポリ
MUNCH
ポリ
MUNCH
HE'S EATING THEM ?!
SO THOSE YELLOW BITS ARE REAL POTATO CHIPS?!
THEY'RE SO TINY I THOUGHT THEY WERE FAKE!
スッ
SFF
A COLA KEYCHAIN ?
カチャン
KACHINK
THAT LOOKS FAKE, TOO, BUT...
ぐびっ
GLUG
HE DRANK IT!
HE PUT REAL COLA IN IT!
ぐびっ
GLUG

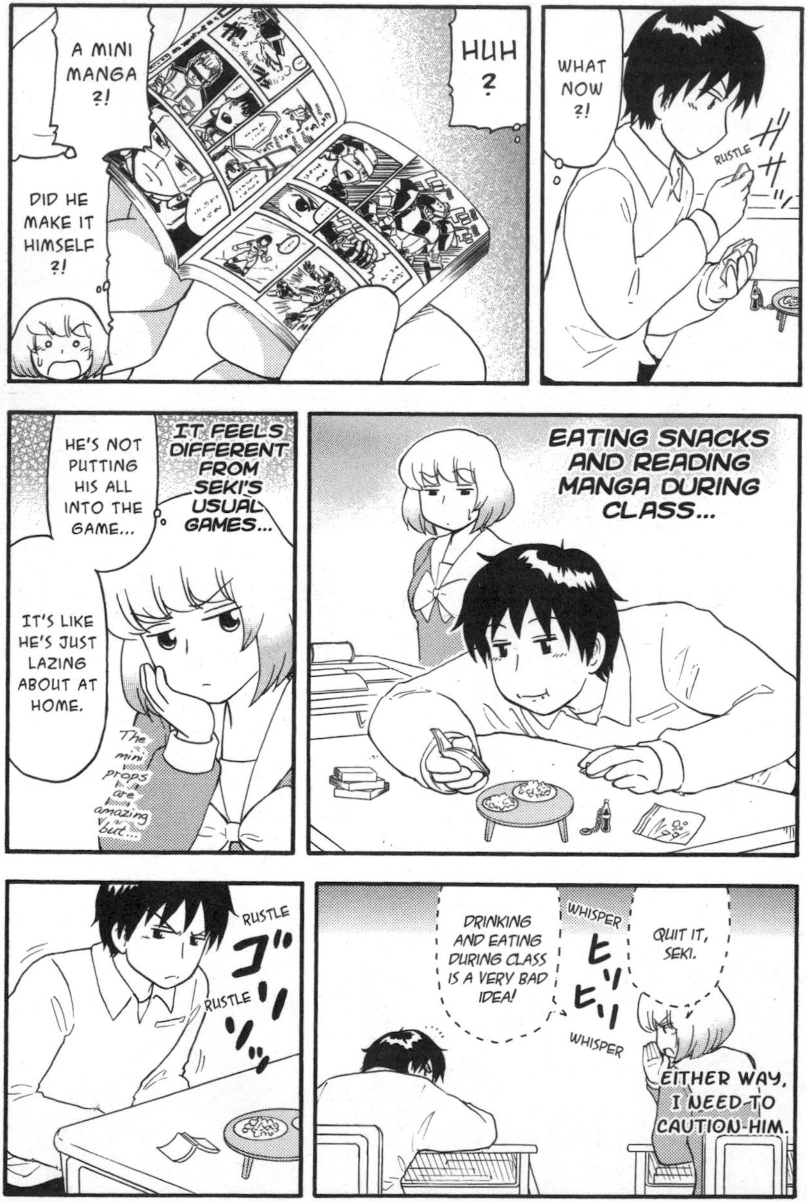
WHAT NOW ?!
RUSTLE
HUH ?
A MINI MANGA ?!
DID HE MAKE IT HIMSELF ?!
EATING SNACKS AND READING MANGA DURING CLASS...
IT FEELS DIFFERENT FROM SEKI'S USUAL GAMES...
HE'S NOT PUTTING HIS ALL INTO THE GAME...
IT'S LIKE HE'S JUST LAZING ABOUT AT HOME.
The mini props are amazing but...
EITHER WAY, I NEED TO CAUTION HIM.
QUIT IT, SEKI.
WHISPER
DRINKING AND EATING DURING CLASS IS A VERY BAD IDEA!
WHISPER
RUSTLE
RUSTLE

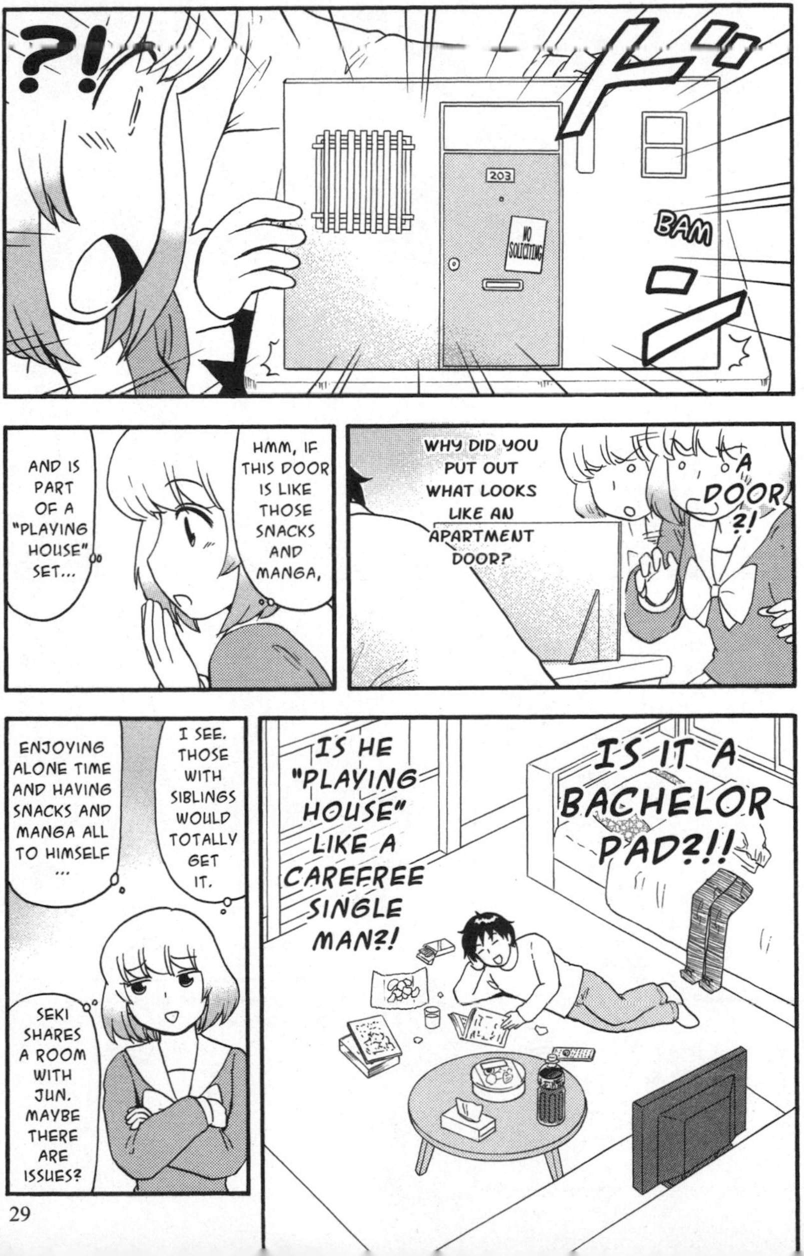
?!
203
NO SOLICITING
BAM
A DOOR?!
WHY DID YOU PUT OUT WHAT LOOKS LIKE AN APARTMENT DOOR?
HMM, IF THIS DOOR IS LIKE THOSE SNACKS AND MANGA,
AND IS PART OF A "PLAYING HOUSE" SET...
IS IT A BACHELOR PAD?!!
IS HE "PLAYING HOUSE" LIKE A CAREFREE SINGLE MAN?!
I SEE. THOSE WITH SIBLINGS WOULD TOTALLY GET IT.
ENJOYING ALONE TIME AND HAVING SNACKS AND MANGA ALL TO HIMSELF...
SEKI SHARES A ROOM WITH JUN. MAYBE THERE ARE ISSUES?

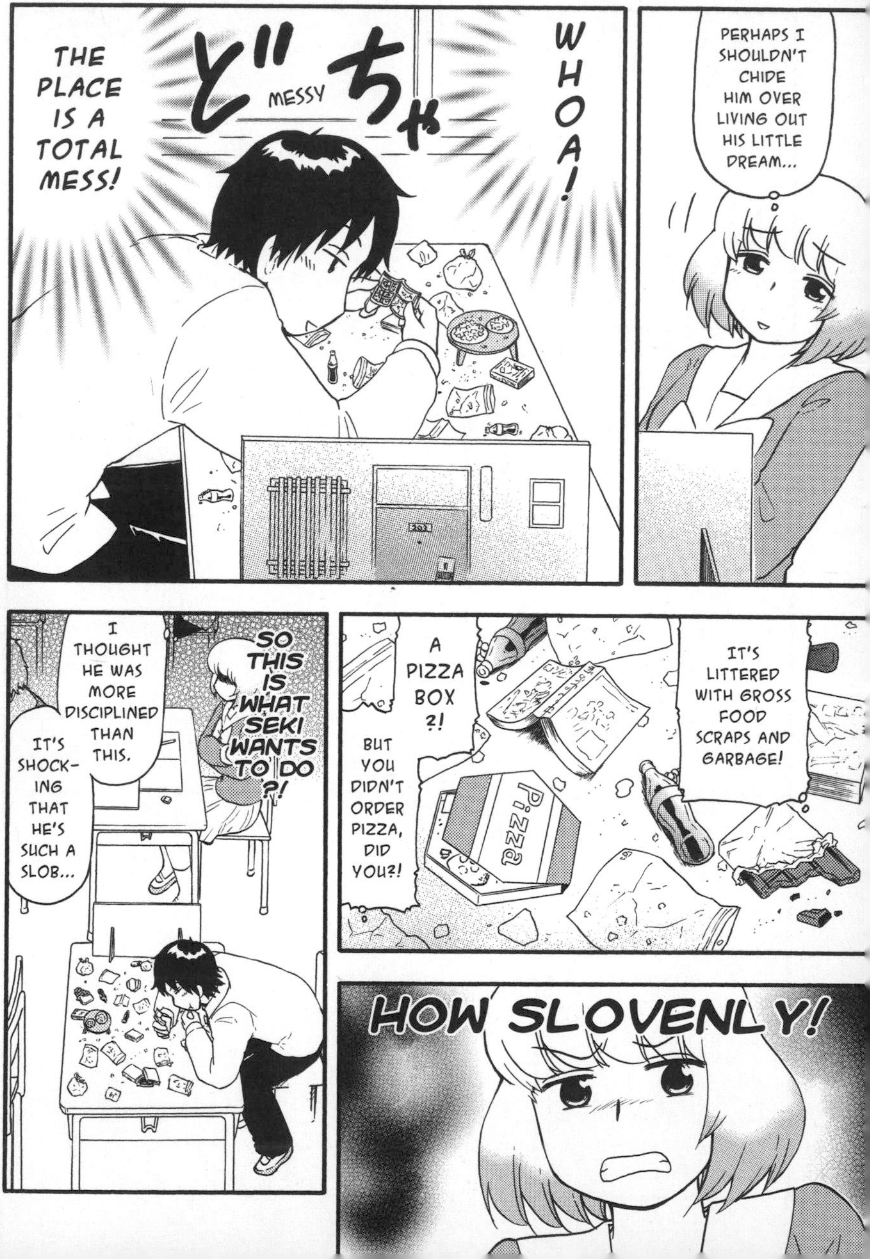
PERHAPS I SHOULDN'T CHIDE HIM OVER LIVING OUT HIS LITTLE DREAM...
WHOA!
どちゃ
MESSY
THE PLACE IS A TOTAL MESS!
IT'S LITTERED WITH GROSS FOOD SCRAPS AND GARBAGE!
A PIZZA BOX?!
BUT YOU DIDN'T ORDER PIZZA, DID YOU?!
Pizza
SO THIS IS WHAT SEKI WANTS TO DO?!
I THOUGHT HE WAS MORE DISCIPLINED THAN THIS.
IT'S SHOCKING THAT HE'S SUCH A SLOB...
HOW SLOVENLY!

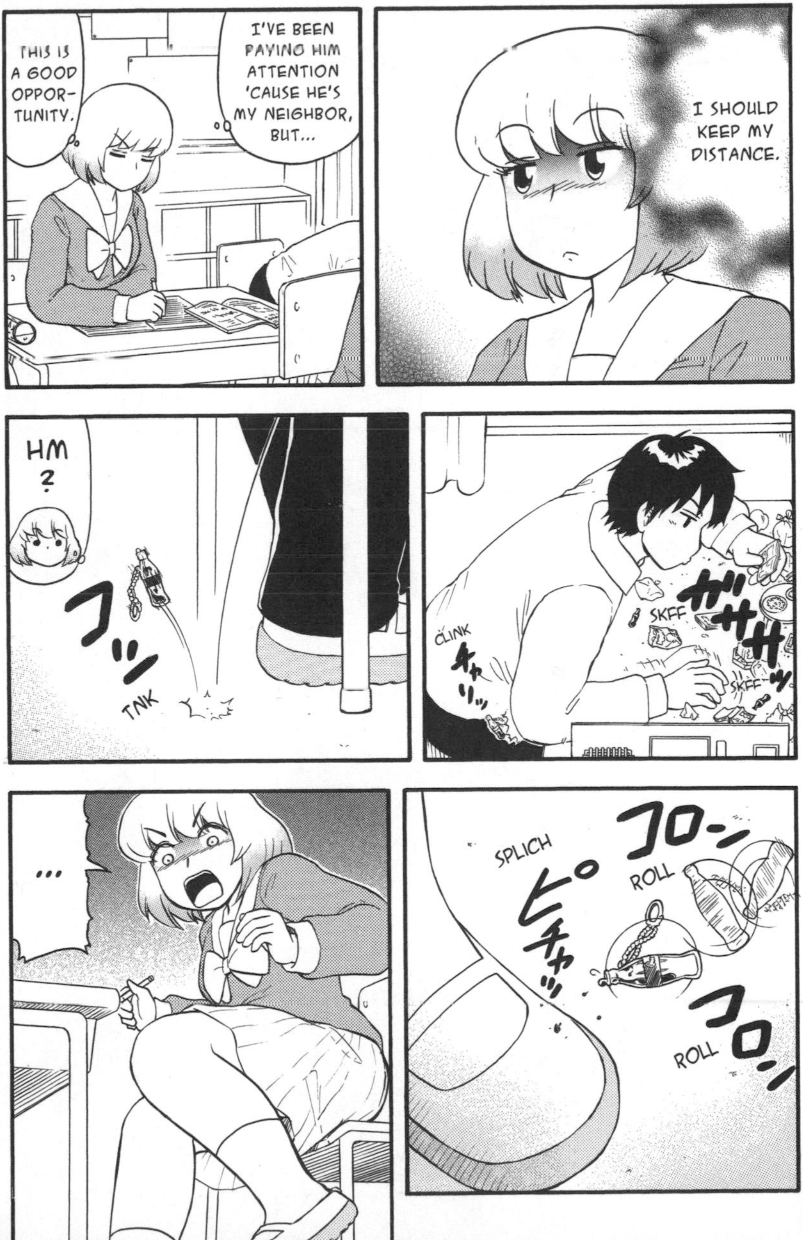
THIS IS A GOOD OPPOR-TUNITY.
I'VE BEEN PAYING HIM ATTENTION 'CAUSE HE'S MY NEIGHBOR, BUT...
I SHOULD KEEP MY DISTANCE.
HM ?
フッ
TNK
CLINK
チャリッ
SKFF
ガサササッ
SKFF
...
SPLICH
ピチャッ
コローン
ROLL
コロン
ROLL

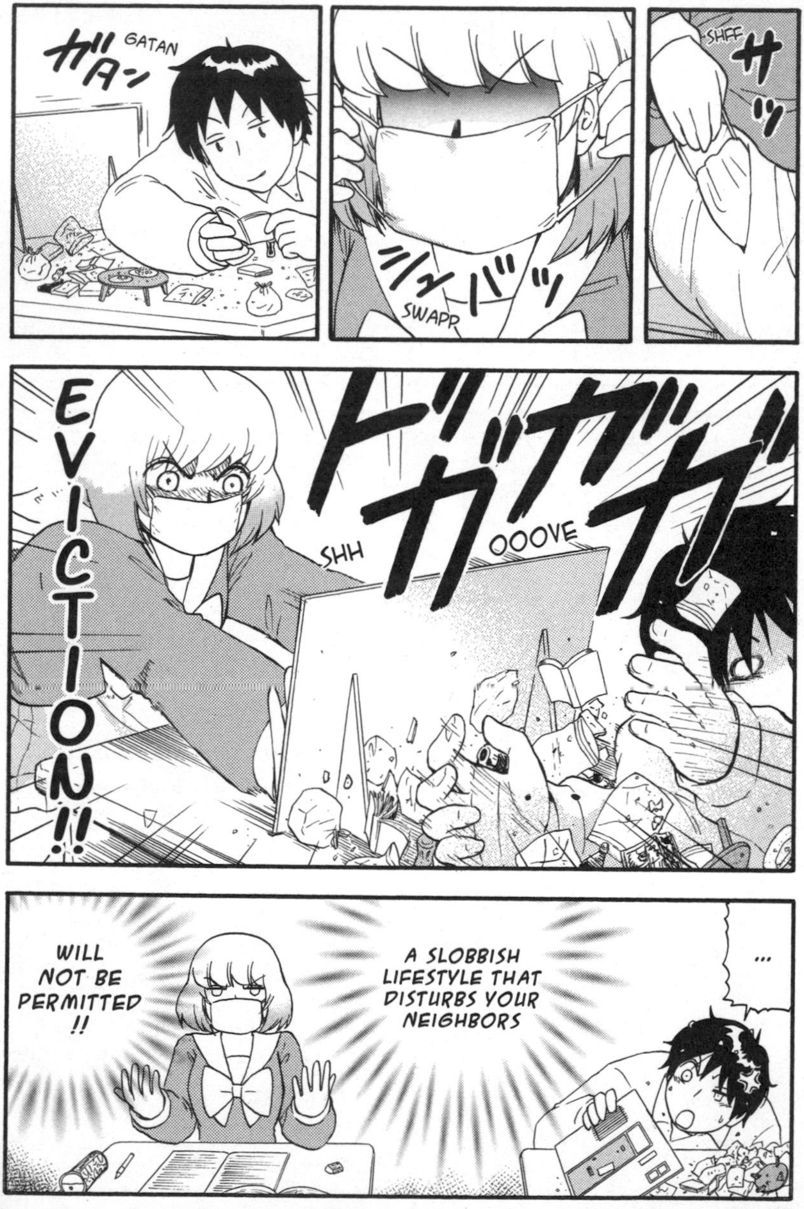
SHFF
サッ
SWAPP
シュバッ
GATAN
ガタン
SHH OOOVE
EVICTION!!
...
A SLOBBISH LIFESTYLE THAT DISTURBS YOUR NEIGHBORS
WILL NOT BE PERMITTED !!

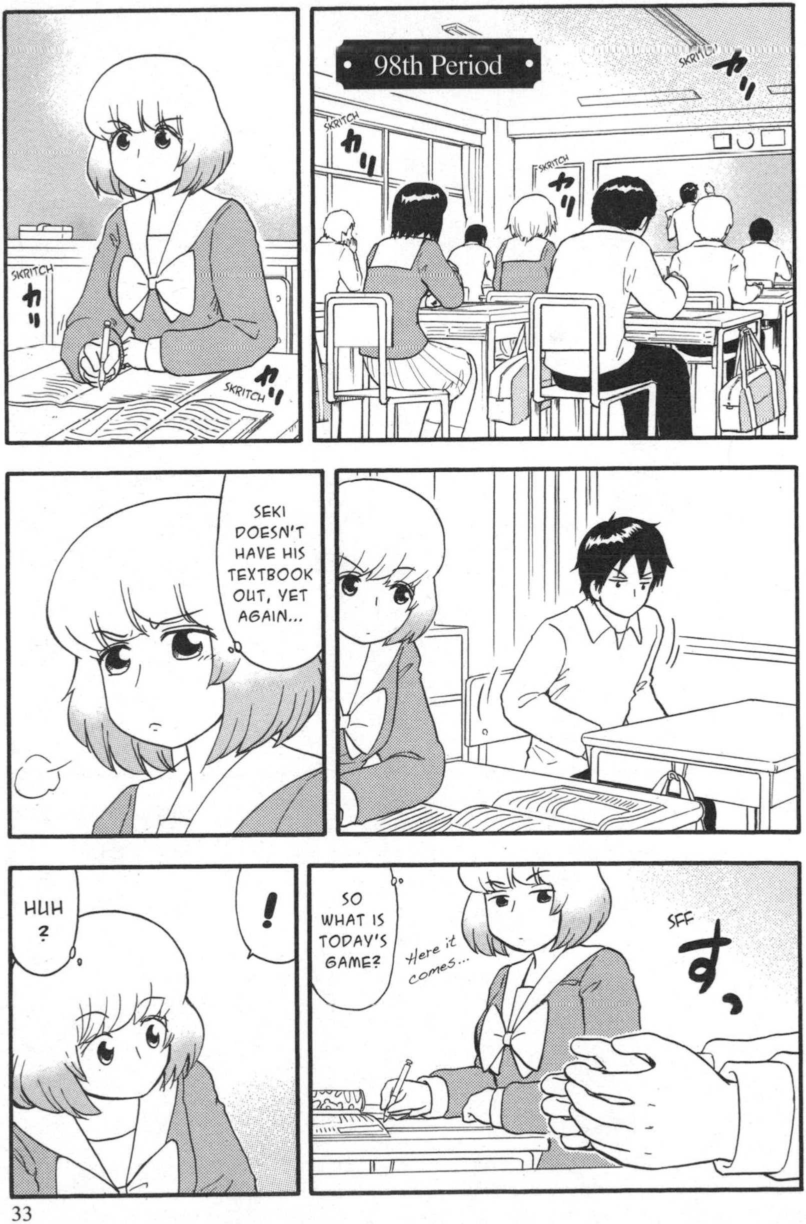
98th Period
SKRITCH
カリ
SKRITCH
カリ
SKRITCH
カリ
SKRITCH
カリ
SKRITCH
カリ
SEKI DOESN'T HAVE HIS TEXTBOOK OUT, YET AGAIN...
SO WHAT IS TODAY'S GAME?
Here it comes...
SFF
すっ
!
HUH?

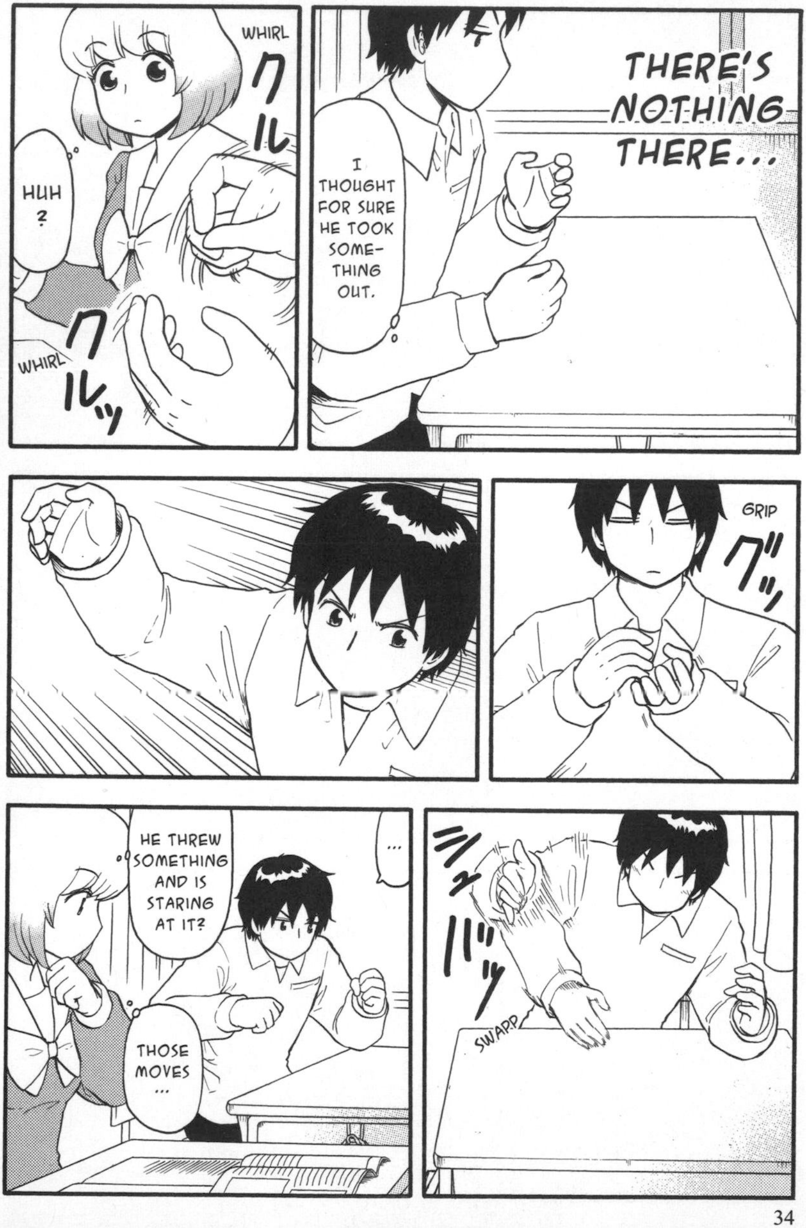
THERE'S NOTHING THERE...
I THOUGHT FOR SURE HE TOOK SOME-THING OUT.
WHIRL
クル
HUH ?
WHIRL
クルッ
GRIP
グッ
...
HE THREW SOMETHING AND IS STARING AT IT?
THOSE MOVES ...
シュ
バッ
SWAPP

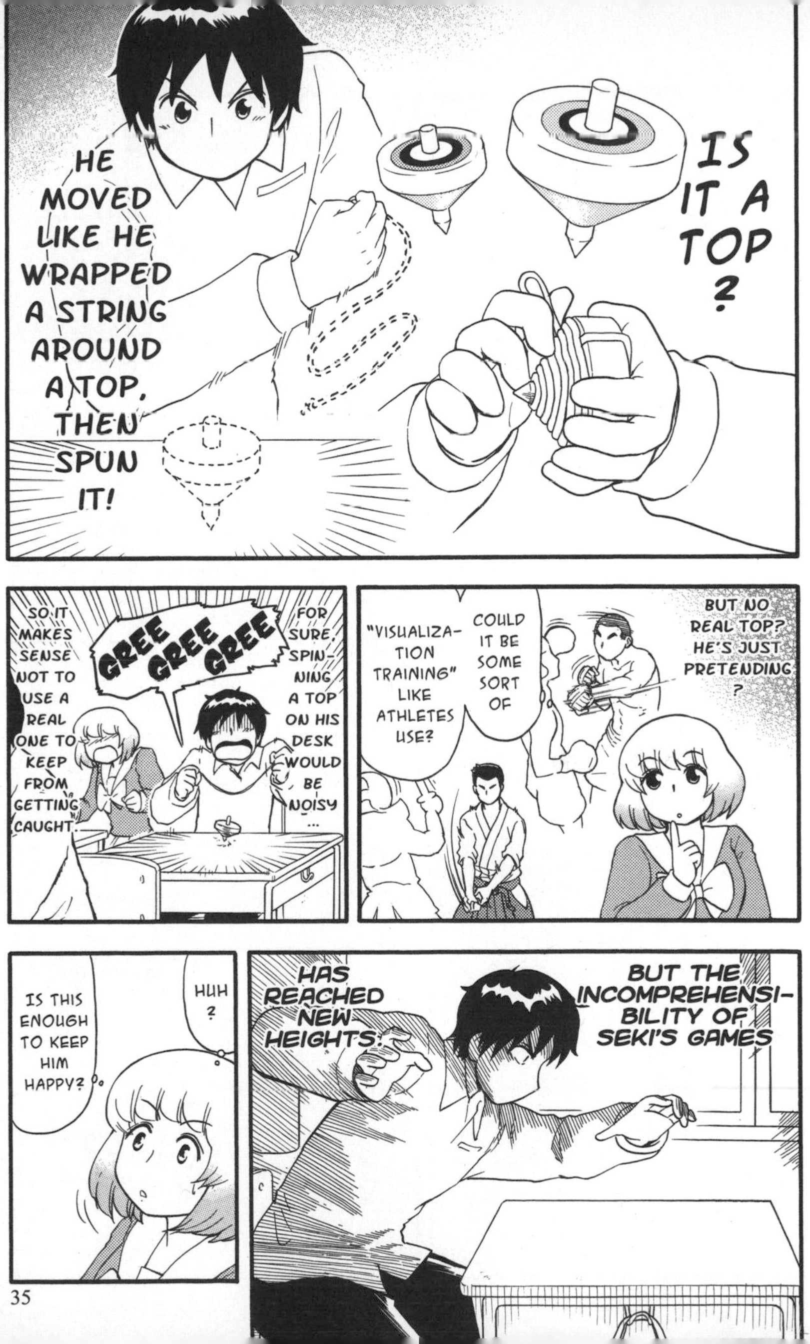
IS IT A TOP?
HE MOVED LIKE HE WRAPPED A STRING AROUND A TOP, THEN SPUN IT!
BUT NO REAL TOP? HE'S JUST PRETENDING?
COULD IT BE SOME SORT OF
"VISUALIZATION TRAINING" LIKE ATHLETES USE?
FOR SURE, SPINNING A TOP ON HIS DESK WOULD BE NOISY...
GREE GREE GREE
SO IT MAKES SENSE NOT TO USE A REAL ONE TO KEEP FROM GETTING CAUGHT.
BUT THE INCOMPREHENSIBILITY OF SEKI'S GAMES
HAS REACHED NEW HEIGHTS.
HUH?
IS THIS ENOUGH TO KEEP HIM HAPPY?

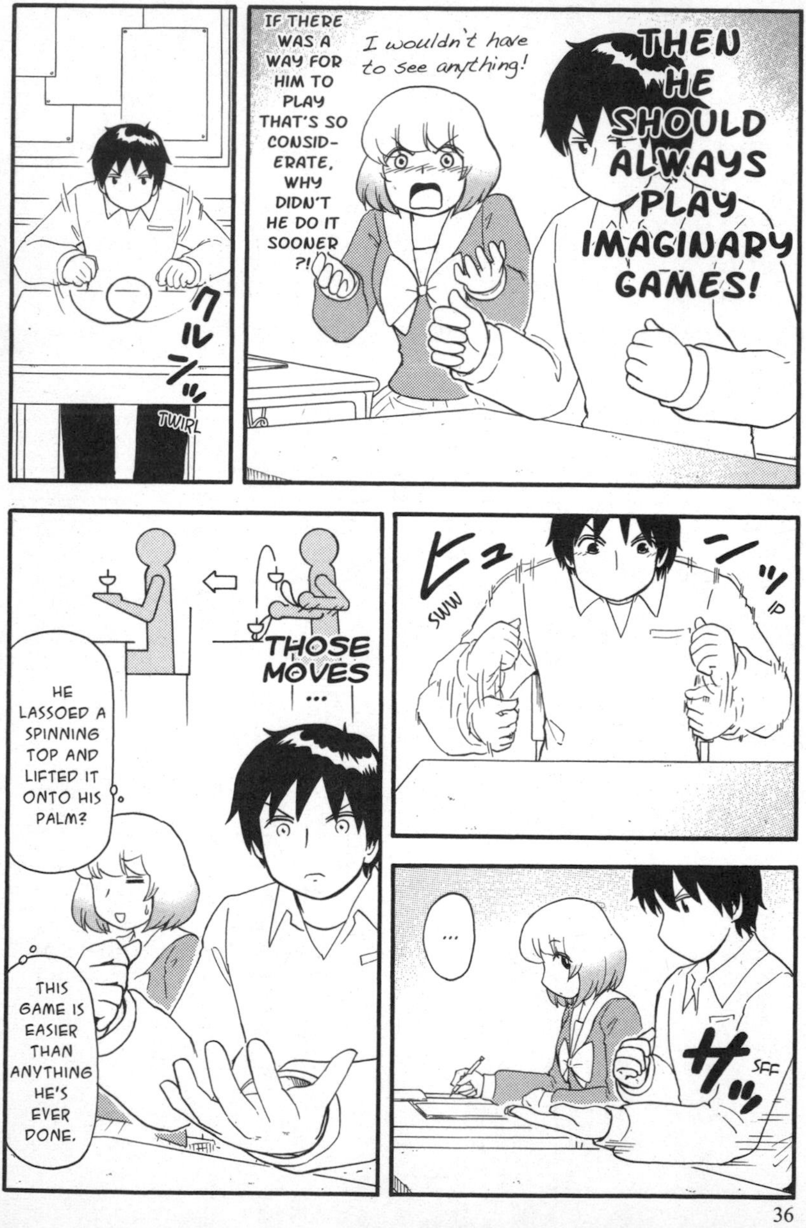

IF THERE WAS A WAY FOR HIM TO PLAY THAT'S SO CONSID-ERATE, WHY DIDN'T HE DO IT SOONER ?!
I wouldn't have to see anything!
THEN HE SHOULD ALWAYS PLAY IMAGINARY GAMES!
クルンッ
TWIRL
ヒュンッ
SWW IP
THOSE MOVES ...
HE LASSOED A SPINNING TOP AND LIFTED IT ONTO HIS PALM?
THIS GAME IS EASIER THAN ANYTHING HE'S EVER DONE.
...
サッ
SFF

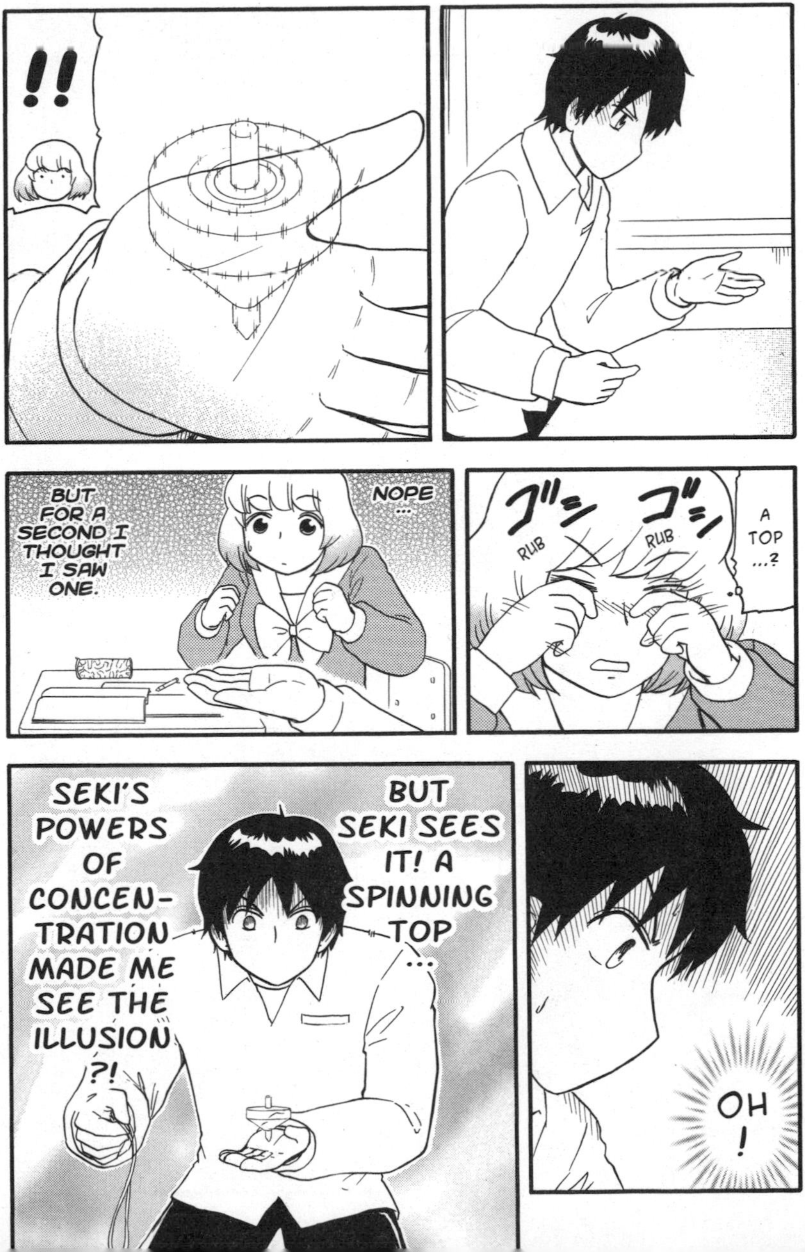
!!
A TOP ...?
RUB RUB
NOPE ...
BUT FOR A SECOND I THOUGHT I SAW ONE.
OH !
BUT SEKI SEES IT! A SPINNING TOP ...
SEKI'S POWERS OF CONCEN-TRATION MADE ME SEE THE ILLUSION ?!

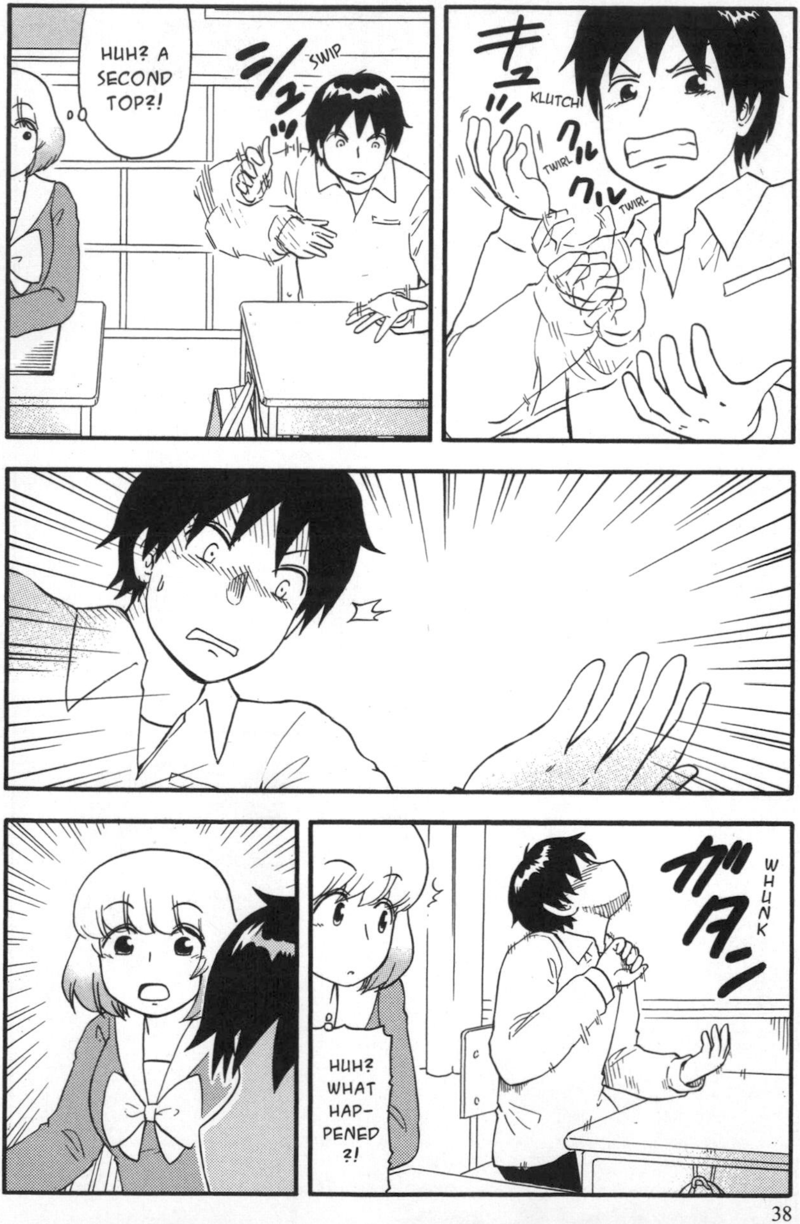

キュッ
KLUTCH
クルクル
TWIRL
TWIRL
シュッ
SWIP
HUH? A SECOND TOP?!
ガタン
WHUNK
HUH? WHAT HAP-PENED ?!

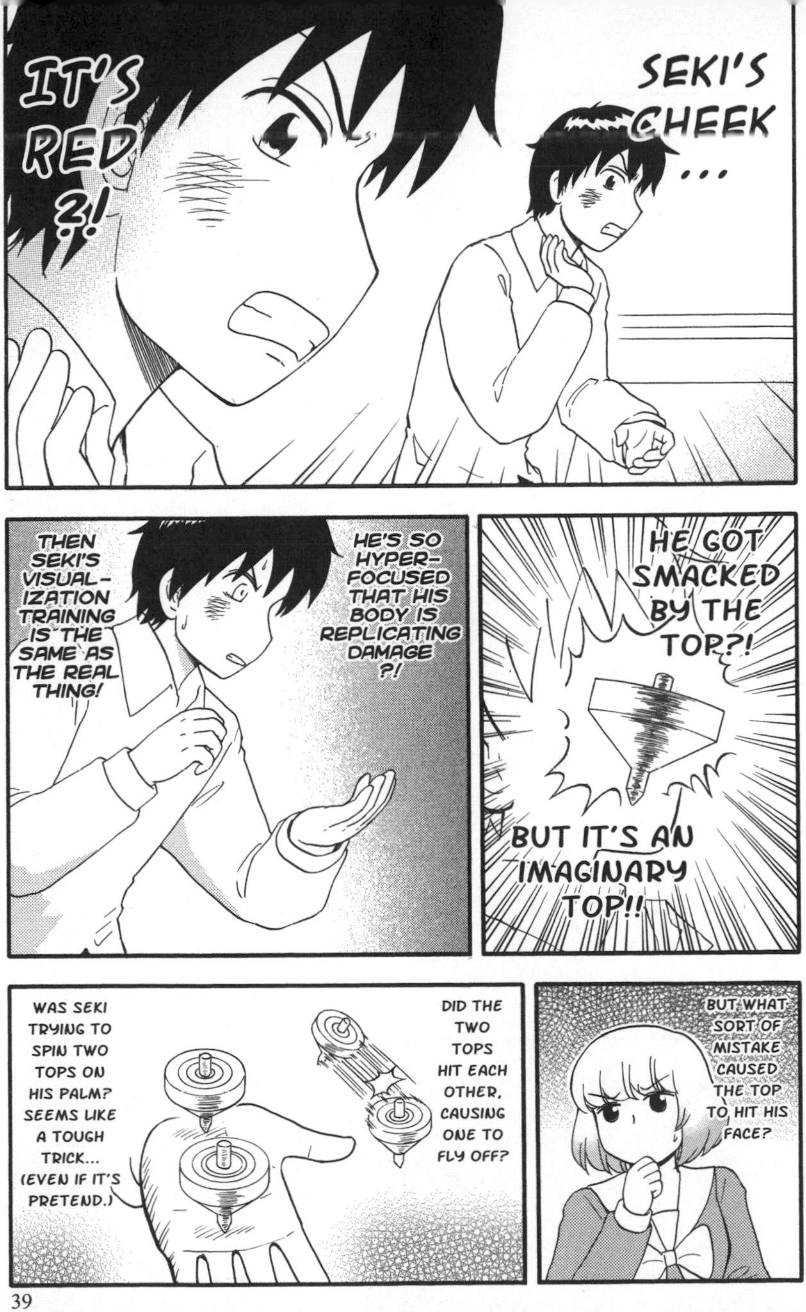
SEKI'S CHEEK...
IT'S RED?!
HE GOT SMACKED BY THE TOP?!
BUT IT'S AN IMAGINARY TOP!!
HE'S SO HYPER-FOCUSED THAT HIS BODY IS REPLICATING DAMAGE?!
THEN SEKI'S VISUAL-IZATION TRAINING IS THE SAME AS THE REAL THING!
BUT WHAT SORT OF MISTAKE CAUSED THE TOP TO HIT HIS FACE?
DID THE TWO TOPS HIT EACH OTHER, CAUSING ONE TO FLY OFF?
WAS SEKI TRYING TO SPIN TWO TOPS ON HIS PALM? SEEMS LIKE A TOUGH TRICK... (EVEN IF IT'S PRETEND.)

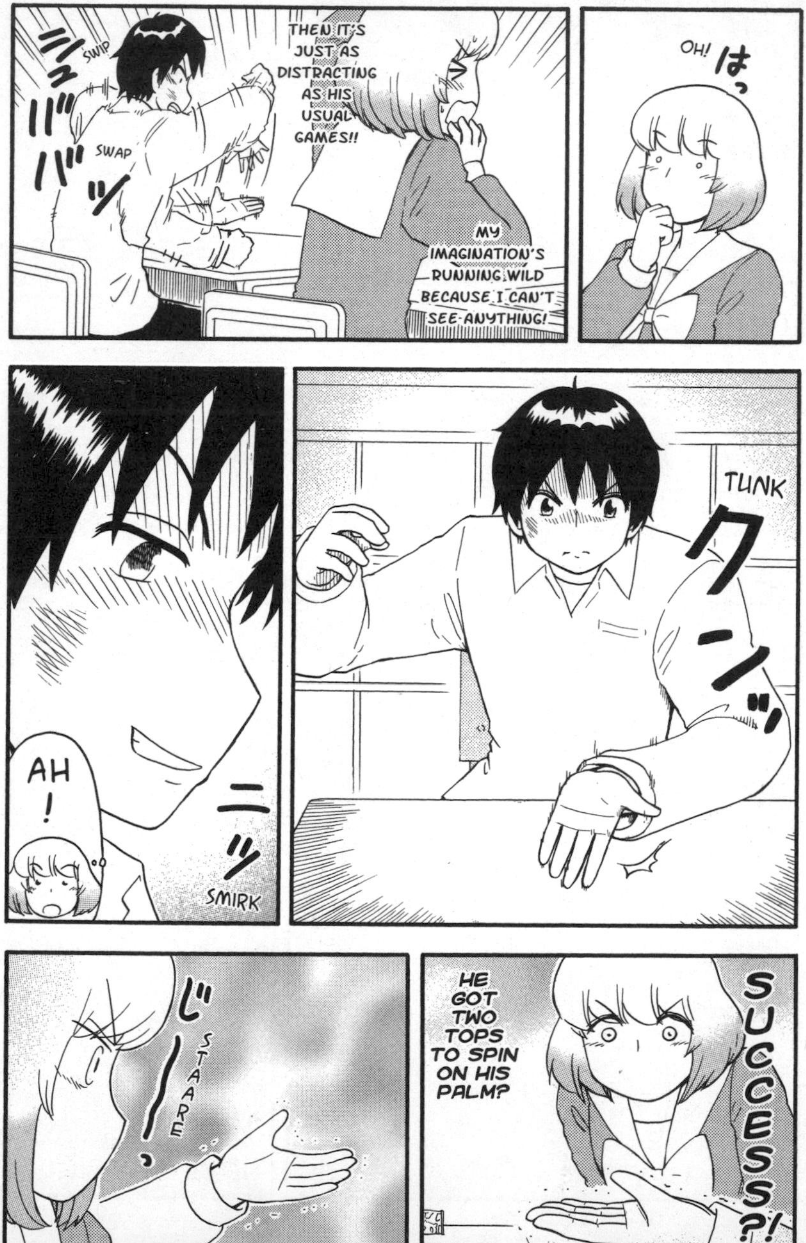

OH!
はっ
SWIP
SWAP
シュババッ
THEN IT'S JUST AS DISTRACTING AS HIS USUAL GAMES!!
MY IMAGINATION'S RUNNING WILD BECAUSE I CAN'T SEE ANYTHING!
TUNK
クンッ
ニッ
SMIRK
AH!
HE GOT TWO TOPS TO SPIN ON HIS PALM?
SUCCESS?!
じーー
STAARE

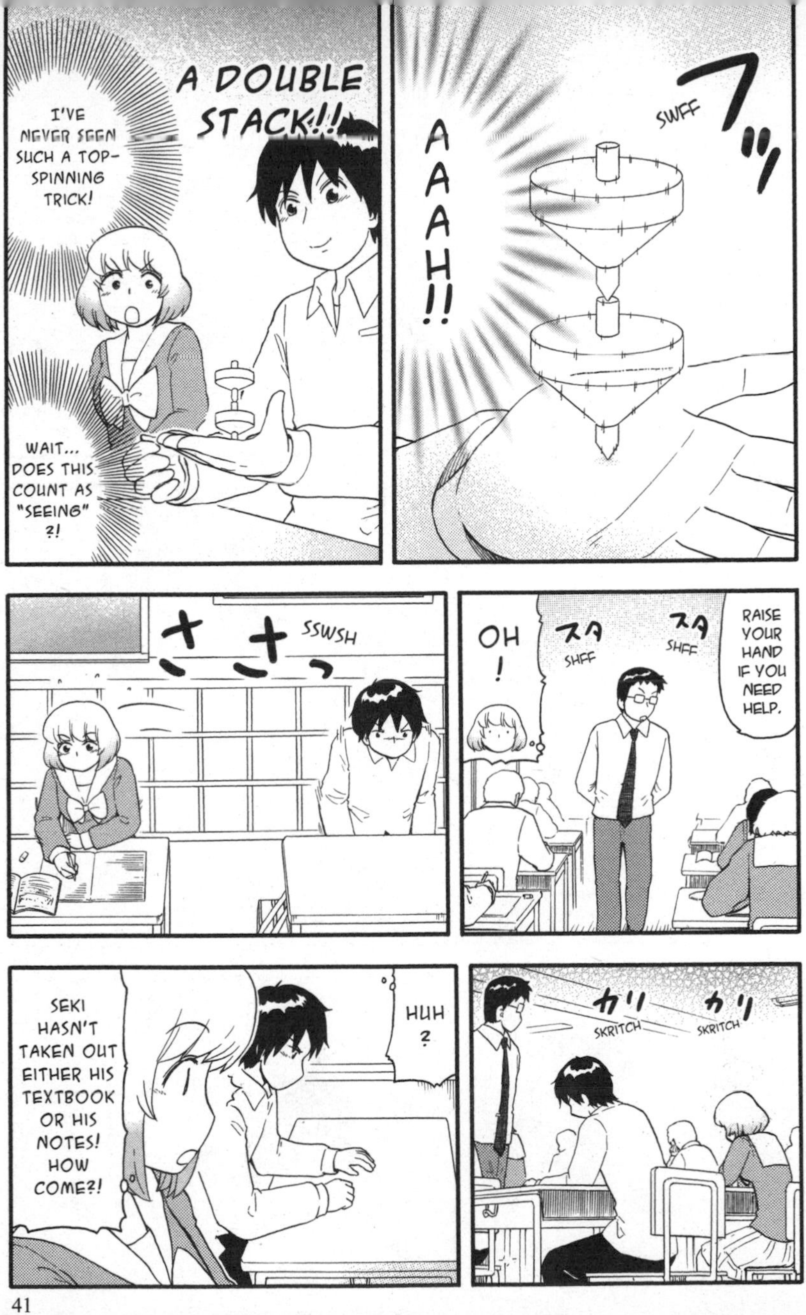

フッ
SWFF
AAAAH!!
A DOUBLE STACK!!
I'VE NEVER SEEN SUCH A TOP-SPINNING TRICK!
WAIT... DOES THIS COUNT AS "SEEING"?!
RAISE YOUR HAND IF YOU NEED HELP.
スタ
SHFF
スタ
SHFF
OH!
ささっ
SSWSH
カリ
SKRITCH
カリ
SKRITCH
HUH?
SEKI HASN'T TAKEN OUT EITHER HIS TEXTBOOK OR HIS NOTES! HOW COME?!

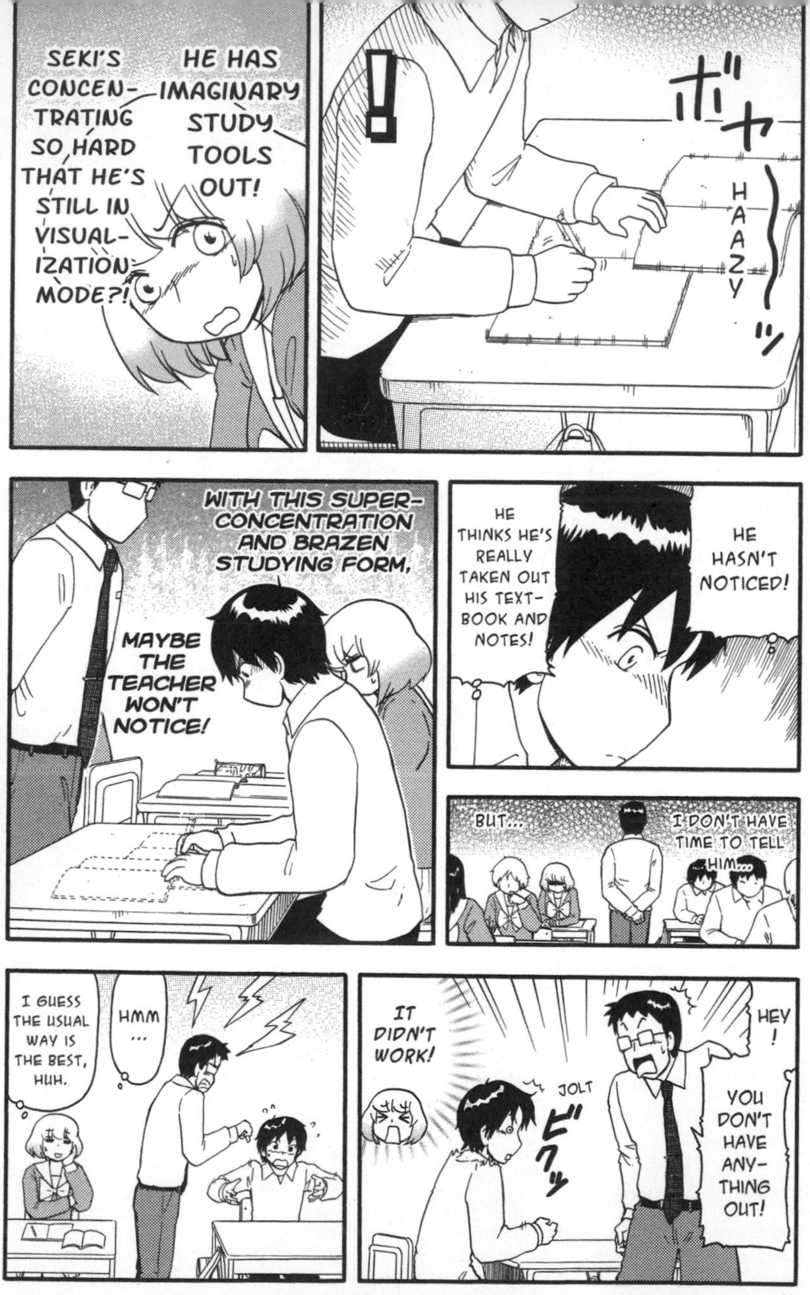
HAAZY
HE HAS IMAGINARY STUDY TOOLS OUT!
SEKI'S CONCEN-TRATING SO HARD THAT HE'S STILL IN VISUAL-IZATION MODE?!
HE HASN'T NOTICED!
HE THINKS HE'S REALLY TAKEN OUT HIS TEXT-BOOK AND NOTES!
I DON'T HAVE TIME TO TELL HIM...
BUT...
WITH THIS SUPER-CONCENTRATION AND BRAZEN STUDYING FORM,
MAYBE THE TEACHER WON'T NOTICE!
HEY!
YOU DON'T HAVE ANY-THING OUT!
JOLT
IT DIDN'T WORK!
HMM ...
I GUESS THE USUAL WAY IS THE BEST, HUH.

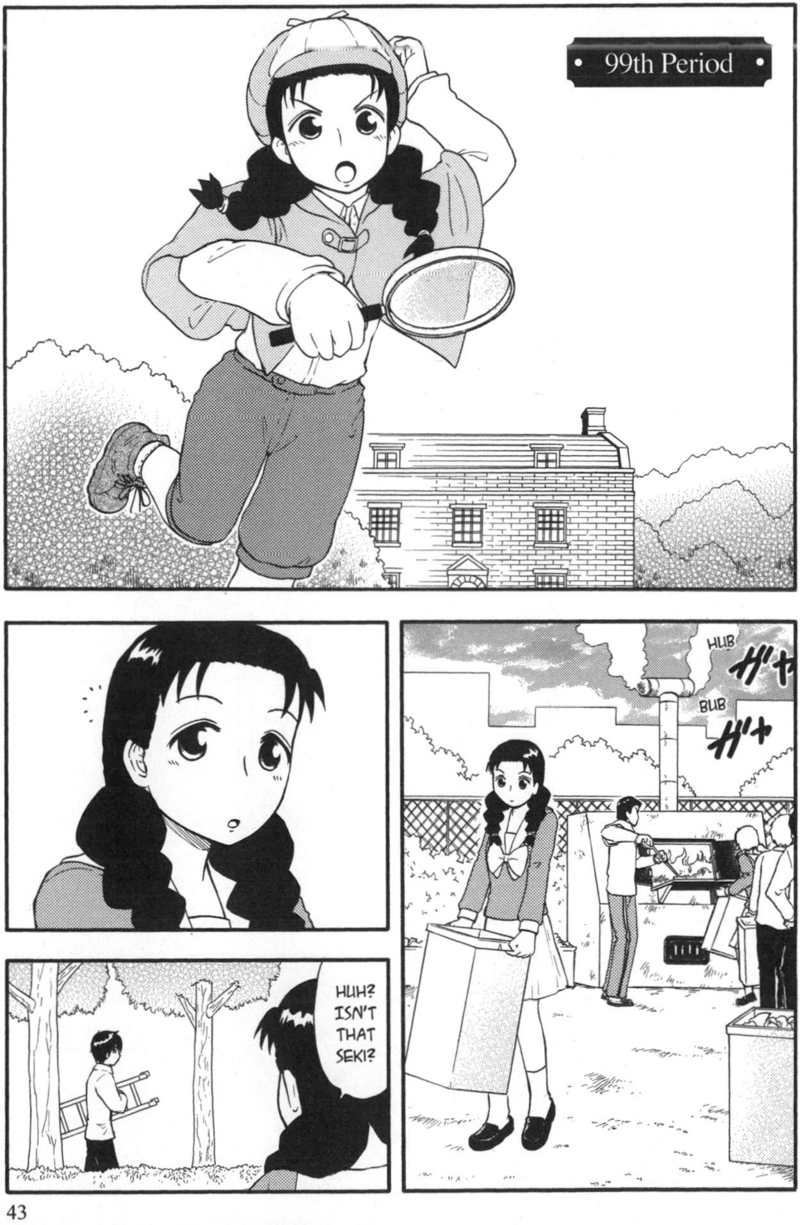
99th Period
HUB
ガヤ
BUB
ガヤ
HUH? ISN'T THAT SEKI?

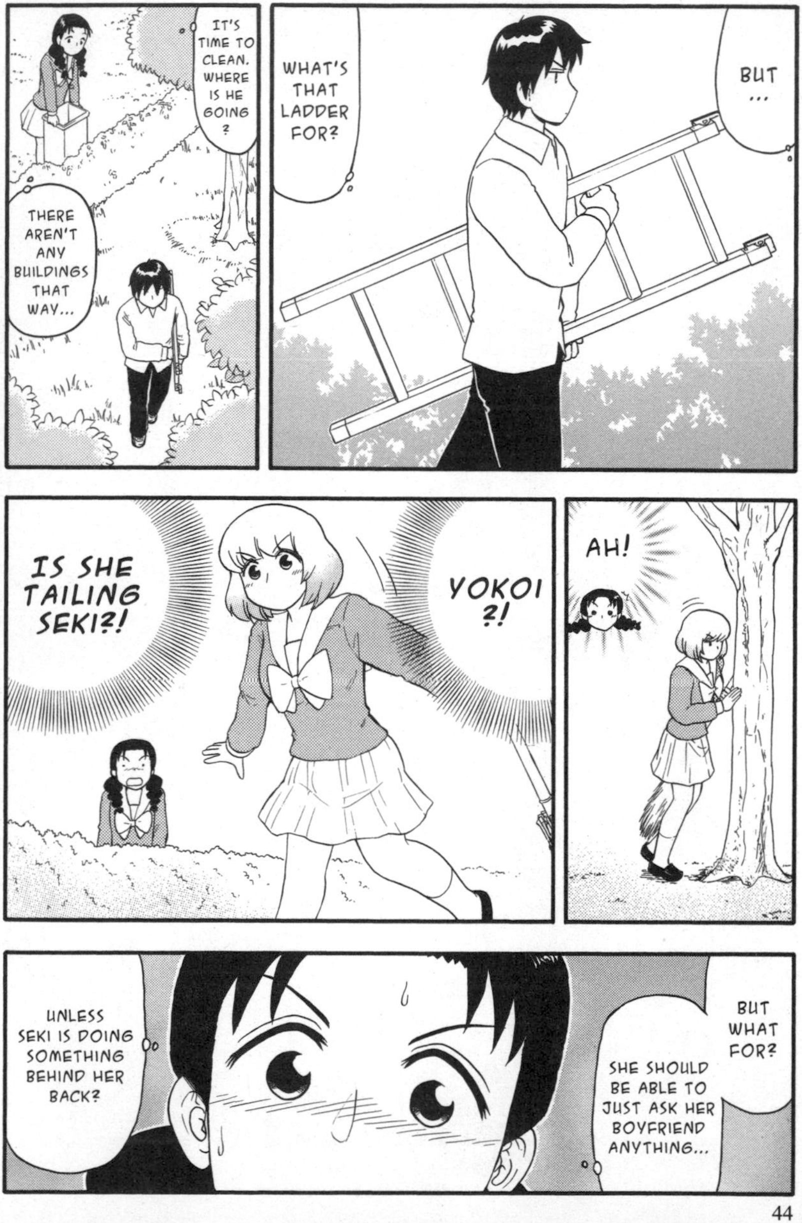
BUT ...
WHAT'S THAT LADDER FOR?
IT'S TIME TO CLEAN. WHERE IS HE GOING?
THERE AREN'T ANY BUILDINGS THAT WAY...
AH!
YOKOI?!
IS SHE TAILING SEKI?!
BUT WHAT FOR?
SHE SHOULD BE ABLE TO JUST ASK HER BOYFRIEND ANYTHING...
UNLESS SEKI IS DOING SOMETHING BEHIND HER BACK?

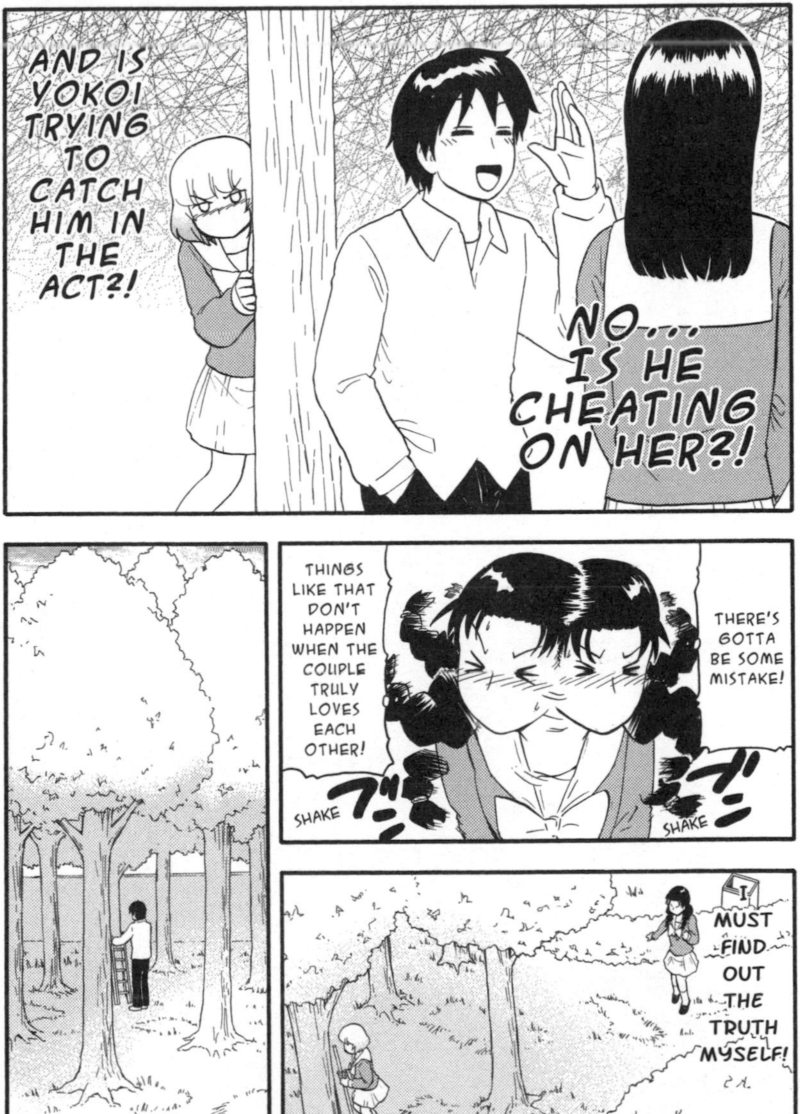
AND IS YOKOI TRYING TO CATCH HIM IN THE ACT?!
NO... IS HE CHEATING ON HER?!
THERE'S GOTTA BE SOME MISTAKE!
THINGS LIKE THAT DON'T HAPPEN WHEN THE COUPLE TRULY LOVES EACH OTHER!
SHAKE
SHAKE
I MUST FIND OUT THE TRUTH MYSELF!

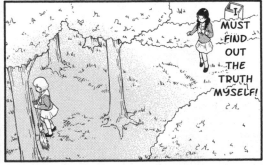

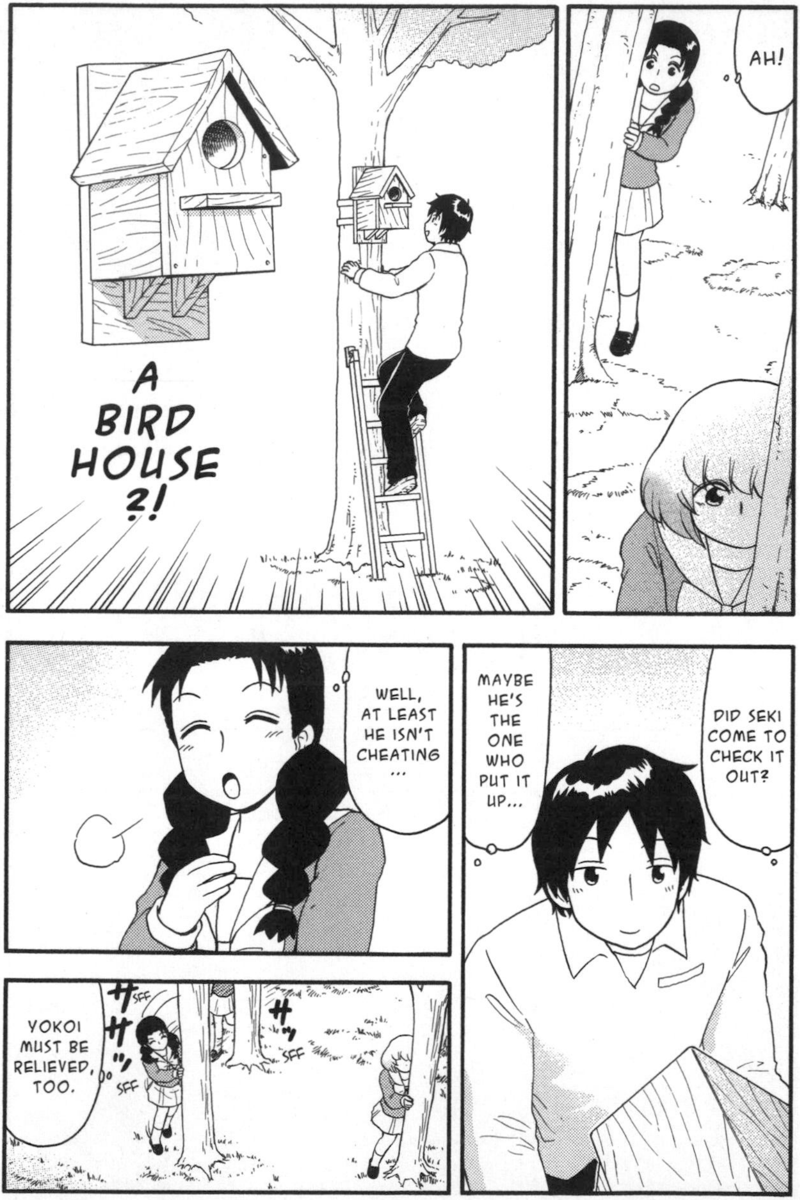
AH!
A BIRD HOUSE ?!
DID SEKI COME TO CHECK IT OUT?
MAYBE HE'S THE ONE WHO PUT IT UP...
WELL, AT LEAST HE ISN'T CHEATING ...
SFF
SFF
YOKOI MUST BE RELIEVED, TOO.
SFF

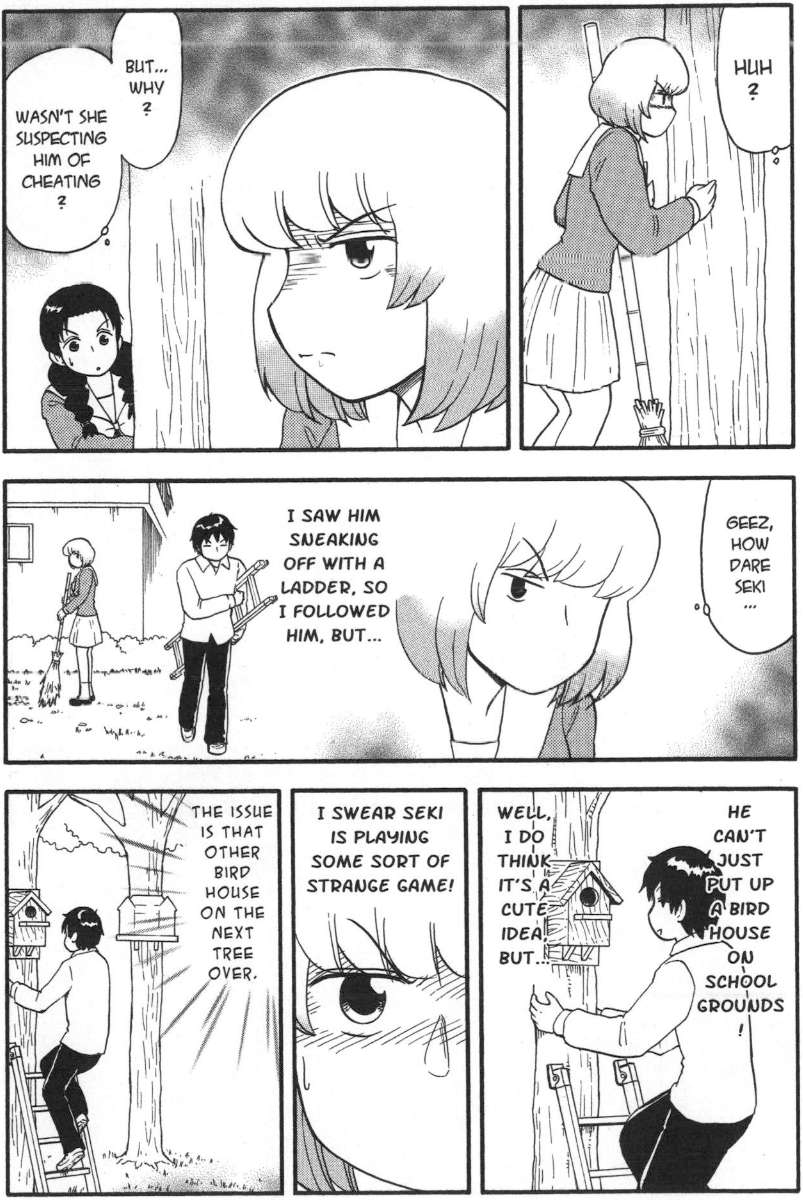
HUH?
BUT... WHY?
WASN'T SHE SUSPECTING HIM OF CHEATING?
GEEZ, HOW DARE SEKI...
I SAW HIM SNEAKING OFF WITH A LADDER, SO I FOLLOWED HIM, BUT...
WELL, I DO THINK IT'S A CUTE IDEA, BUT...
HE CAN'T JUST PUT UP A BIRD HOUSE ON SCHOOL GROUNDS!
I SWEAR SEKI IS PLAYING SOME SORT OF STRANGE GAME!
THE ISSUE IS THAT OTHER BIRD HOUSE ON THE NEXT TREE OVER.

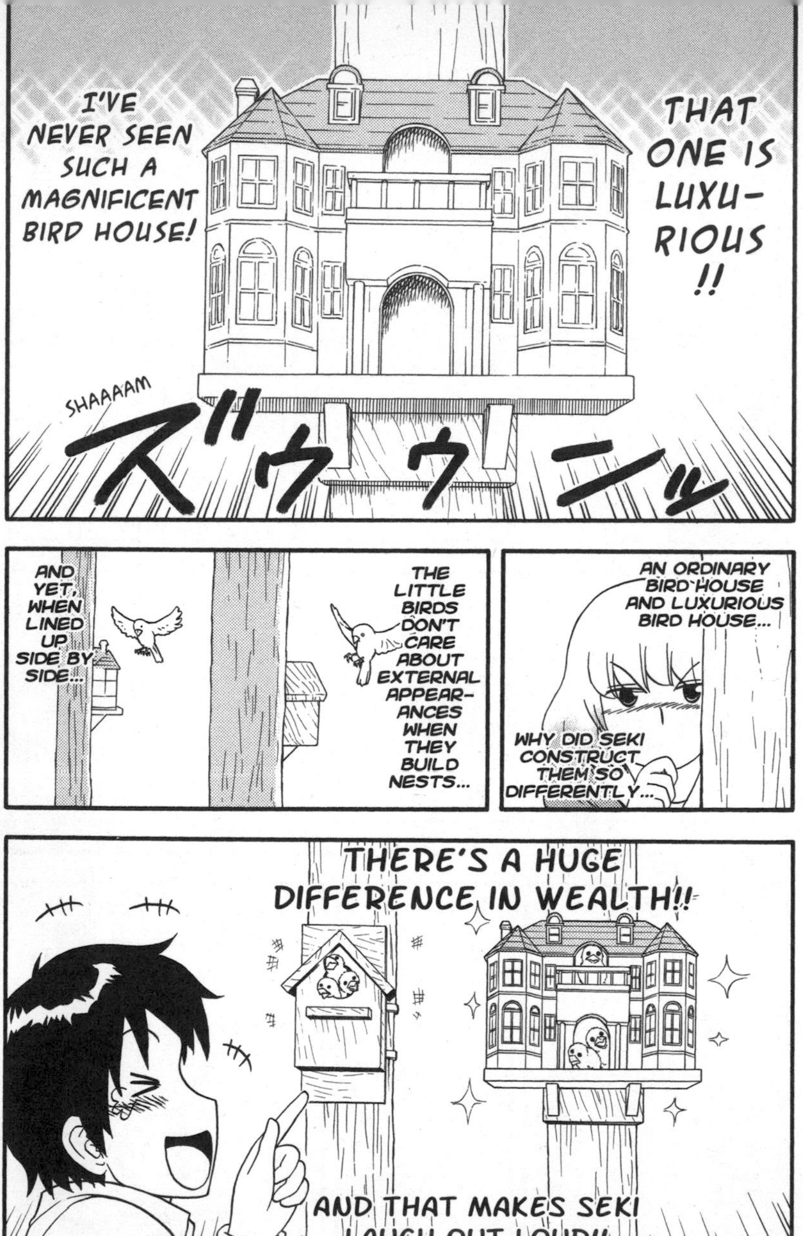
THAT ONE IS LUXURIOUS!!
I'VE NEVER SEEN SUCH A MAGNIFICENT BIRD HOUSE!
SHAAAAM
ズウウーンッ
AN ORDINARY BIRD HOUSE AND LUXURIOUS BIRD HOUSE...
WHY DID SEKI CONSTRUCT THEM SO DIFFERENTLY...
THE LITTLE BIRDS DON'T CARE ABOUT EXTERNAL APPEARANCES WHEN THEY BUILD NESTS...
AND YET, WHEN LINED UP SIDE BY SIDE...
THERE'S A HUGE DIFFERENCE IN WEALTH!!
AND THAT MAKES SEKI LAUGH OUT LOUD!!

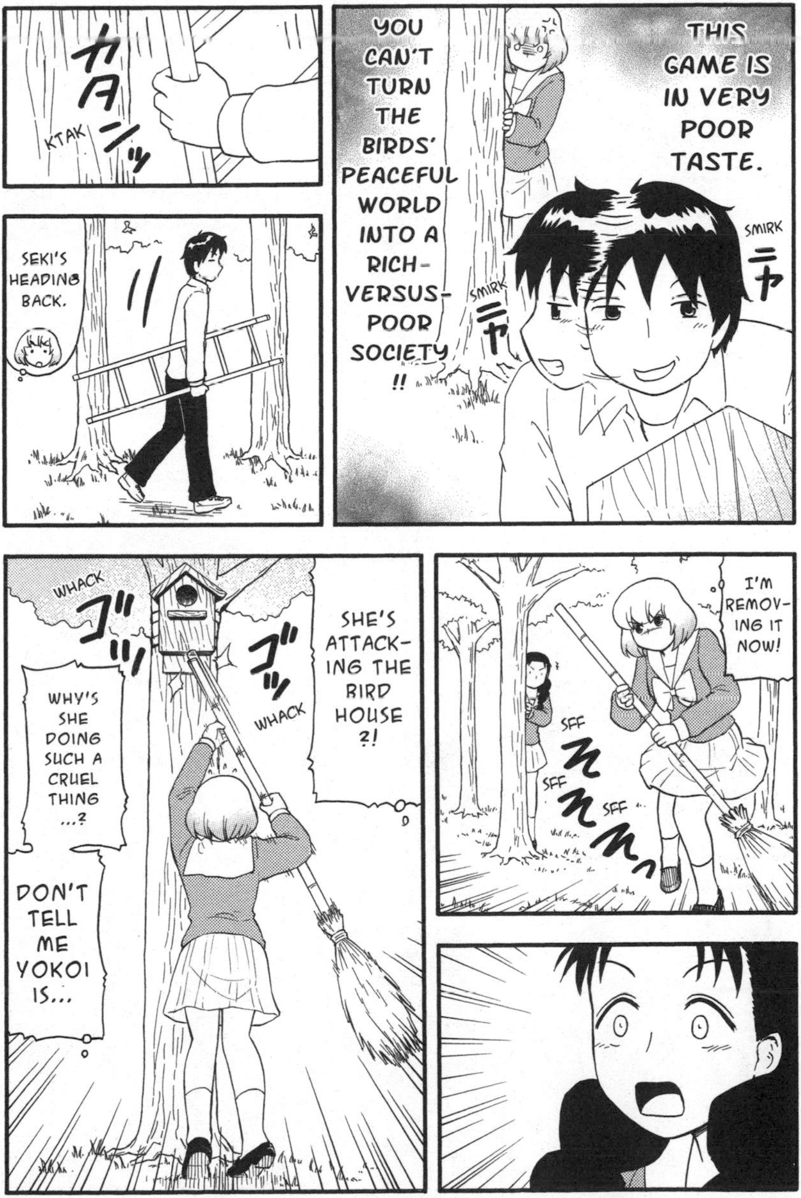
THIS GAME IS IN VERY POOR TASTE.
YOU CAN'T TURN THE BIRDS' PEACEFUL WORLD INTO A RICH-VERSUS-POOR SOCIETY!!
SMIRK
ニヤ
SMIRK
ニヤ
カタンッ
KTAK
SEKI'S HEADING BACK.
I'M REMOVING IT NOW!
SFF
SFF
SFF
WHACK
ゴッ
ゴッ
WHACK
SHE'S ATTACKING THE BIRD HOUSE?!
WHY'S SHE DOING SUCH A CRUEL THING...?
DON'T TELL ME YOKOI IS...

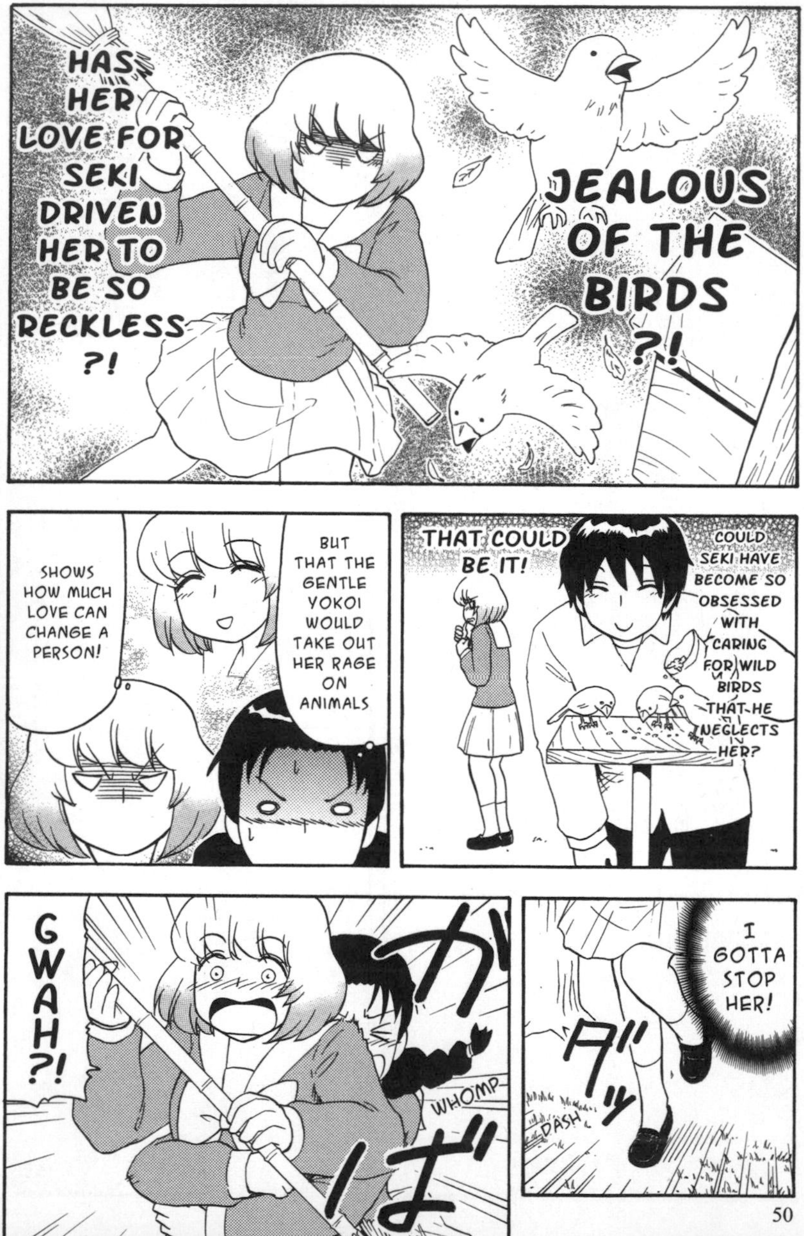
JEALOUS OF THE BIRDS ?!
HAS HER LOVE FOR SEKI DRIVEN HER TO BE SO RECKLESS ?!
COULD SEKI HAVE BECOME SO OBSESSED WITH CARING FOR WILD BIRDS THAT HE NEGLECTS HER?
THAT COULD BE IT!
BUT THAT THE GENTLE YOKOI WOULD TAKE OUT HER RAGE ON ANIMALS
SHOWS HOW MUCH LOVE CAN CHANGE A PERSON!
I GOTTA STOP HER!
DASH
GWAH?!
WHOMP

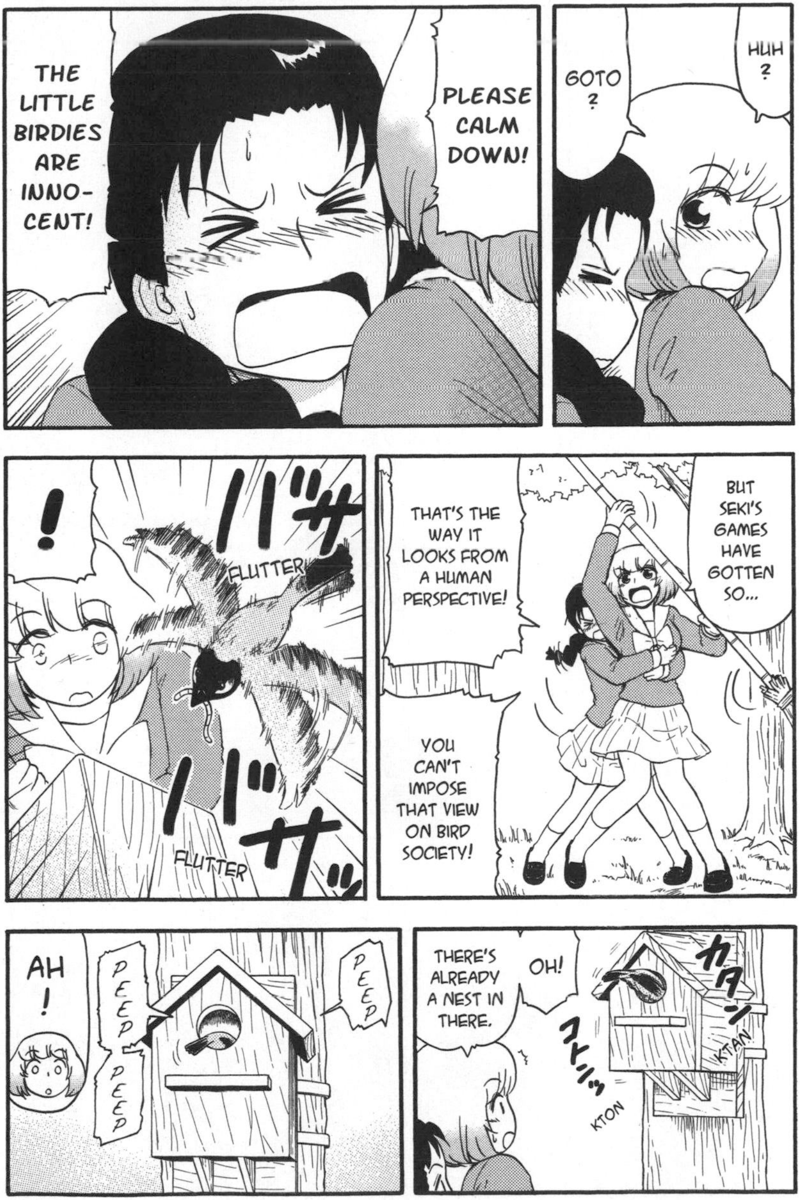
HUH?
GOTO?
PLEASE CALM DOWN!
THE LITTLE BIRDIES ARE INNO-CENT!
BUT SEKI'S GAMES HAVE GOTTEN SO...
THAT'S THE WAY IT LOOKS FROM A HUMAN PERSPECTIVE!
YOU CAN'T IMPOSE THAT VIEW ON BIRD SOCIETY!
!
FLUTTER
FLUTTER
OH!
THERE'S ALREADY A NEST IN THERE.
KTAN
KTON
PEEP
PEEP
PEEP
PEEP
AH!

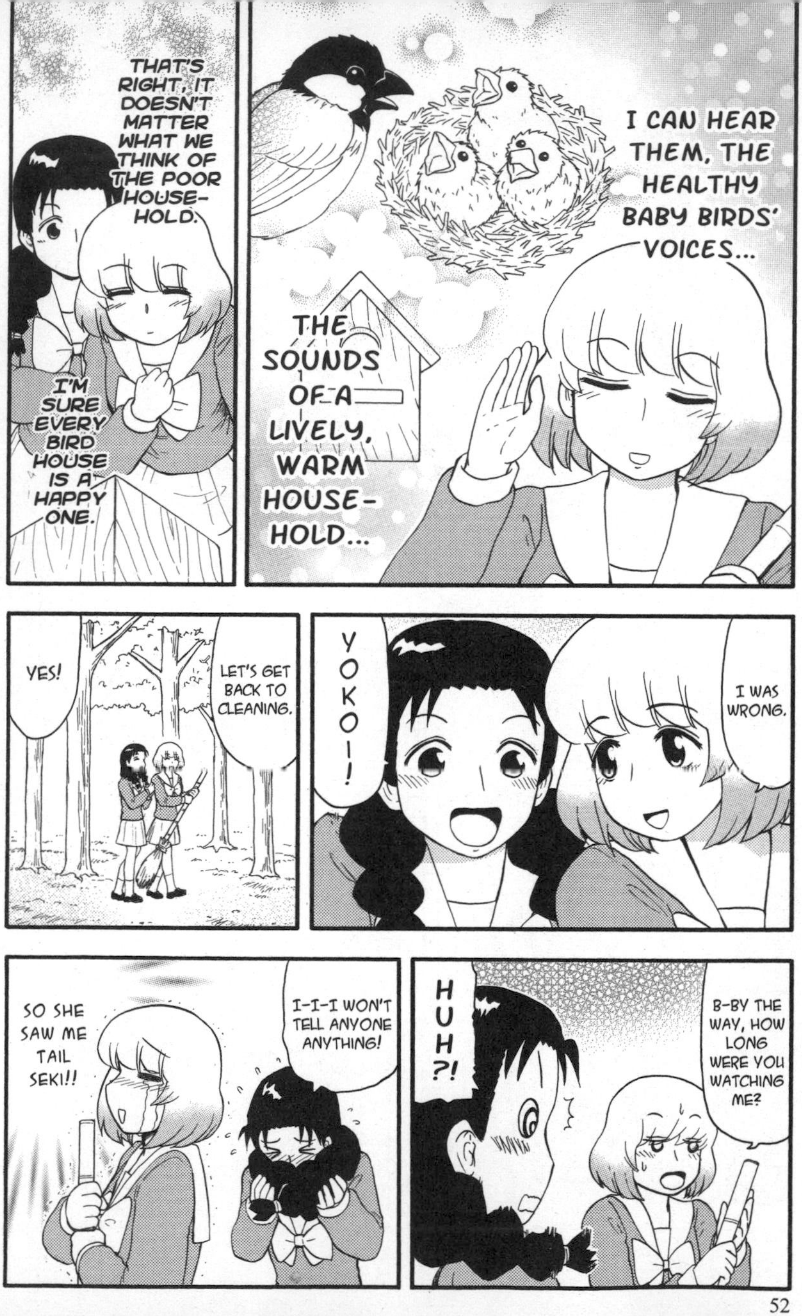
I CAN HEAR THEM, THE HEALTHY BABY BIRDS' VOICES...
THE SOUNDS OF A LIVELY, WARM HOUSE-HOLD...
THAT'S RIGHT, IT DOESN'T MATTER WHAT WE THINK OF THE POOR HOUSE-HOLD.
I'M SURE EVERY BIRD HOUSE IS A HAPPY ONE.
I WAS WRONG.
YOKO!!
LET'S GET BACK TO CLEANING.
YES!
B-BY THE WAY, HOW LONG WERE YOU WATCHING ME?
HUH?!
I-I-I WON'T TELL ANYONE ANYTHING!
SO SHE SAW ME TAIL SEKI!!

My Neighbor Seki

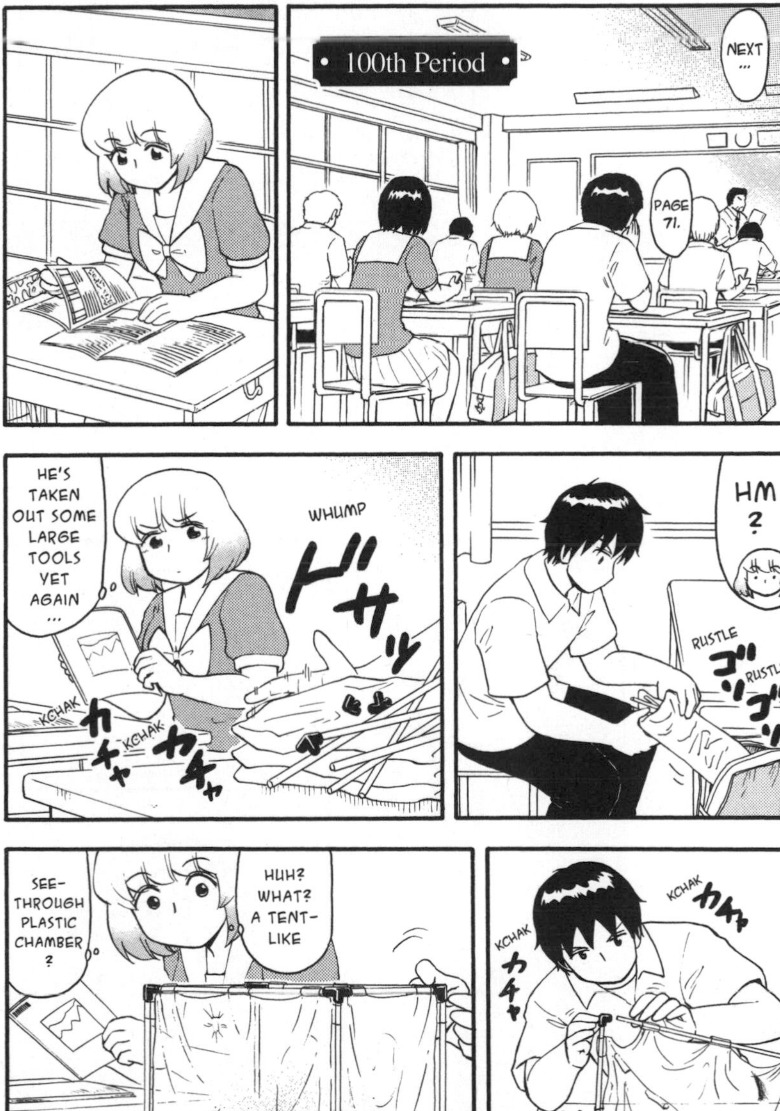

100th Period
NEXT ...
PAGE 71.
HM ?
RUSTLE RUSTLE
HE'S TAKEN OUT SOME LARGE TOOLS YET AGAIN ...
WHUMP
KCHAK KCHAK
KCHAK KCHAK
HUH? WHAT? A TENT-LIKE
SEE-THROUGH PLASTIC CHAMBER ?

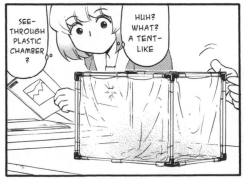

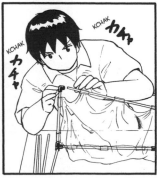

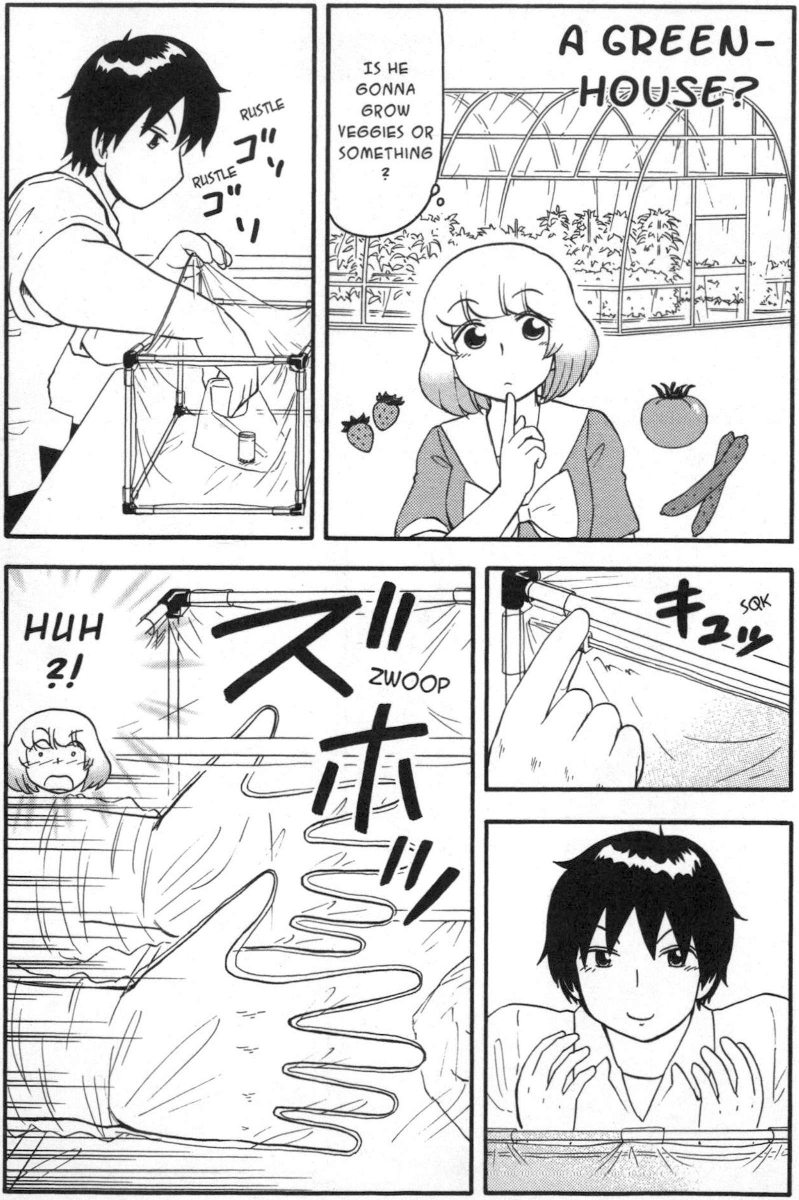
A GREEN-HOUSE?
IS HE GONNA GROW VEGGIES OR SOMETHING?
ゴッ RUSTLE
ゴッ RUSTLE
キュッ SQK
HUH?!
スポッ ZWOOP

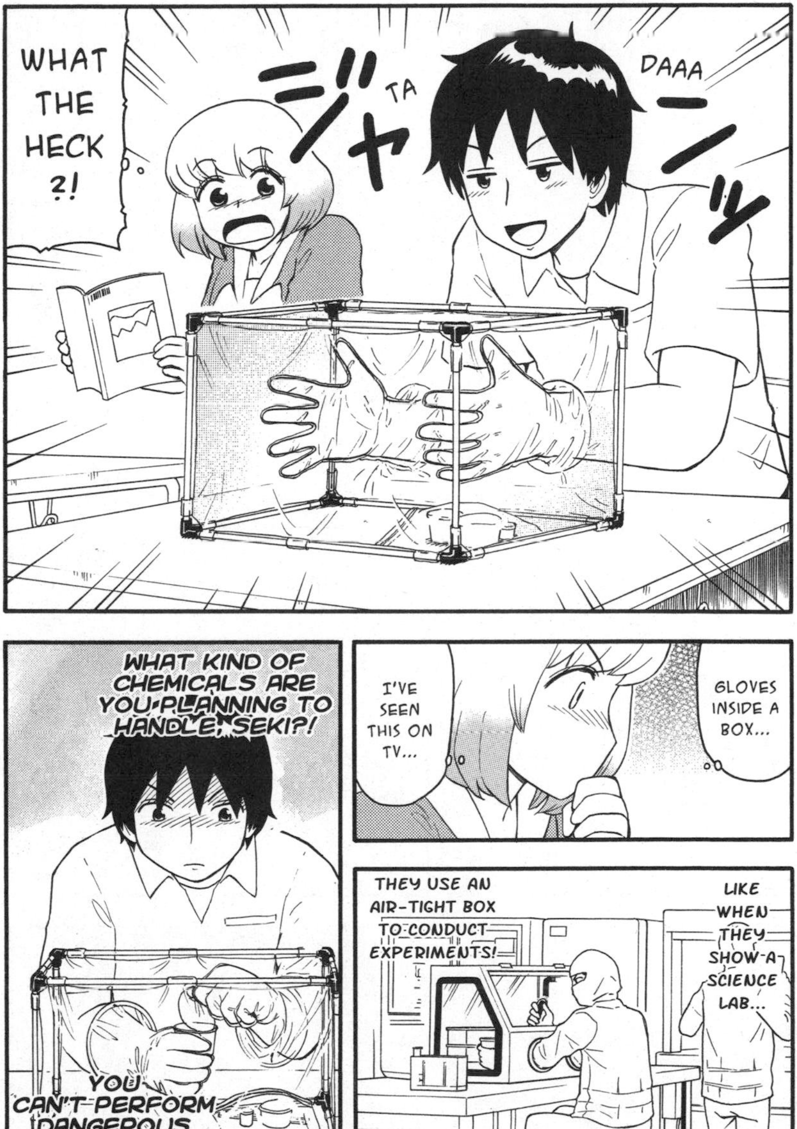

ジャーンッ
TA
DAAA
WHAT THE HECK ?!
GLOVES INSIDE A BOX...
I'VE SEEN THIS ON TV...
LIKE WHEN THEY SHOW A SCIENCE LAB...
THEY USE AN AIR-TIGHT BOX TO CONDUCT EXPERIMENTS!
WHAT KIND OF CHEMICALS ARE YOU PLANNING TO HANDLE, SEKI?!
YOU CAN'T PERFORM DANGEROUS EXPERIMENTS DURING CLASS!

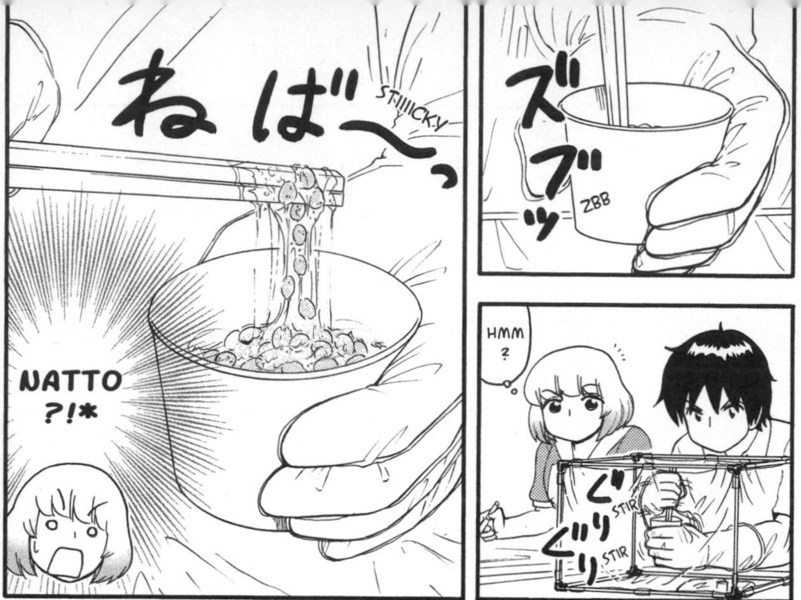
ねばーっ
STIIIICKY
NATTO ?!*
ズブッ
ZBB
HMM ?
ぐりぐり
STIR STIR

*PUNGENT FERMENTED SOYBEANS THAT TURN STICKY WHEN STIRRED.

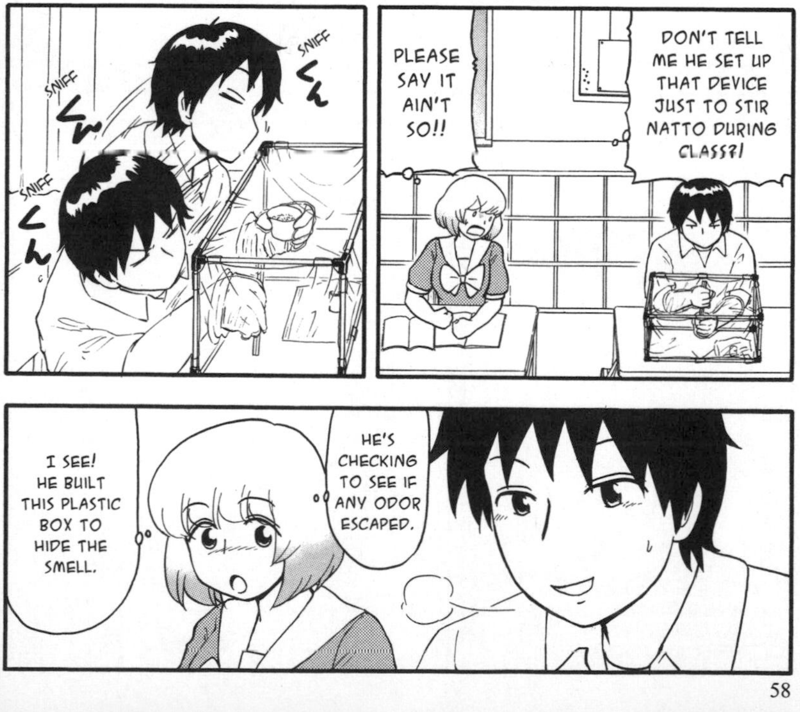
SNIFF
くん
SNIFF
くん
SNIFF
くん
PLEASE SAY IT AIN'T SO!!
DON'T TELL ME HE SET UP THAT DEVICE JUST TO STIR NATTO DURING CLASS?!
I SEE! HE BUILT THIS PLASTIC BOX TO HIDE THE SMELL.
HE'S CHECKING TO SEE IF ANY ODOR ESCAPED.

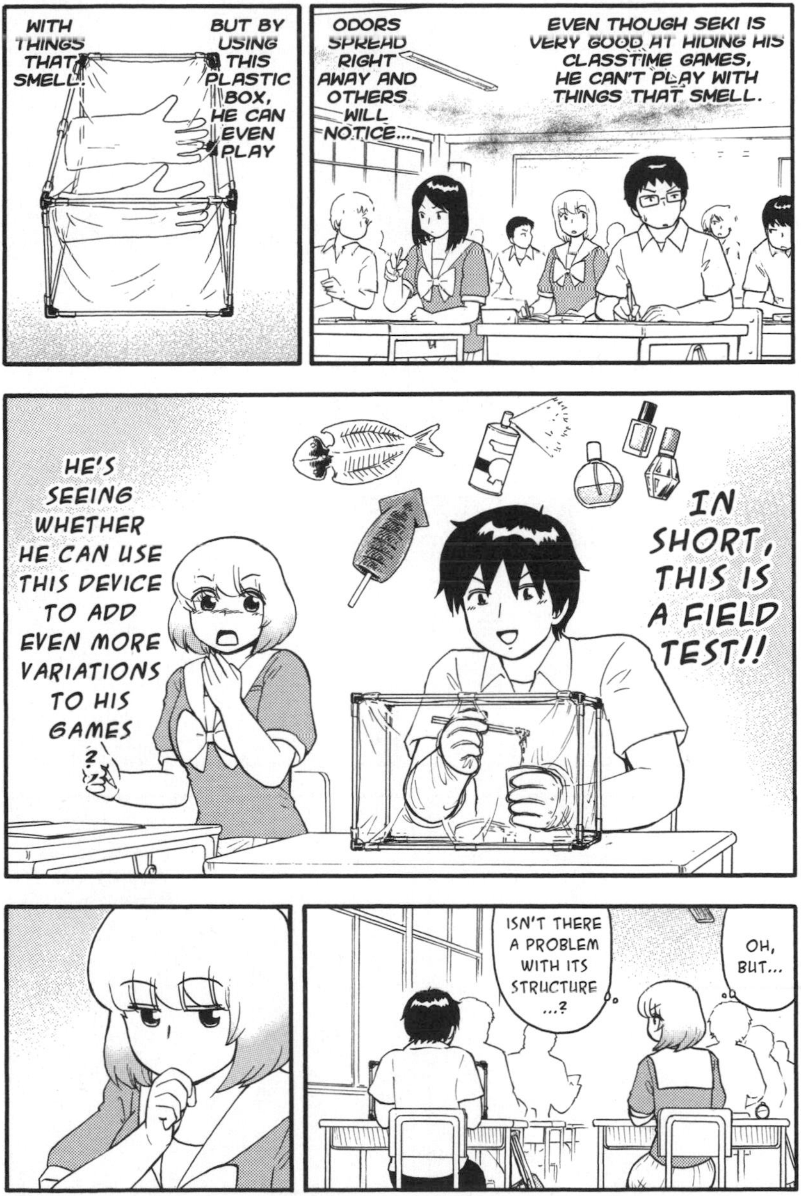
EVEN THOUGH SEKI IS VERY GOOD AT HIDING HIS CLASSTIME GAMES, HE CAN'T PLAY WITH THINGS THAT SMELL.
ODORS SPREAD RIGHT AWAY AND OTHERS WILL NOTICE...
BUT BY USING THIS PLASTIC BOX, HE CAN EVEN PLAY
WITH THINGS THAT SMELL.
IN SHORT, THIS IS A FIELD TEST!!
HE'S SEEING WHETHER HE CAN USE THIS DEVICE TO ADD EVEN MORE VARIATIONS TO HIS GAMES?
OH, BUT...
ISN'T THERE A PROBLEM WITH ITS STRUCTURE ...?

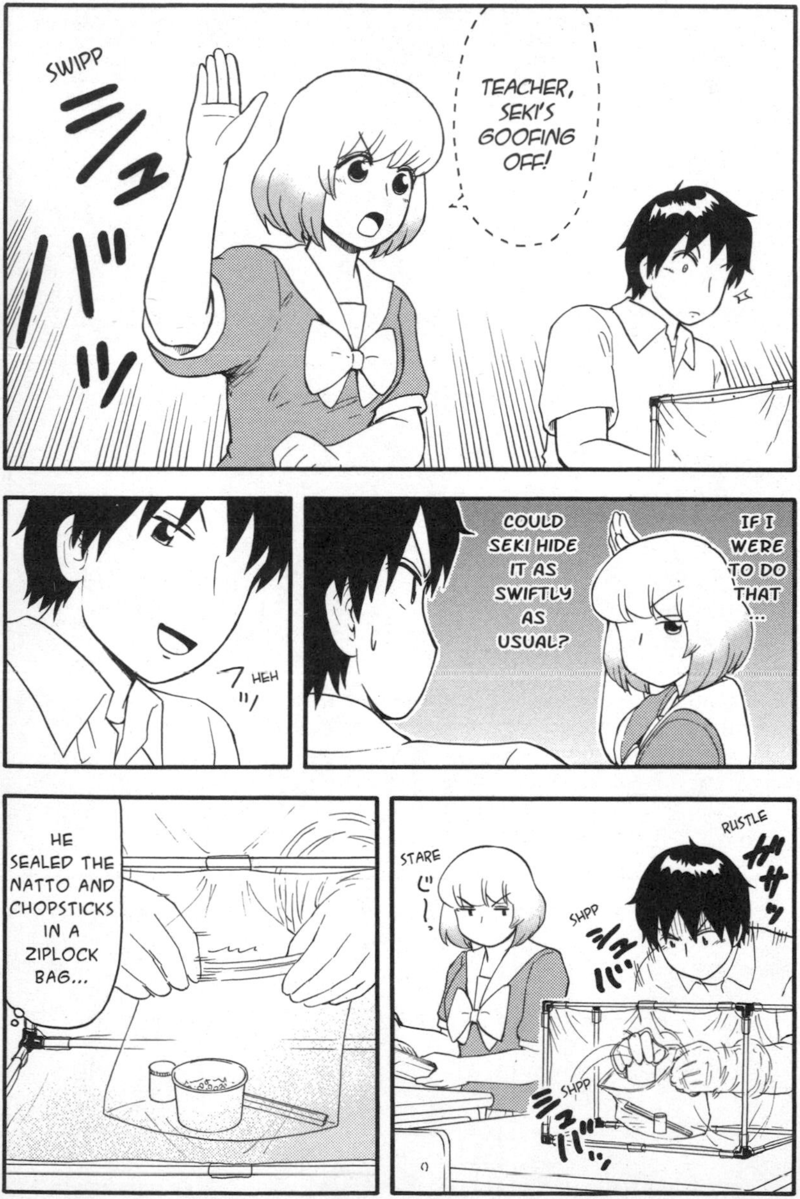
SWIPP
シュバッ
TEACHER, SEKI'S GOOFING OFF!
IF I WERE TO DO THAT...
COULD SEKI HIDE IT AS SWIFTLY AS USUAL?
HEH
フッ
RUSTLE
ガサッ
STARE
じー
SHPP
シュバ
SHPP
シュバッ
HE SEALED THE NATTO AND CHOPSTICKS IN A ZIPLOCK BAG...

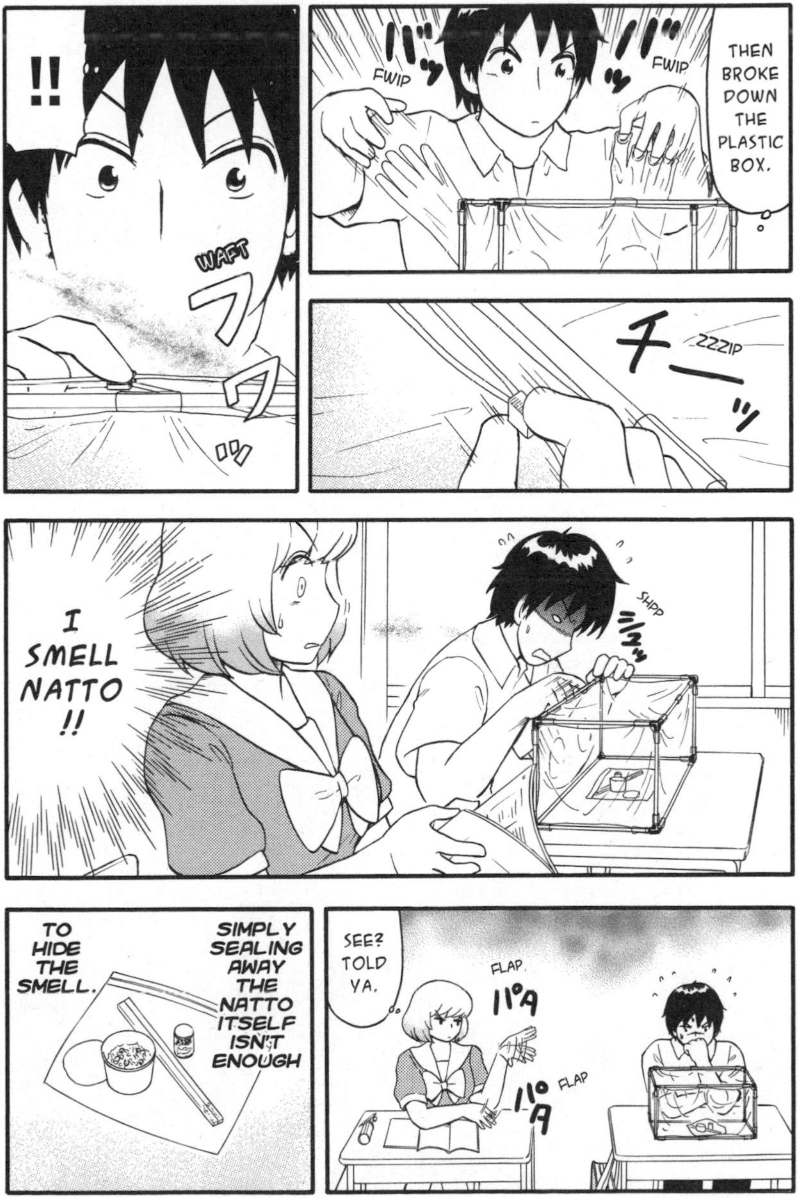
FWIP
FWIP
THEN BROKE DOWN THE PLASTIC BOX.
ZZZIP
!!
WAFT
SHPP
I SMELL NATTO !!
SEE? TOLD YA.
FLAP
FLAP
SIMPLY SEALING AWAY THE NATTO ITSELF ISN'T ENOUGH
TO HIDE THE SMELL.

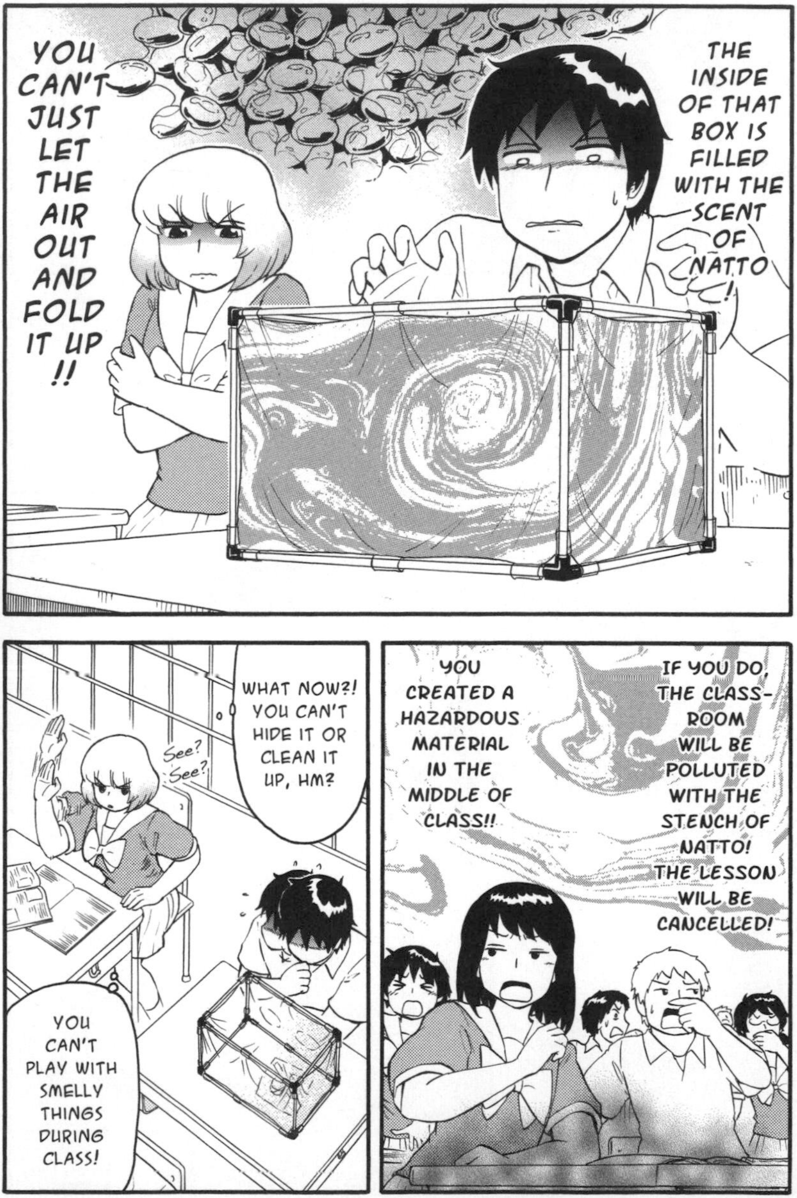
THE INSIDE OF THAT BOX IS FILLED WITH THE SCENT OF NATTO!
YOU CAN'T JUST LET THE AIR OUT AND FOLD IT UP!!
WHAT NOW?! YOU CAN'T HIDE IT OR CLEAN IT UP, HM?
See? See?
YOU CAN'T PLAY WITH SMELLY THINGS DURING CLASS!
IF YOU DO, THE CLASS-ROOM WILL BE POLLUTED WITH THE STENCH OF NATTO! THE LESSON WILL BE CANCELLED!
YOU CREATED A HAZARDOUS MATERIAL IN THE MIDDLE OF CLASS!!

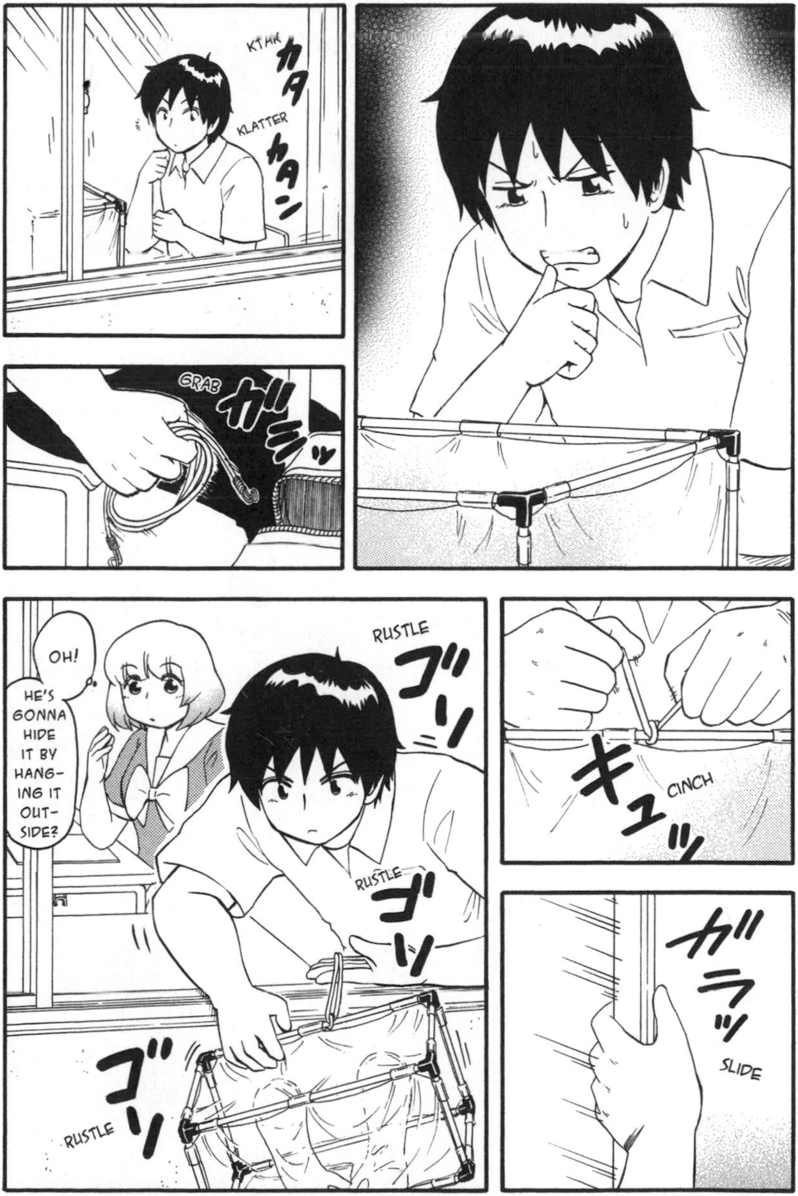
KTAK
カタ
KLATTER
カタン
GRAB
ガシッ
CINCH
キュッ
ガラッ
SLIDE
OH!
HE'S GONNA HIDE IT BY HANG-ING IT OUT-SIDE?
RUSTLE
ゴソ
RUSTLE
ゴソ
ゴソ
RUSTLE

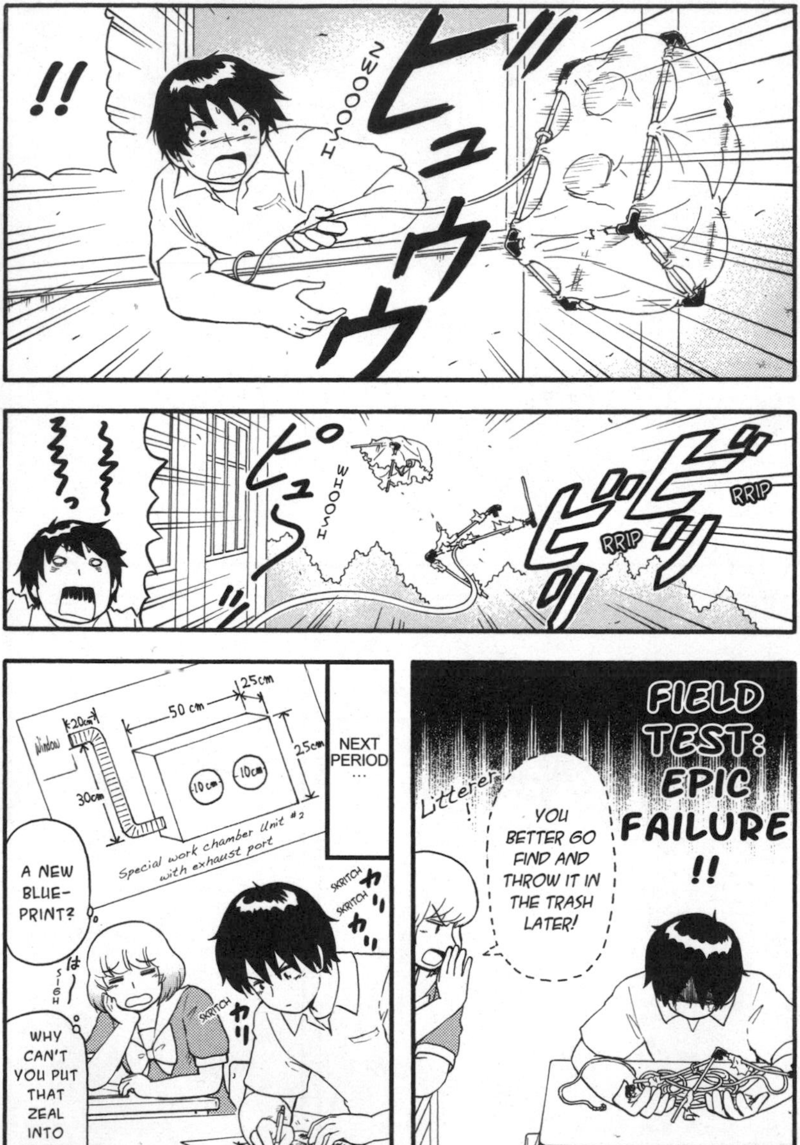
!!
ZWOOOSH
WHOOSH
RRIP
RRIP
FIELD TEST: EPIC FAILURE !!
Litterer!
YOU BETTER GO FIND AND THROW IT IN THE TRASH LATER!
NEXT PERIOD …
50 cm
25cm
25cm
20cm
window
30cm
10cm
10cm
Special work chamber Unit #2 with exhaust port
A NEW BLUE-PRINT?
SKRITCH
SKRITCH
SKRITCH
SIGH
WHY CAN'T YOU PUT THAT ZEAL INTO STUDY-ING?

• 101st Period •

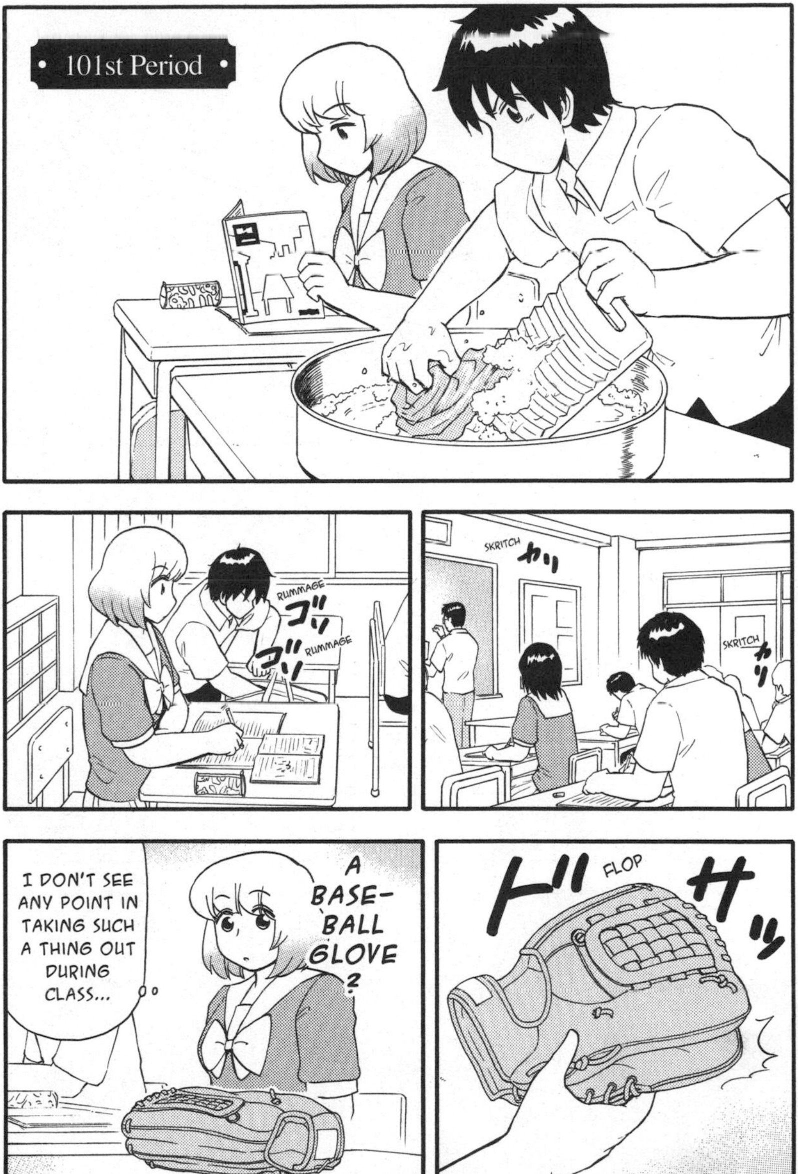

SKRITCH
SKRITCH
RUMMAGE
RUMMAGE
FLOP
A BASE-BALL GLOVE?
I DON'T SEE ANY POINT IN TAKING SUCH A THING OUT DURING CLASS...

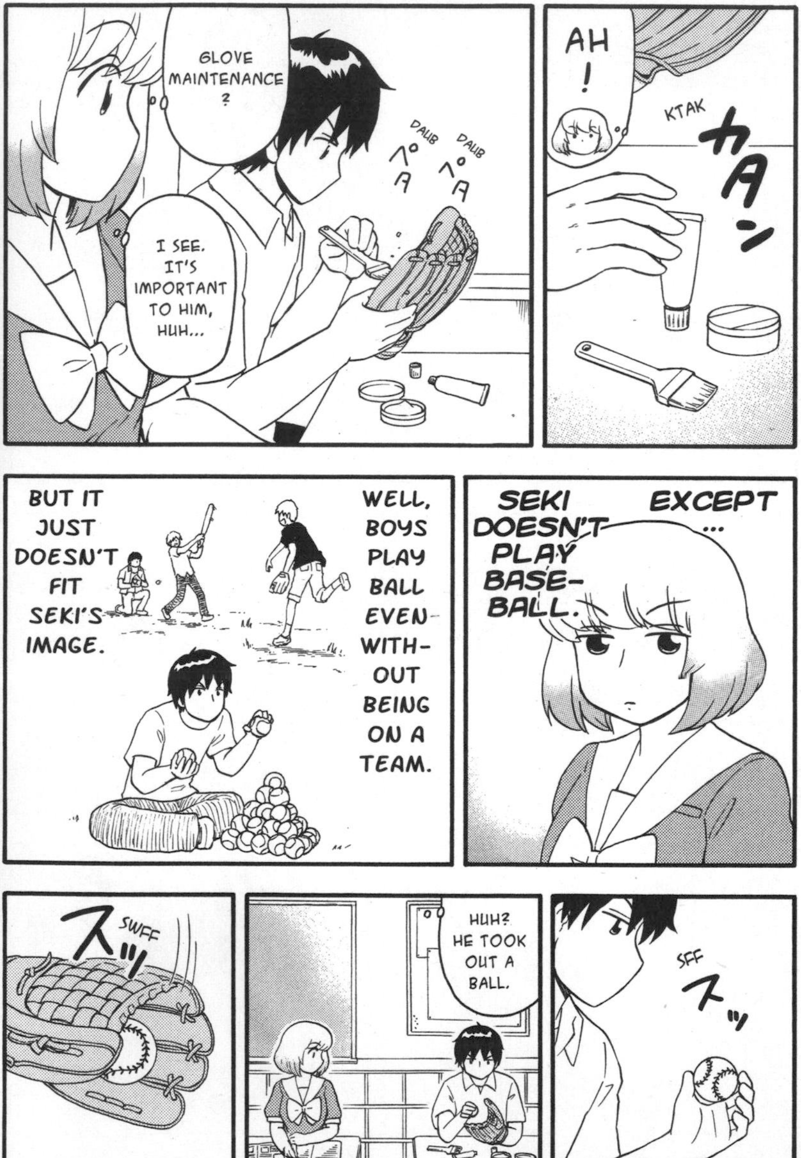
GLOVE MAINTENANCE?
DAUB DAUB
I SEE. IT'S IMPORTANT TO HIM, HUH...
AH!
KTAK
WELL, BOYS PLAY BALL EVEN WITHOUT BEING ON A TEAM.
BUT IT JUST DOESN'T FIT SEKI'S IMAGE.
EXCEPT...
SEKI DOESN'T PLAY BASEBALL.
SWFF
HUH? HE TOOK OUT A BALL.
SFF

DANGLE
DANGLE
OH !
THE BALL IS STICKING TO THE GLOVE!
HOW ?!
OH, I SEE.
SPLICH
SPLICH
SPLICH
HE PUT SOMETHING STICKY ON THE INNER SURFACE OF THE GLOVE.
AH. SOME-TIMES A PLAYER WILL DROP A BALL DURING A GAME, BUT...
TH
PP
YOU WOULDN'T HAVE TO WORRY ABOUT THAT WITH A STICKY GLOVE!! HANDY!
BUT ISN'T THAT...
KIND OF CHEATING ...?

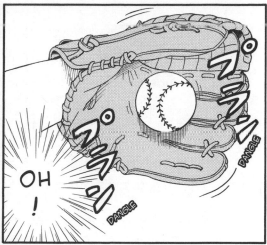

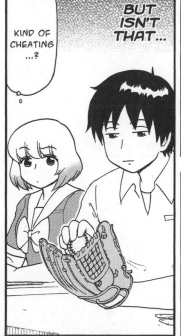

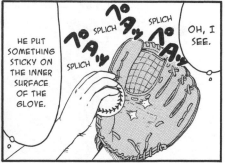

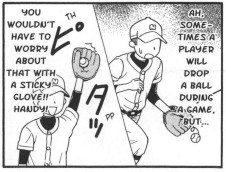

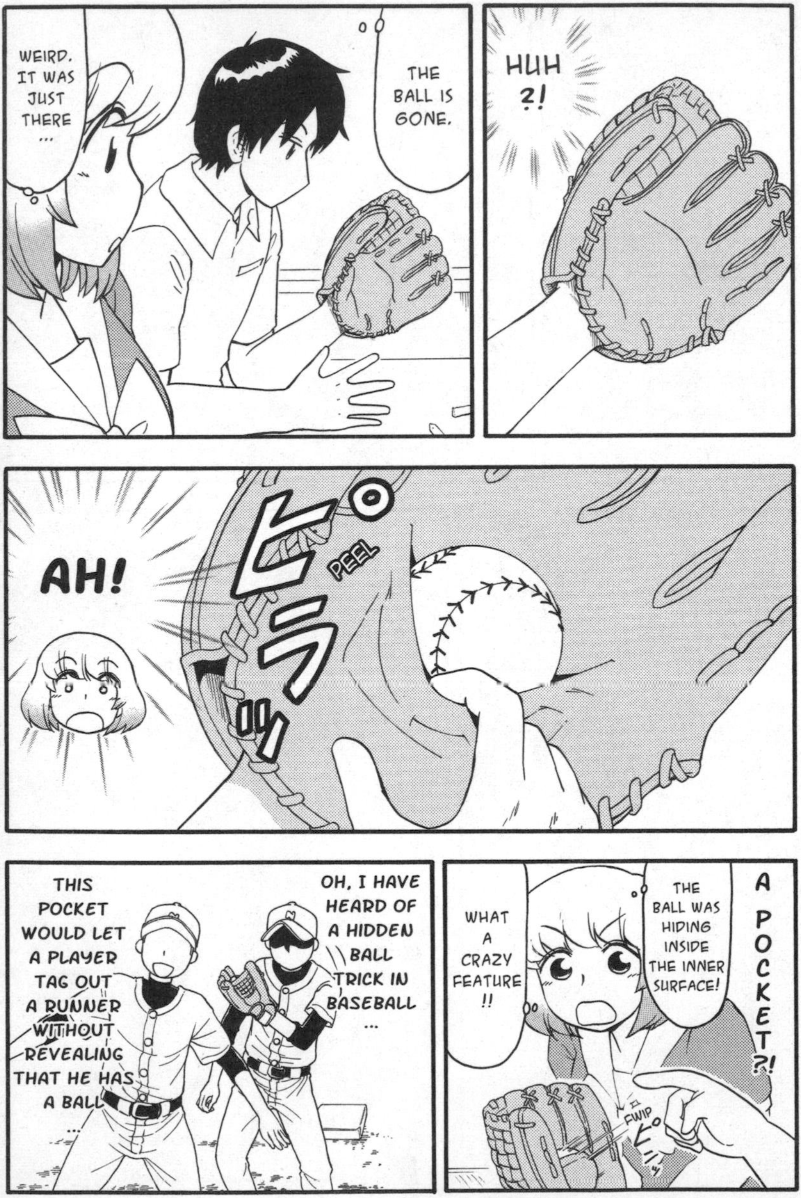
HUH ?!
THE BALL IS GONE.
WEIRD. IT WAS JUST THERE ...
AH!
ピラっ
PEEL
A POCKET?!
THE BALL WAS HIDING INSIDE THE INNER SURFACE!
WHAT A CRAZY FEATURE !!
FWIP
OH, I HAVE HEARD OF A HIDDEN BALL TRICK IN BASEBALL ...
THIS POCKET WOULD LET A PLAYER TAG OUT A RUNNER WITHOUT REVEALING THAT HE HAS A BALL ...

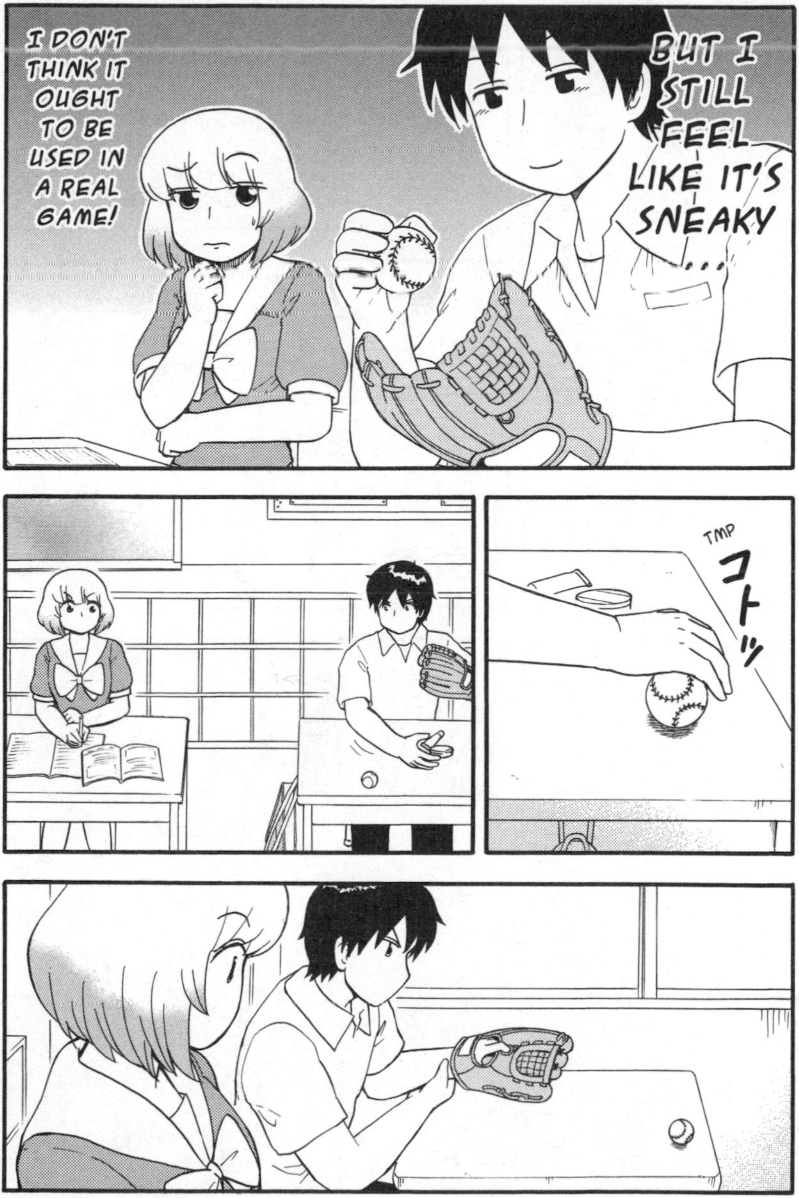
BUT I STILL FEEL LIKE IT'S SNEAKY...
I DON'T THINK IT OUGHT TO BE USED IN A REAL GAME!
TMP
コトッ

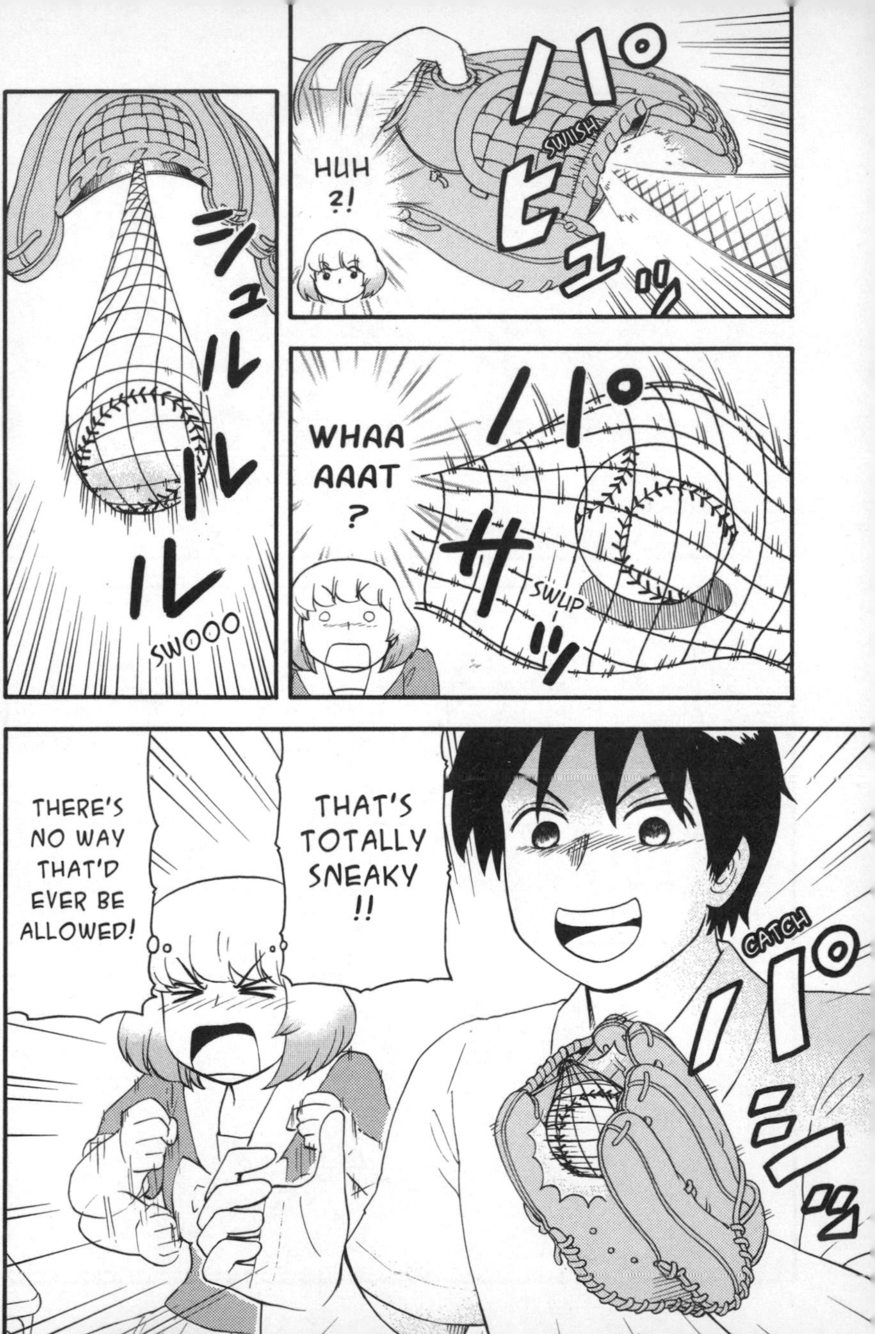
SWIISH
HUH ?!
WHAA AAAT ?
SWUP
SWOOO
CATCH
THAT'S TOTALLY SNEAKY !!
THERE'S NO WAY THAT'D EVER BE ALLOWED!

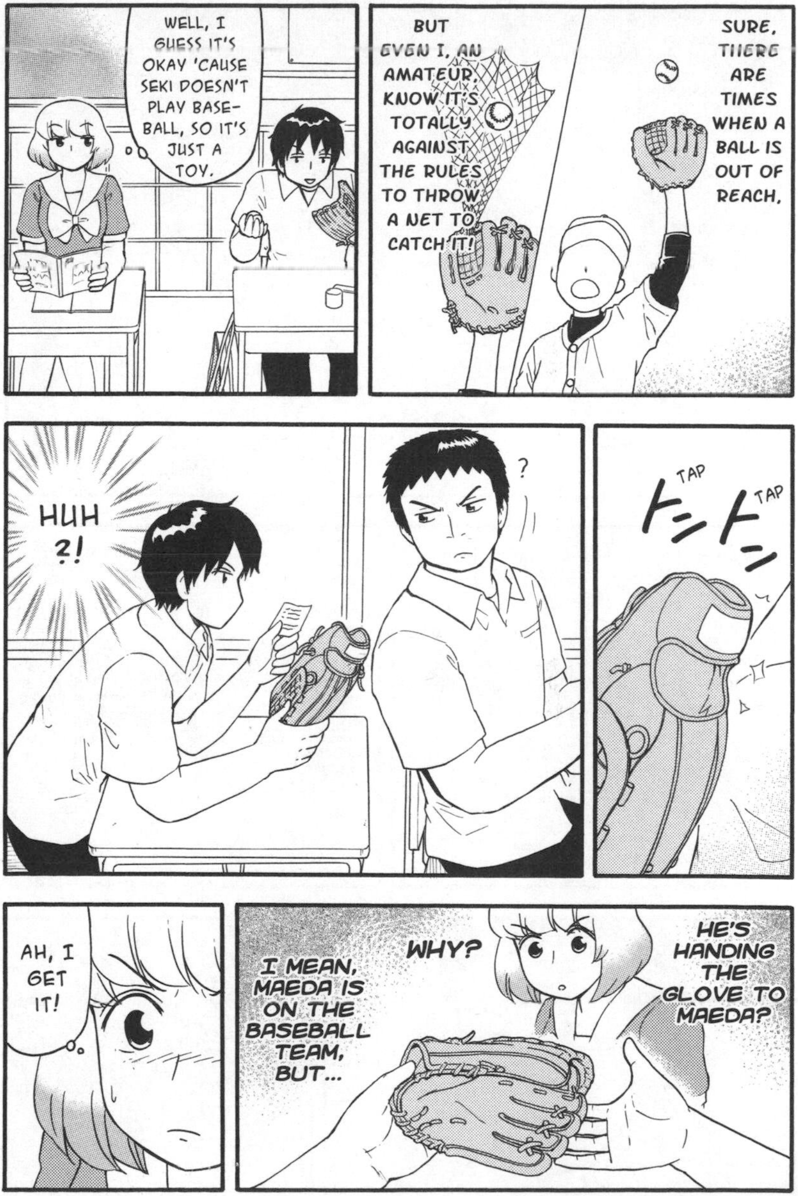
SURE, THERE ARE TIMES WHEN A BALL IS OUT OF REACH.
BUT EVEN I, AN AMATEUR, KNOW IT'S TOTALLY AGAINST THE RULES TO THROW A NET TO CATCH IT!
WELL, I GUESS IT'S OKAY 'CAUSE SEKI DOESN'T PLAY BASE-BALL, SO IT'S JUST A TOY.
TAP
TAP
?
HUH ?!
HE'S HANDING THE GLOVE TO MAEDA?
WHY?
I MEAN, MAEDA IS ON THE BASEBALL TEAM, BUT...
AH, I GET IT!

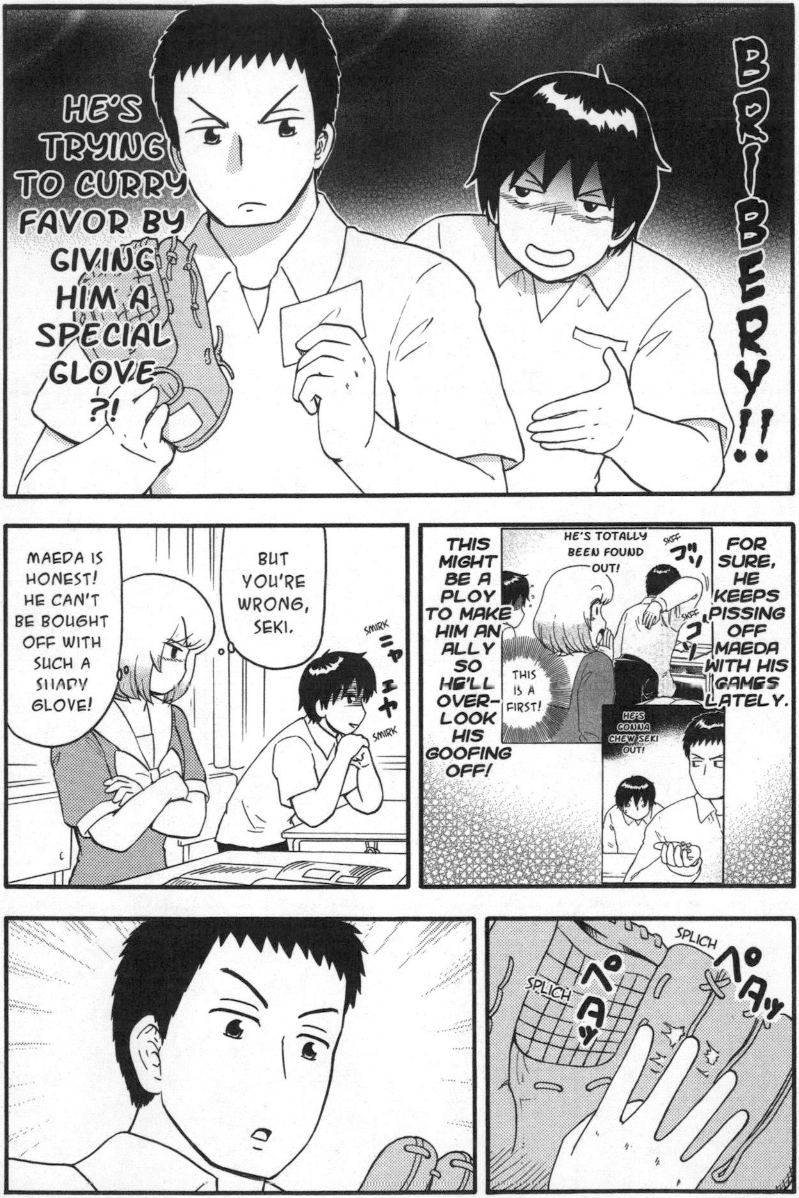
BRIBERY!!
HE'S TRYING TO CURRY FAVOR BY GIVING HIM A SPECIAL GLOVE ?!
FOR SURE, HE KEEPS PISSING OFF MAEDA WITH HIS GAMES LATELY.
SKFF
SKFF
HE'S TOTALLY BEEN FOUND OUT!
THIS IS A FIRST!
HE'S GONNA CHEW SEKI OUT!
THIS MIGHT BE A PLOY TO MAKE HIM AN ALLY SO HE'LL OVERLOOK HIS GOOFING OFF!
BUT YOU'RE WRONG, SEKI.
SMIRK
SMIRK
MAEDA IS HONEST! HE CAN'T BE BOUGHT OFF WITH SUCH A SHADY GLOVE!
SPLICH
SPLICH

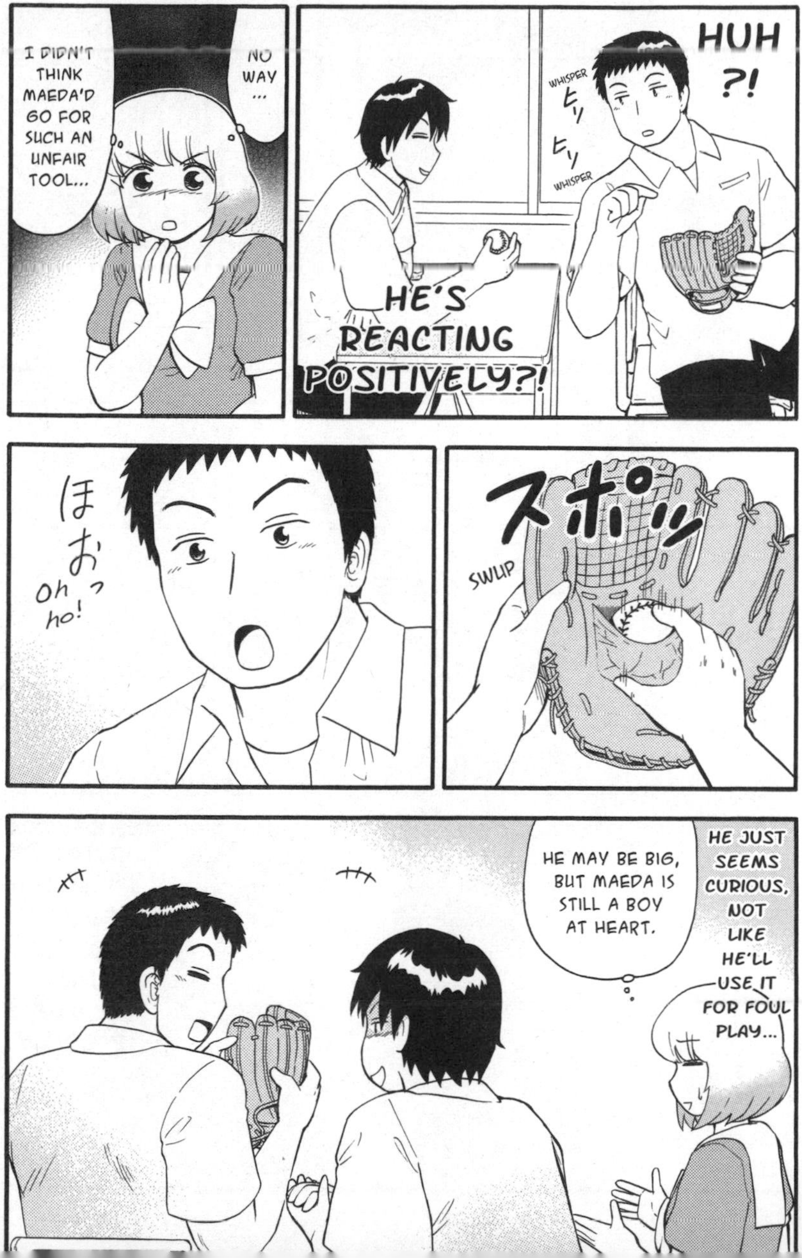
HUH ?!
ヒソ WHISPER
ヒソ WHISPER
HE'S REACTING POSITIVELY?!
NO WAY ...
I DIDN'T THINK MAEDA'D GO FOR SUCH AN UNFAIR TOOL...
スポッ
SWUP
ほおっ
Oh ho!
HE JUST SEEMS CURIOUS, NOT LIKE HE'LL USE IT FOR FOUL PLAY...
HE MAY BE BIG, BUT MAEDA IS STILL A BOY AT HEART.

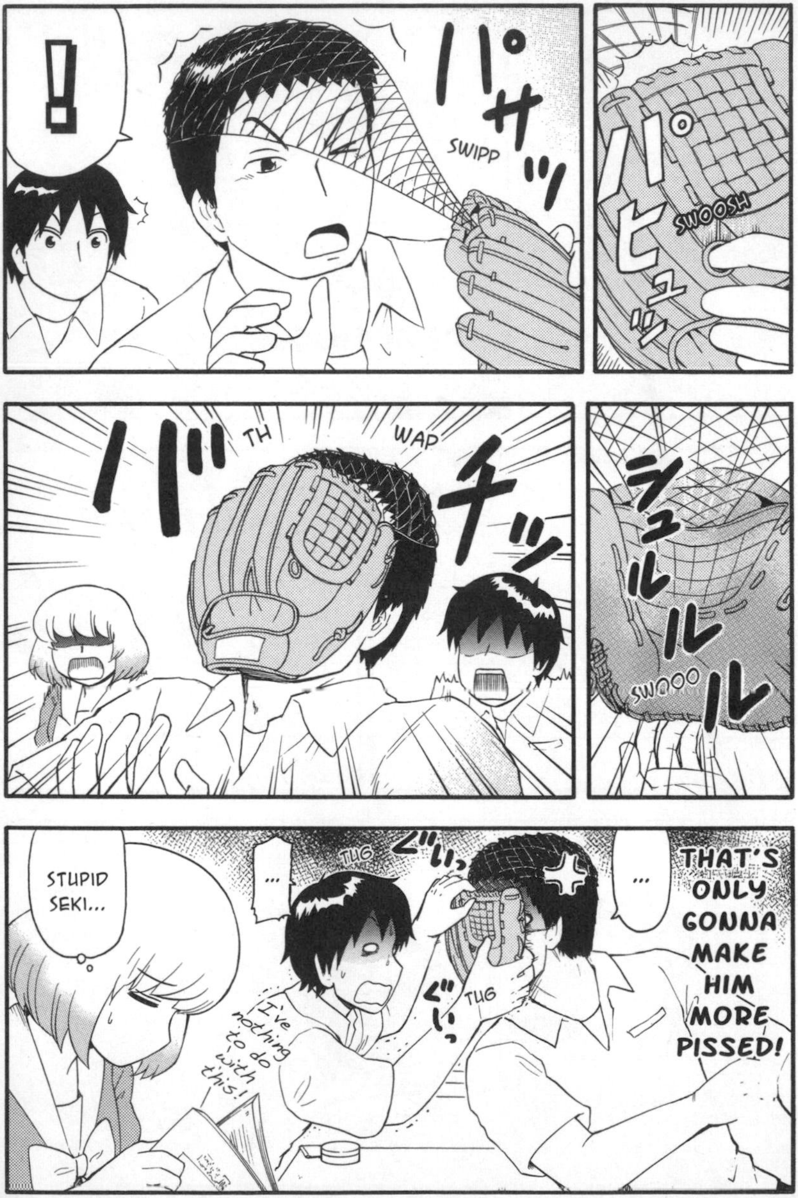
パヒュッ
SWOOSH
パサッ
SWIPP
!
シュルルル
SWOOO
バチッ
TH WAP
THAT'S ONLY GONNA MAKE HIM MORE PISSED!
...
ぐいっ
TUG
...
ぐいっ
TUG
I've nothing to do with this!
STUPID SEKI...

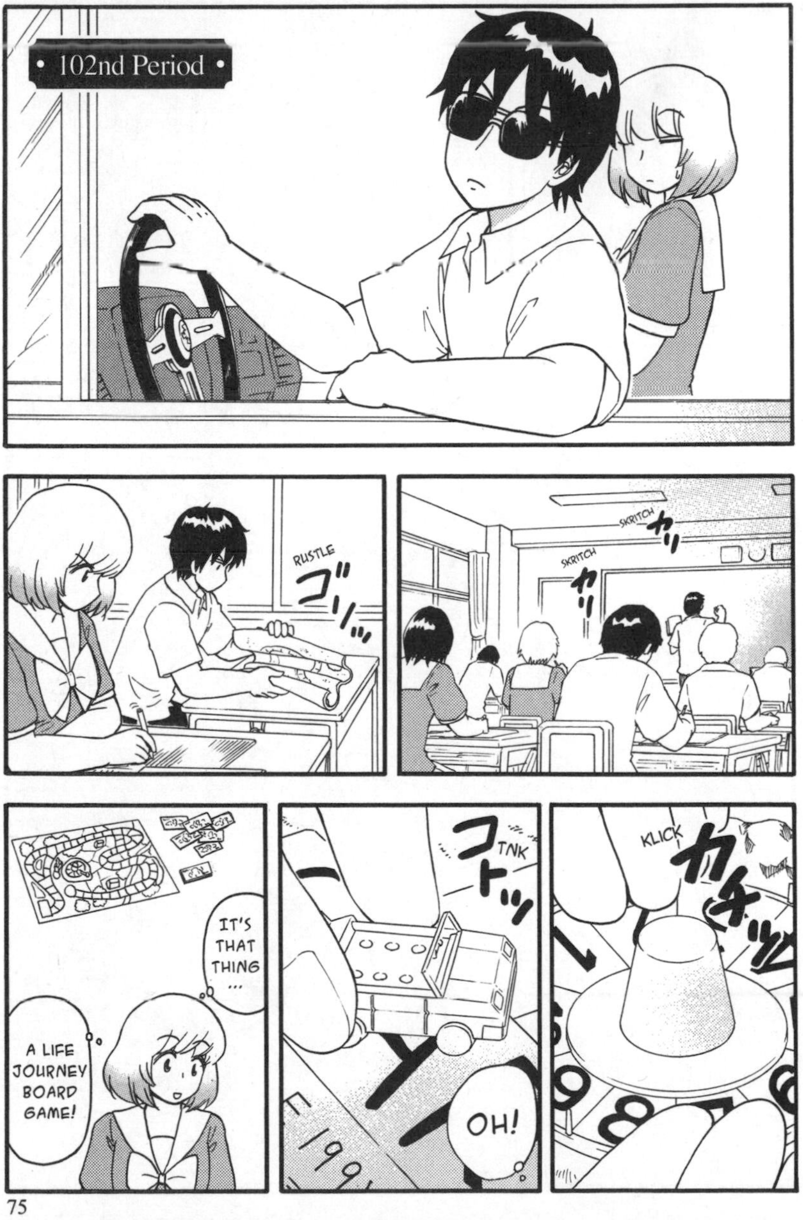
• 102nd Period •
SKRITCH
SKRITCH
RUSTLE
KLICK
TNK
OH!
IT'S THAT THING ...
A LIFE JOURNEY BOARD GAME!

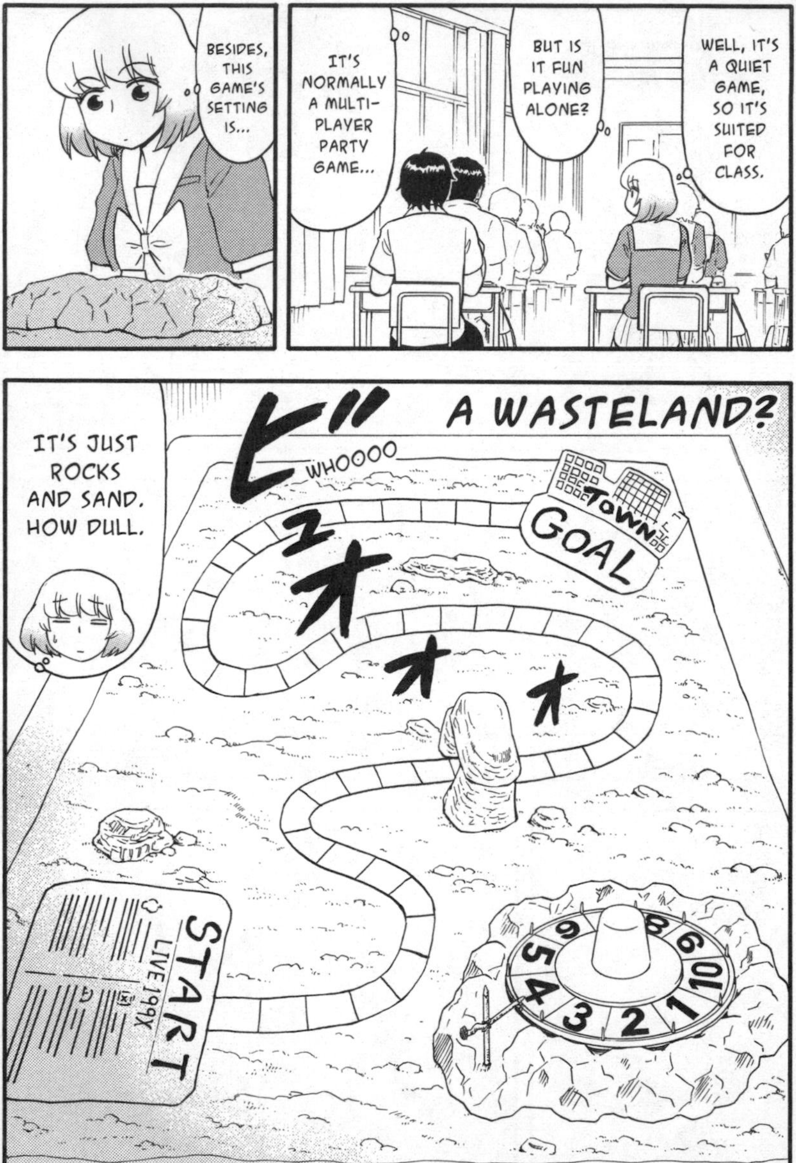
WELL, IT'S A QUIET GAME, SO IT'S SUITED FOR CLASS.
BUT IS IT FUN PLAYING ALONE?
IT'S NORMALLY A MULTI-PLAYER PARTY GAME...
BESIDES, THIS GAME'S SETTING IS...
A WASTELAND?
WHOOOO
IT'S JUST ROCKS AND SAND. HOW DULL.
TOWN
GOAL
START
LIVE 199X
1 2 3 4 5 6 7 8 9 10

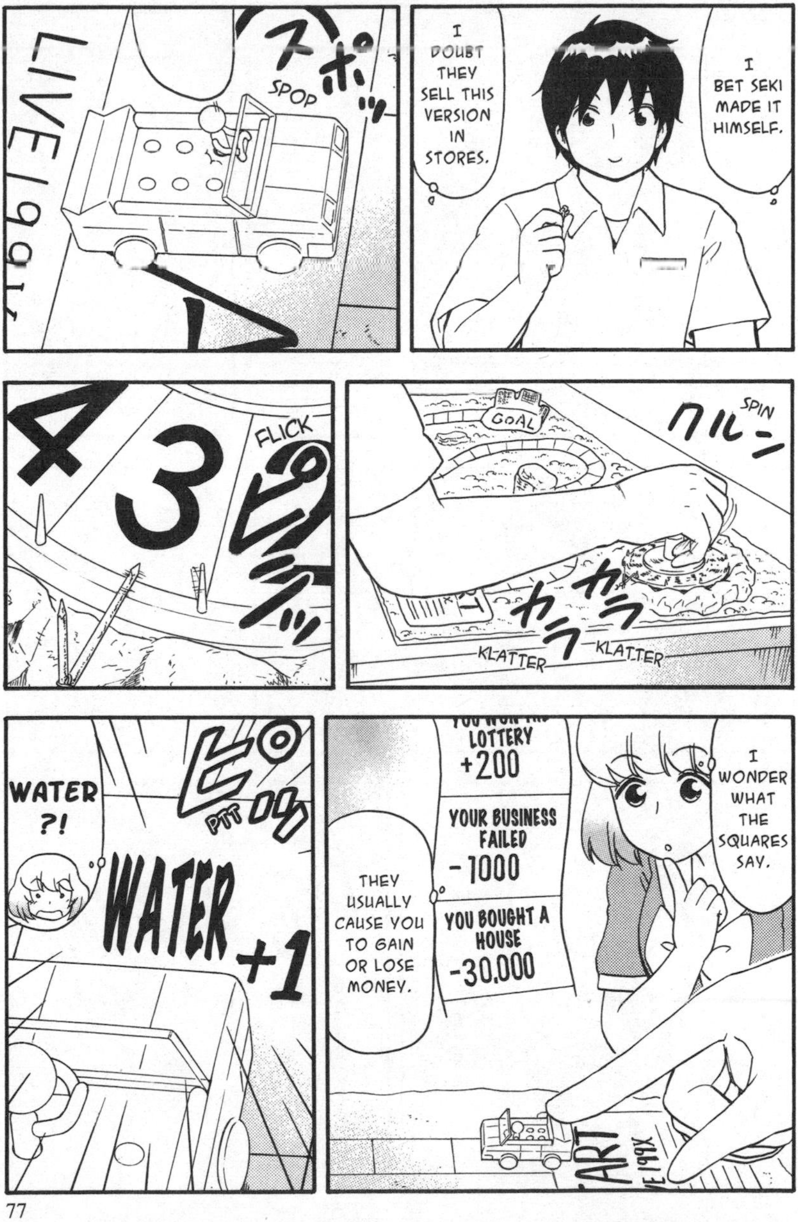
I BET SEKI MADE IT HIMSELF.
I DOUBT THEY SELL THIS VERSION IN STORES.
SPOP
SPIN
GOAL
KLATTER
KLATTER
FLICK
4
3
I WONDER WHAT THE SQUARES SAY.
LOTTERY +200
YOUR BUSINESS FAILED -1000
YOU BOUGHT A HOUSE -30,000
THEY USUALLY CAUSE YOU TO GAIN OR LOSE MONEY.
WATER ?!
PIT
WATER +1

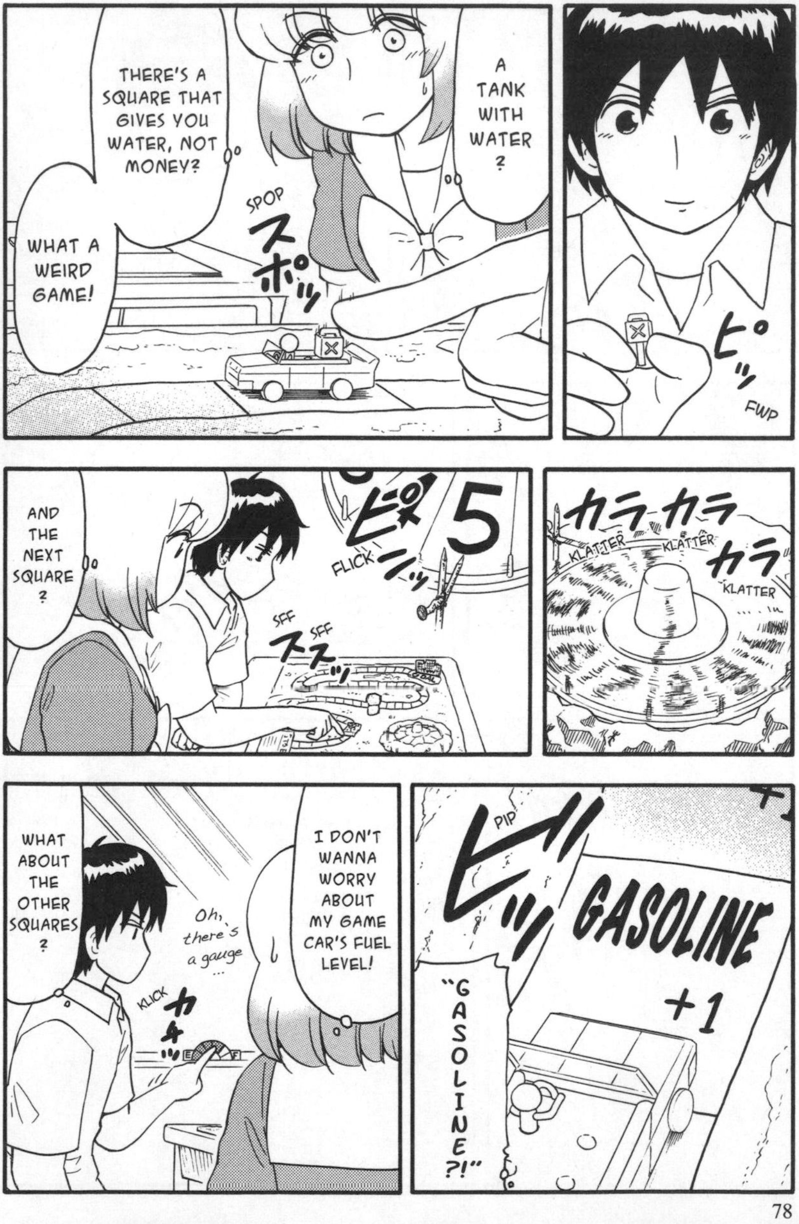
ピッ
FWP
A TANK WITH WATER?
THERE'S A SQUARE THAT GIVES YOU WATER, NOT MONEY?
SPOP
スポッ
WHAT A WEIRD GAME!
カラ カラ カラ
KLATTER KLATTER KLATTER
5
ピシッ
FLICK
SFF SFF
ススッ
AND THE NEXT SQUARE?
PIP
ピッ
GASOLINE
+1
"GASOLINE?!"
I DON'T WANNA WORRY ABOUT MY GAME CAR'S FUEL LEVEL!
Oh, there's a gauge...
KLICK
カチッ
WHAT ABOUT THE OTHER SQUARES?

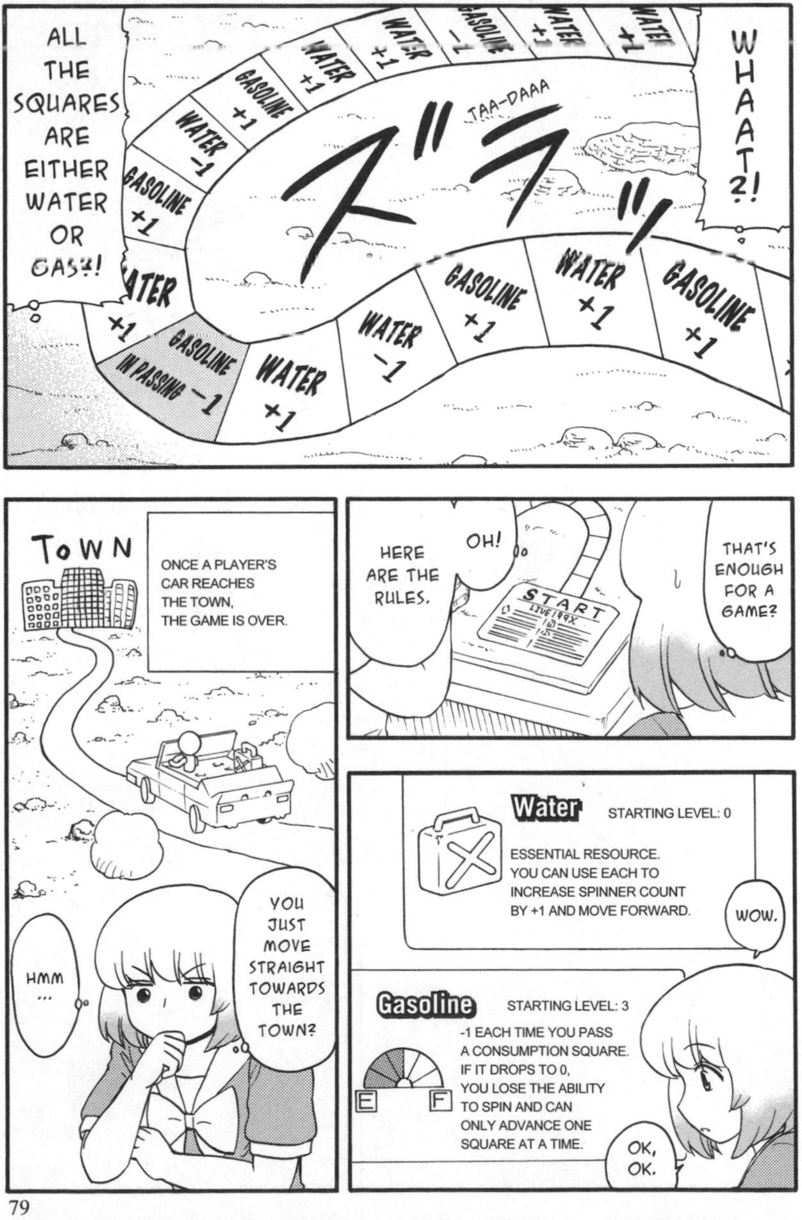
WHAAT?!
TAA-DAAA
ズラッ
ALL THE SQUARES ARE EITHER WATER OR GAS?!
WATER +1
WATER +1
GASOLINE -1
WATER +1
WATER +1
GASOLINE +1
WATER -1
GASOLINE +1
WATER +1
GASOLINE IN PASSING -1
WATER +1
WATER -1
GASOLINE +1
WATER +1
GASOLINE +1
THAT'S ENOUGH FOR A GAME?
OH!
HERE ARE THE RULES.
START
Water
STARTING LEVEL: 0
ESSENTIAL RESOURCE. YOU CAN USE EACH TO INCREASE SPINNER COUNT BY +1 AND MOVE FORWARD.
WOW.
Gasoline
STARTING LEVEL: 3
-1 EACH TIME YOU PASS A CONSUMPTION SQUARE. IF IT DROPS TO 0, YOU LOSE THE ABILITY TO SPIN AND CAN ONLY ADVANCE ONE SQUARE AT A TIME.
E
F
OK, OK.
TOWN
ONCE A PLAYER'S CAR REACHES THE TOWN, THE GAME IS OVER.
YOU JUST MOVE STRAIGHT TOWARDS THE TOWN?
HMM...

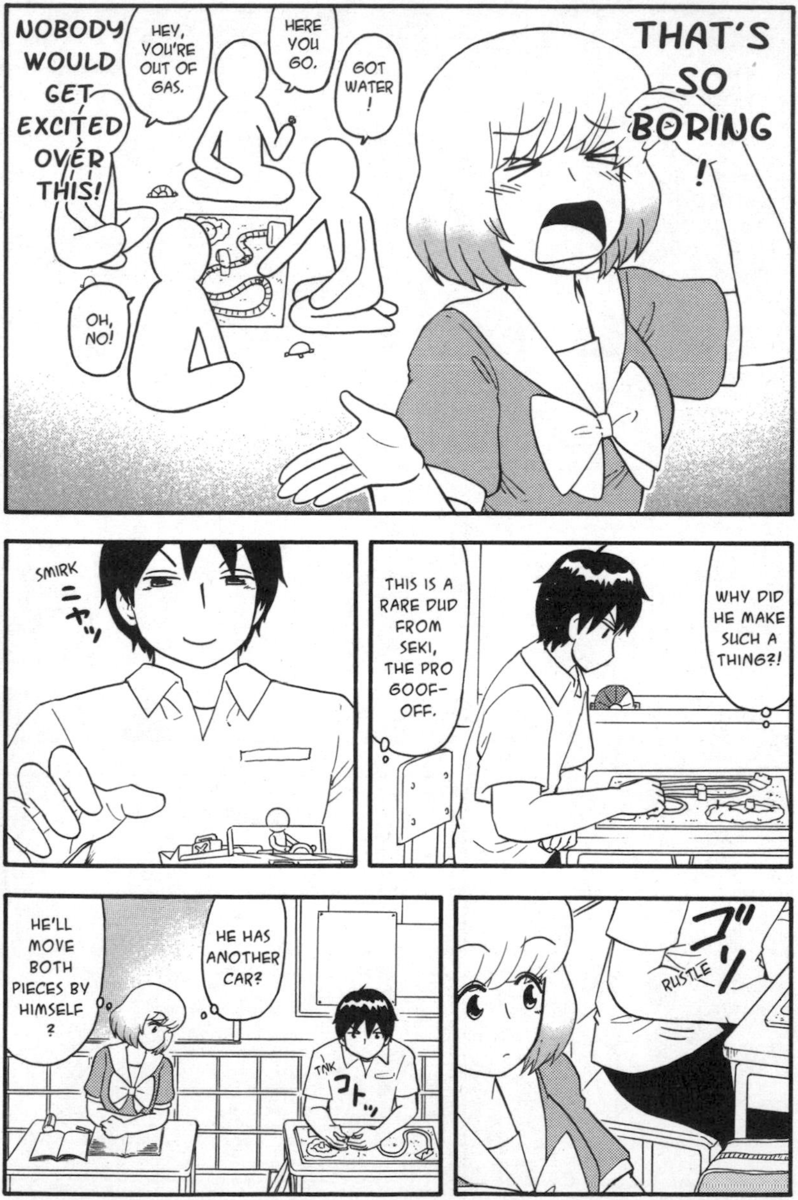
THAT'S SO BORING!
NOBODY WOULD GET EXCITED OVER THIS!
GOT WATER!
HERE YOU GO.
HEY, YOU'RE OUT OF GAS.
OH, NO!
WHY DID HE MAKE SUCH A THING?!
THIS IS A RARE DUD FROM SEKI, THE PRO GOOF-OFF.
SMIRK
ニヤッ
ゴソ
RUSTLE
HE HAS ANOTHER CAR?
HE'LL MOVE BOTH PIECES BY HIMSELF?
TNK
コトッ

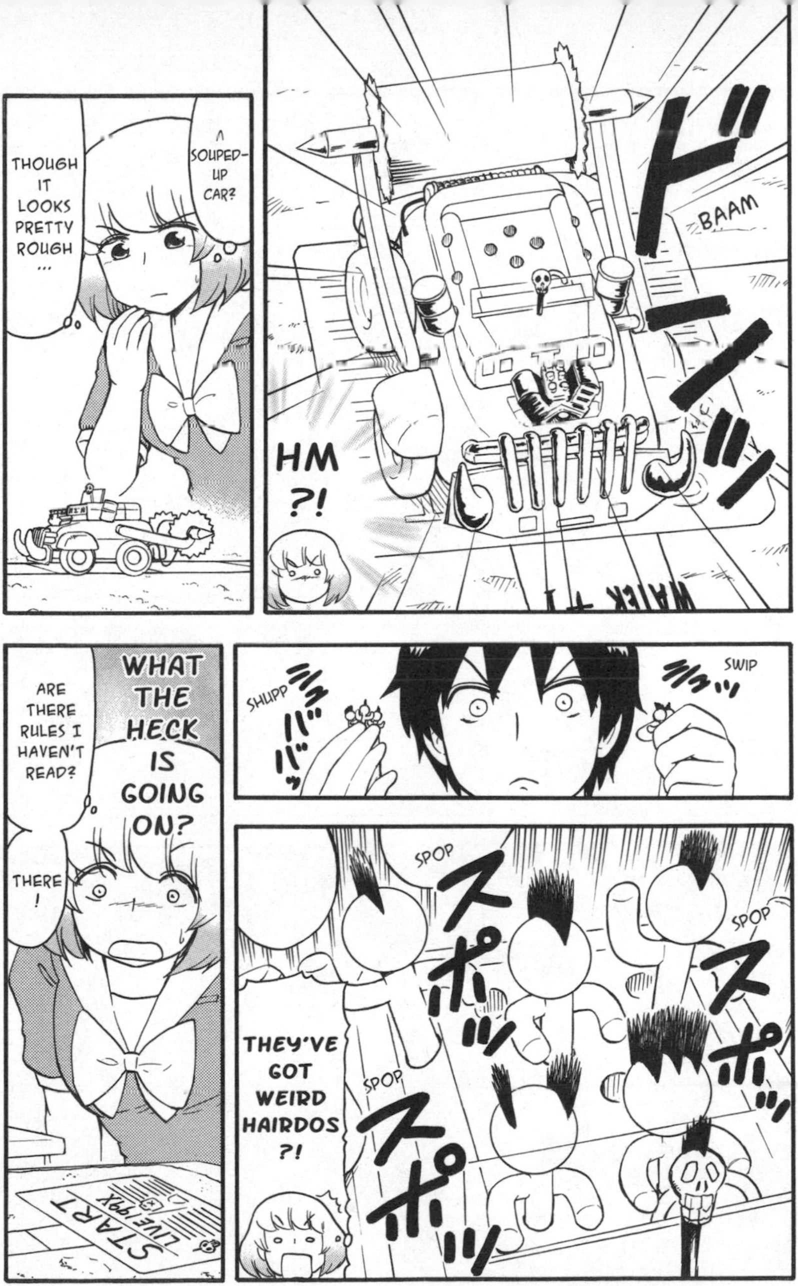

HM ?!
BAAM
ドーン
A SOUPED-UP CAR?
THOUGH IT LOOKS PRETTY ROUGH ...
SWIP
シュッ
SHUPP
シュバババッ
SPOP
スポッ
SPOP
スポッ
SPOP
スポッ
THEY'VE GOT WEIRD HAIRDOS ?!
WHAT THE HECK IS GOING ON?
ARE THERE RULES I HAVEN'T READ?
THERE !
START
LIVE 199X

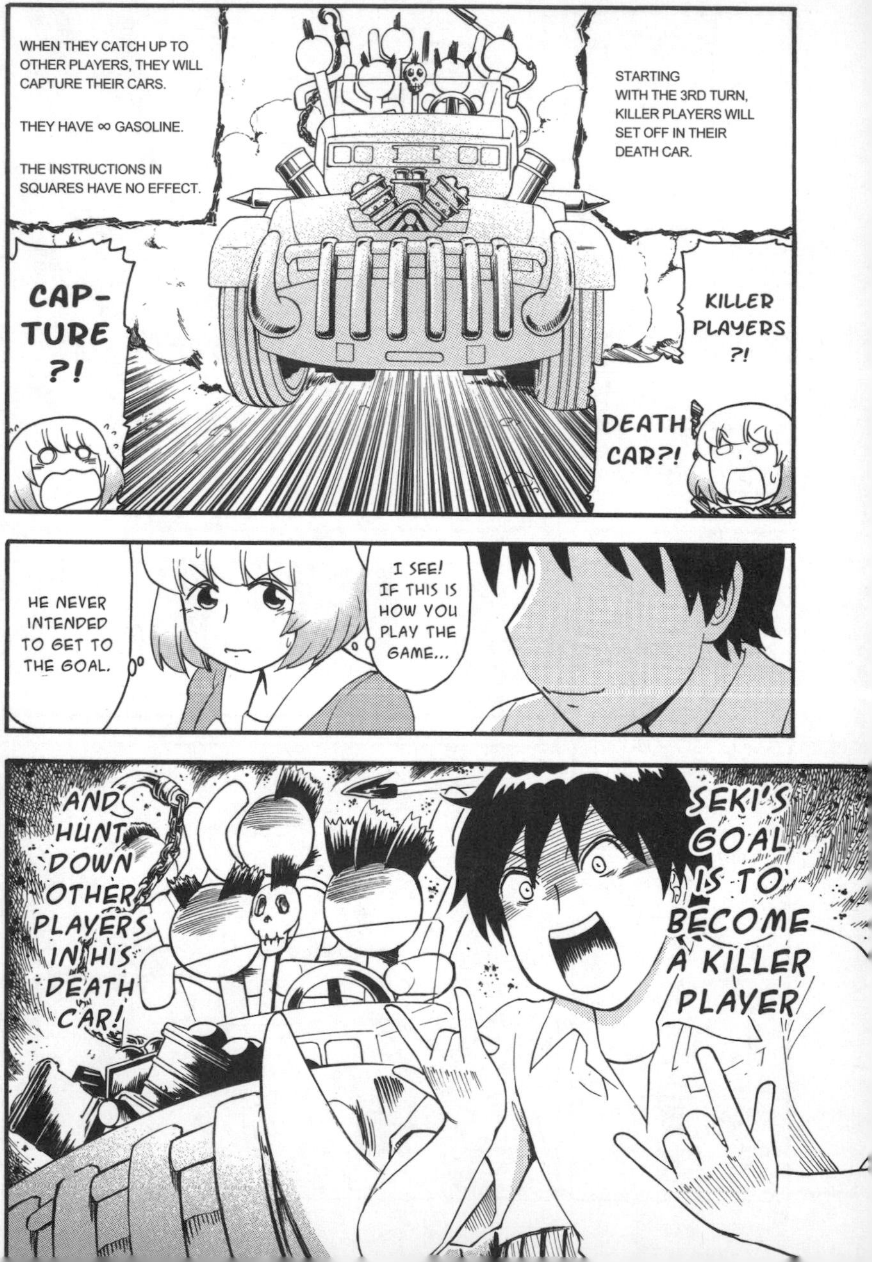
STARTING WITH THE 3RD TURN, KILLER PLAYERS WILL SET OFF IN THEIR DEATH CAR.
WHEN THEY CATCH UP TO OTHER PLAYERS, THEY WILL CAPTURE THEIR CARS.
THEY HAVE ∞ GASOLINE.
THE INSTRUCTIONS IN SQUARES HAVE NO EFFECT.
KILLER PLAYERS ?!
DEATH CAR?!
CAP-TURE ?!
I SEE! IF THIS IS HOW YOU PLAY THE GAME...
HE NEVER INTENDED TO GET TO THE GOAL.
SEKI'S GOAL IS TO BECOME A KILLER PLAYER
AND HUNT DOWN OTHER PLAYERS IN HIS DEATH CAR!

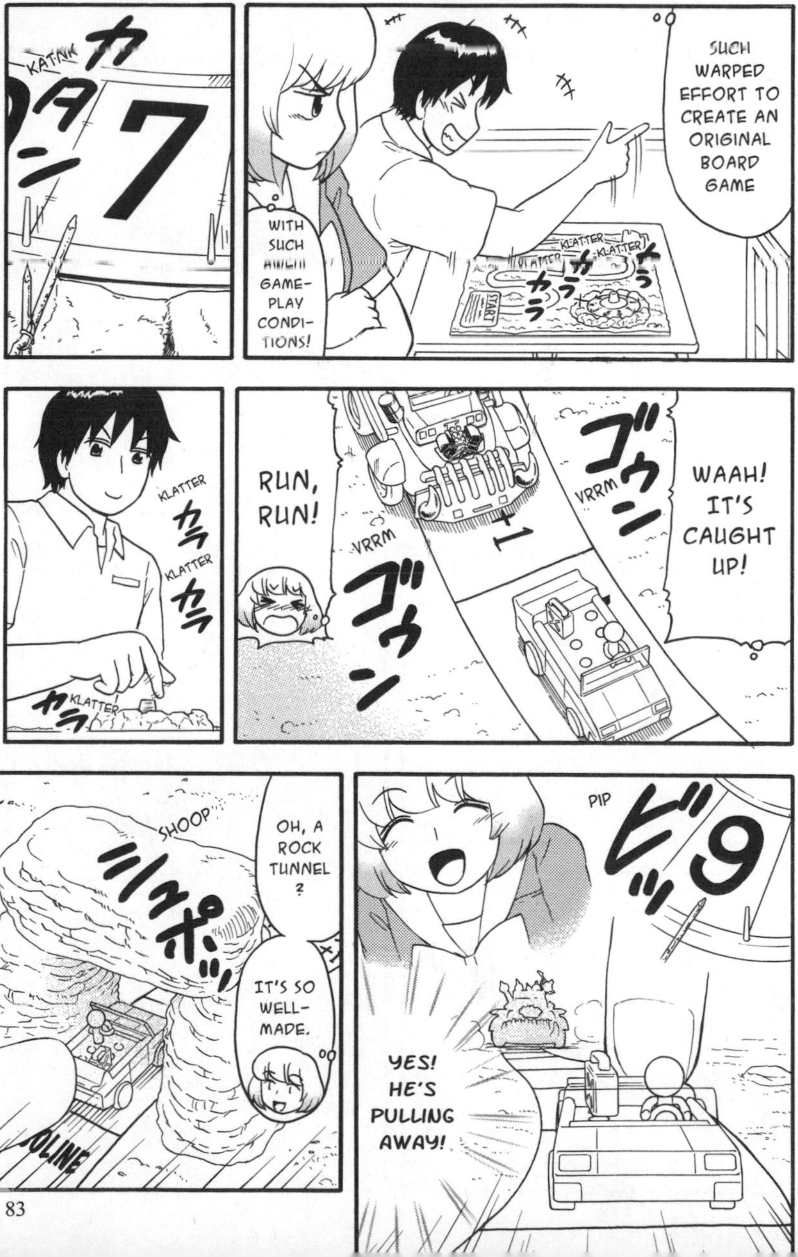
SUCH WARPED EFFORT TO CREATE AN ORIGINAL BOARD GAME
WITH SUCH GAME-PLAY CONDI-TIONS!
KLATTER
KLATTER
KLATTER
カラ カラ カラ
START
KAT-NK
カタン
7
WAAH! IT'S CAUGHT UP!
VRRM
ゴウン
RUN, RUN!
VRRM
ゴウン
+1
KLATTER
カラ
KLATTER
カラ
KLATTER
カラ
PIP
ピッ
9
YES! HE'S PULLING AWAY!
OH, A ROCK TUNNEL?
IT'S SO WELL-MADE.
SHOOP
シュポッ
OLINE

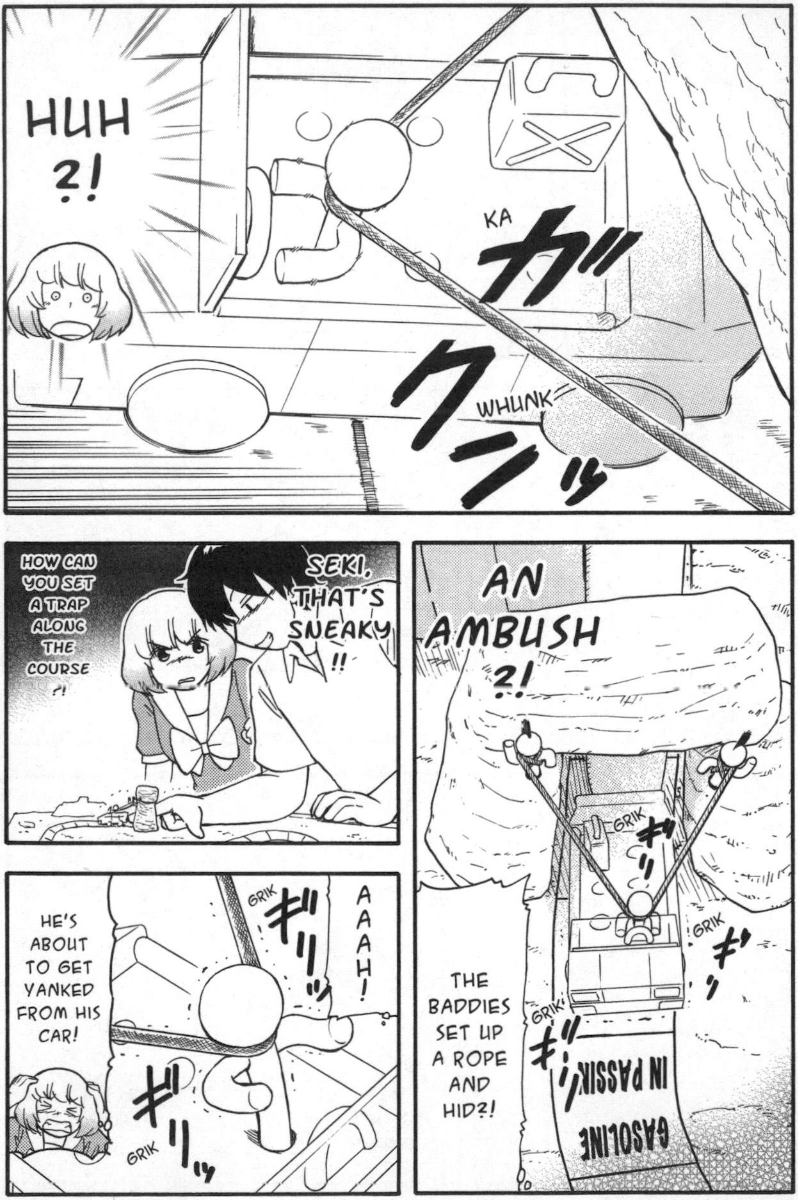
HUH?!
KA
WHUNK
AN AMBUSH?!
GRIK
GRIK
GRIK
THE BADDIES SET UP A ROPE AND HID?!
SEKI, THAT'S SNEAKY!!
HOW CAN YOU SET A TRAP ALONG THE COURSE?!
AAAAH!
GRIK
HE'S ABOUT TO GET YANKED FROM HIS CAR!
GRIK

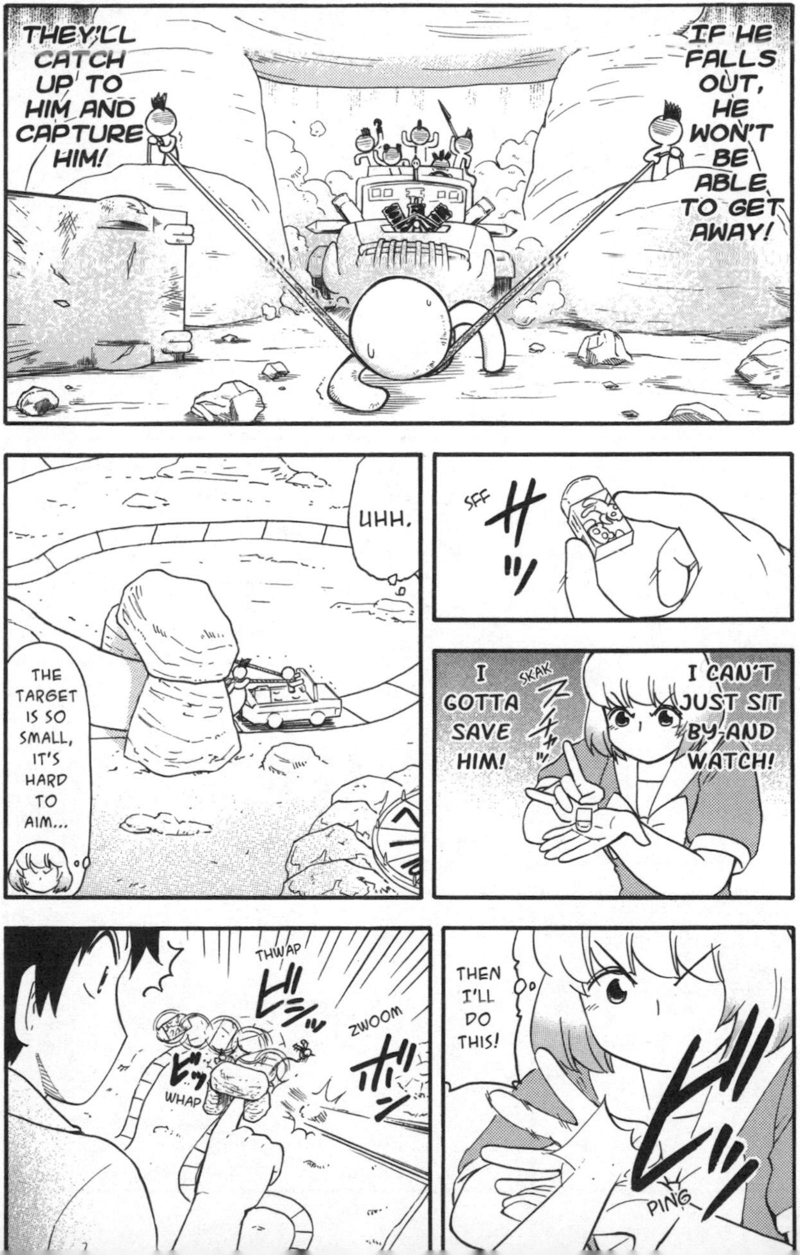

IF HE FALLS OUT, HE WON'T BE ABLE TO GET AWAY!
THEY'LL CATCH UP TO HIM AND CAPTURE HIM!
SFF
I CAN'T JUST SIT BY AND WATCH!
SKAK
I GOTTA SAVE HIM!
UHH.
THE TARGET IS SO SMALL, IT'S HARD TO AIM...
THEN I'LL DO THIS!
PING
THWAP
ZWOOM
WHAP

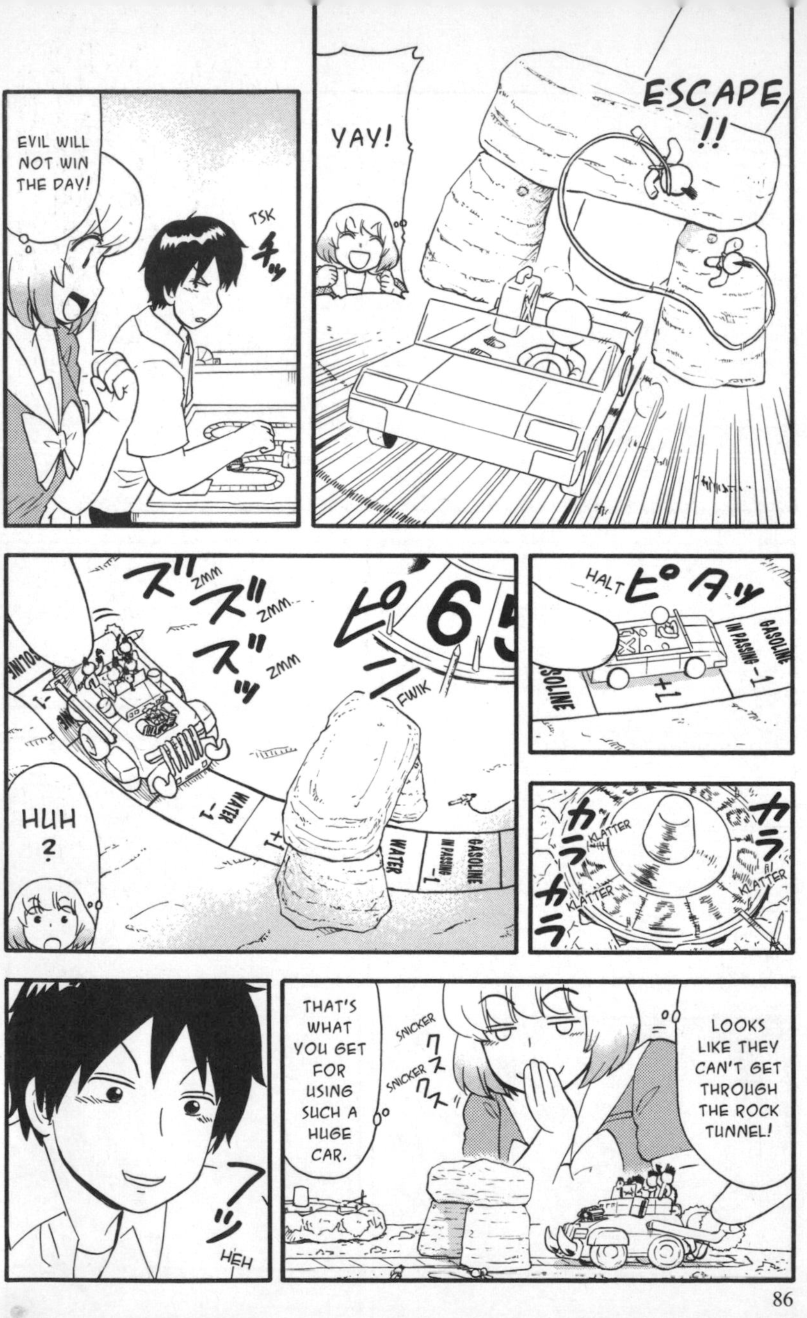
ESCAPE !!
YAY!
EVIL WILL NOT WIN THE DAY!
TSK
チッ
HALT
ピタッ
GASOLINE IN PASSING −1
+1
GASOLINE
カラ
カラ
カラ
KLATTER
KLATTER
KLATTER
ズズズッ
ZMM
ZMM
ZMM
ピ
FWIK
65
GASOLINE IN PASSING −1
WATER
WATER −1
+1
HUH?
LOOKS LIKE THEY CAN'T GET THROUGH THE ROCK TUNNEL!
SNICKER
クス
SNICKER
クス
THAT'S WHAT YOU GET FOR USING SUCH A HUGE CAR.
フッ
HEH

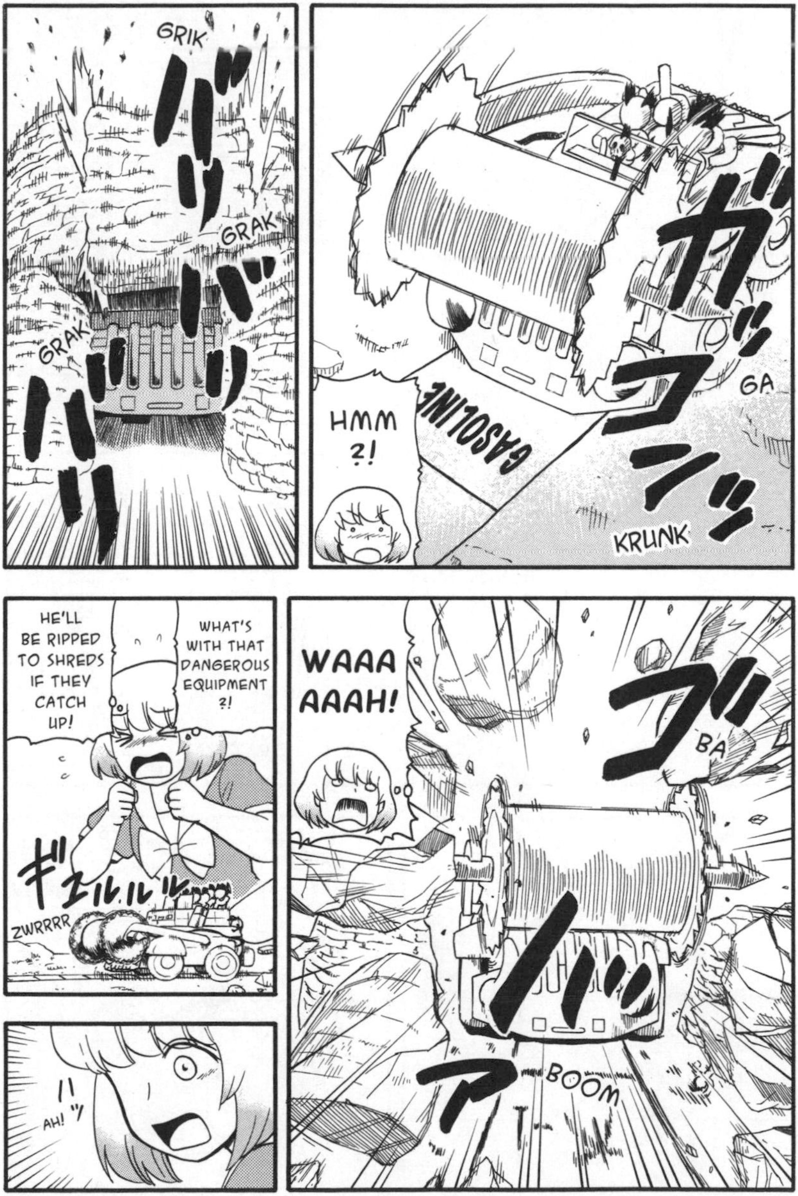
GASOLINE
HMM ?!
ガッコンッ
GA
KRUNK
GRIK
GRAK
GRAK
WAAA AAAH!
ブバッア
BA
BOOM
WHAT'S WITH THAT DANGEROUS EQUIPMENT ?!
HE'LL BE RIPPED TO SHREDS IF THEY CATCH UP!
ギュルルル
ZWRRRR
ハッ
AH!

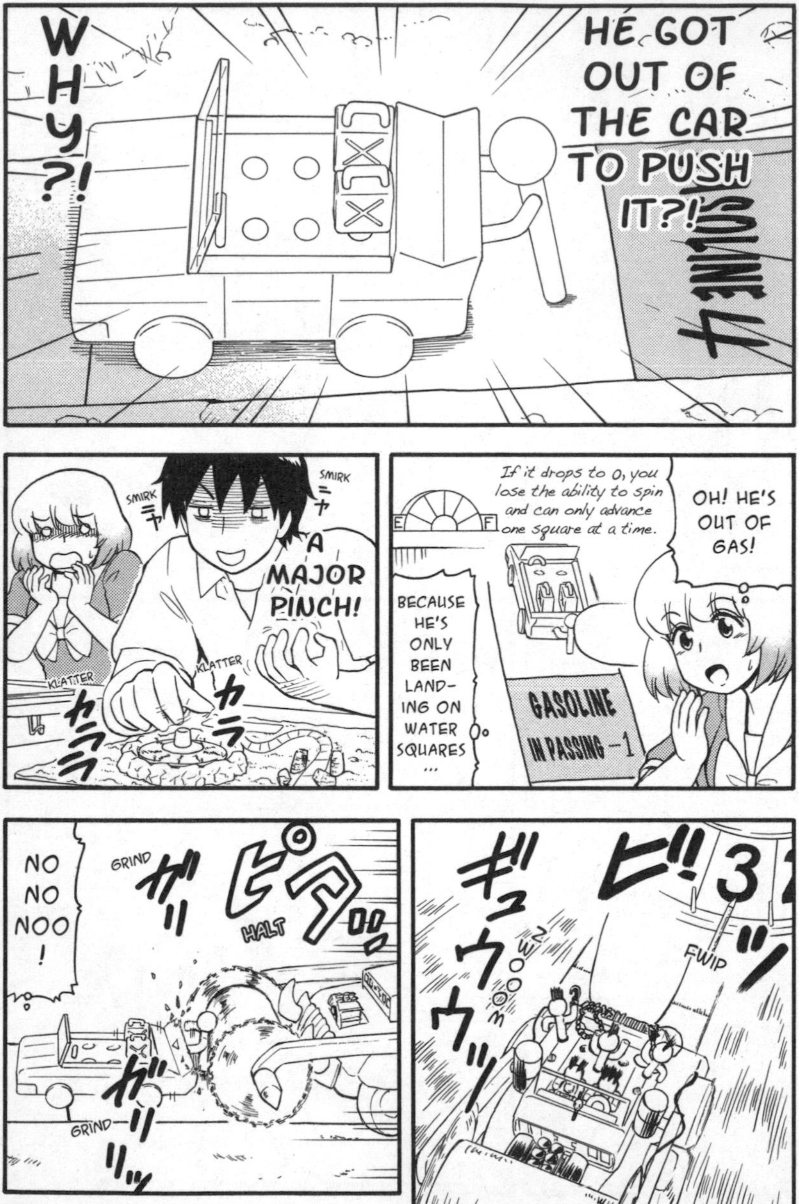
HE GOT OUT OF THE CAR TO PUSH IT?!
WHY?!
OH! HE'S OUT OF GAS!
If it drops to 0, you lose the ability to spin and can only advance one square at a time.
E
F
BECAUSE HE'S ONLY BEEN LAND-ING ON WATER SQUARES ...
GASOLINE IN PASSING -1
SMIRK
ニャ
SMIRK
ニャ
A MAJOR PINCH!
KLATTER
カラ
KLATTER
カラララ
ビ!!
3
ギュウウウッ
FWIP
NO NO NOO!
GRIND
ガリ
ピタ
HALT
GRIND
ガリリッ

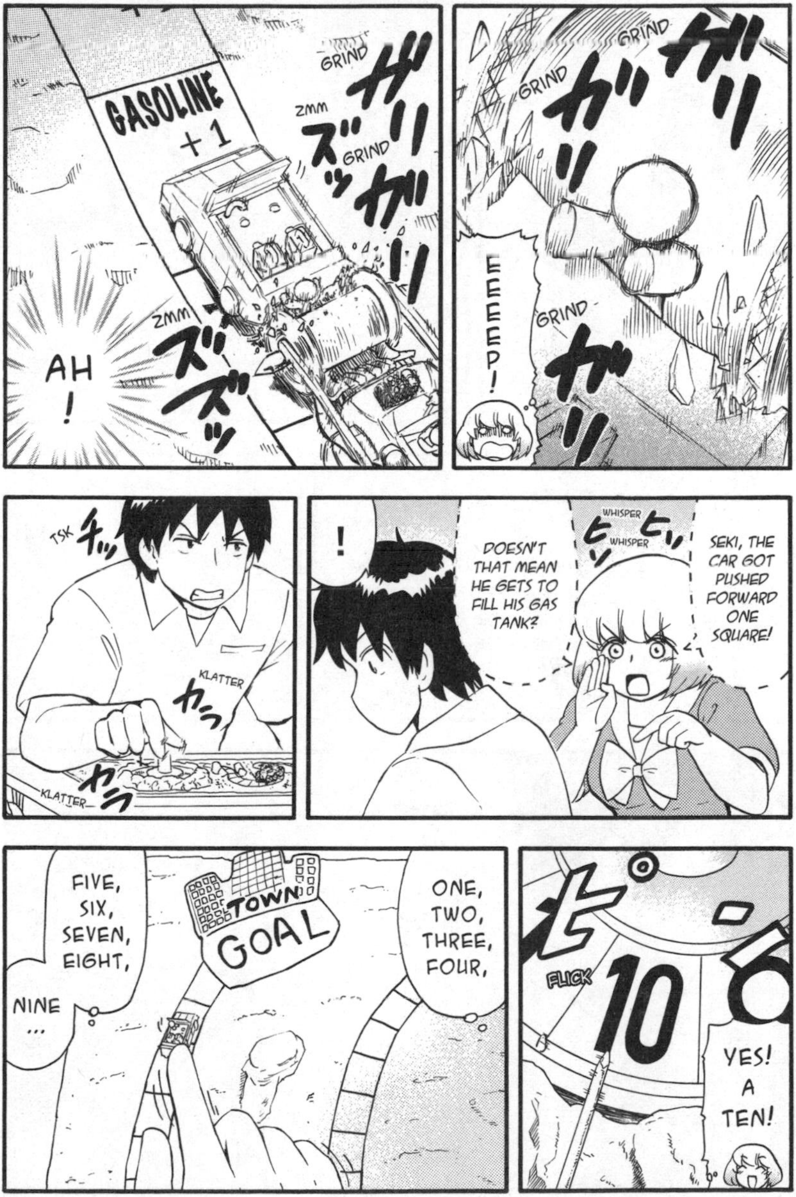
GRIND
GRIND
GRIND
EEEEEP!
GRIND
GASOLINE +1
GRIND
ZMM
GRIND
ZMM
AH!
SEKI, THE CAR GOT PUSHED FORWARD ONE SQUARE!
WHISPER
WHISPER
DOESN'T THAT MEAN HE GETS TO FILL HIS GAS TANK?
!
TSK
KLATTER
KLATTER
FLICK
10
YES! A TEN!
ONE, TWO, THREE, FOUR,
TOWN
GOAL
FIVE, SIX, SEVEN, EIGHT,
NINE ...

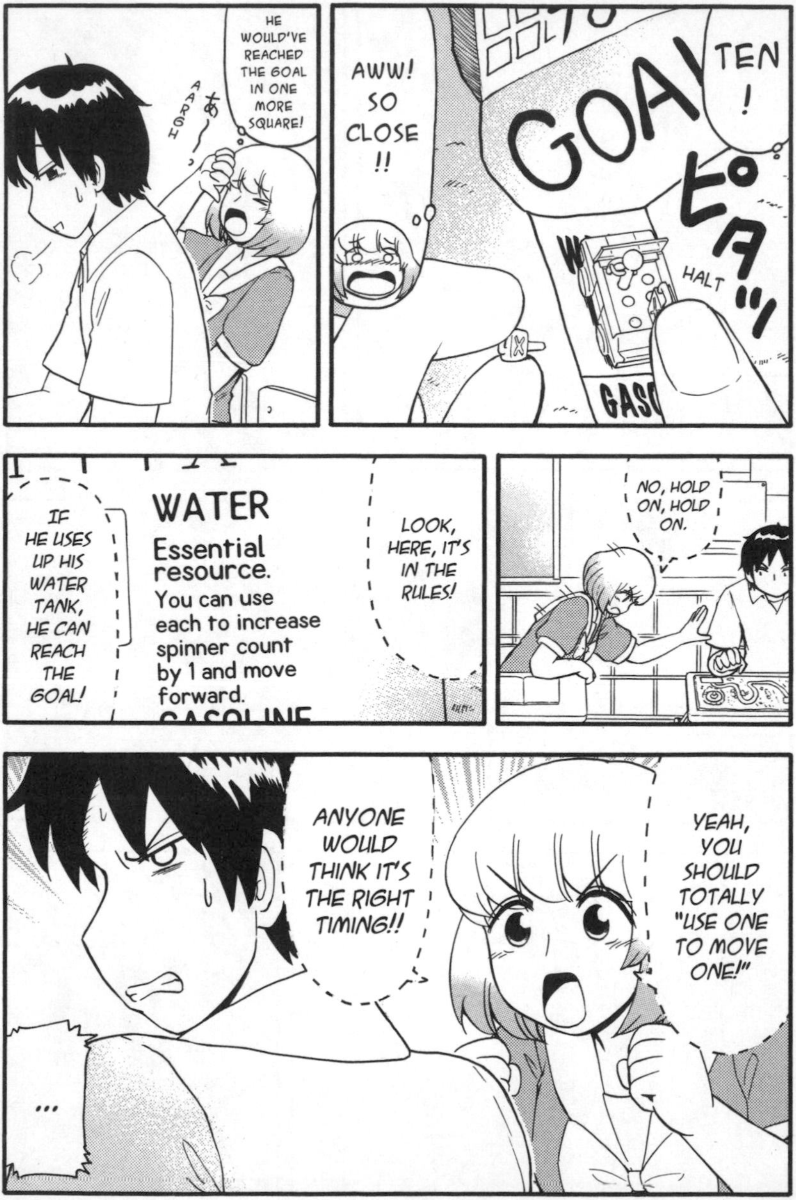
TEN!
ピタッ
HALT
AWW! SO CLOSE!!
HE WOULD'VE REACHED THE GOAL IN ONE MORE SQUARE!
あ～
AARGH
NO, HOLD ON, HOLD ON.
LOOK, HERE, IT'S IN THE RULES!
WATER
Essential resource.
You can use each to increase spinner count by 1 and move forward.
IF HE USES UP HIS WATER TANK, HE CAN REACH THE GOAL!
YEAH, YOU SHOULD TOTALLY "USE ONE TO MOVE ONE!"
ANYONE WOULD THINK IT'S THE RIGHT TIMING!!
...

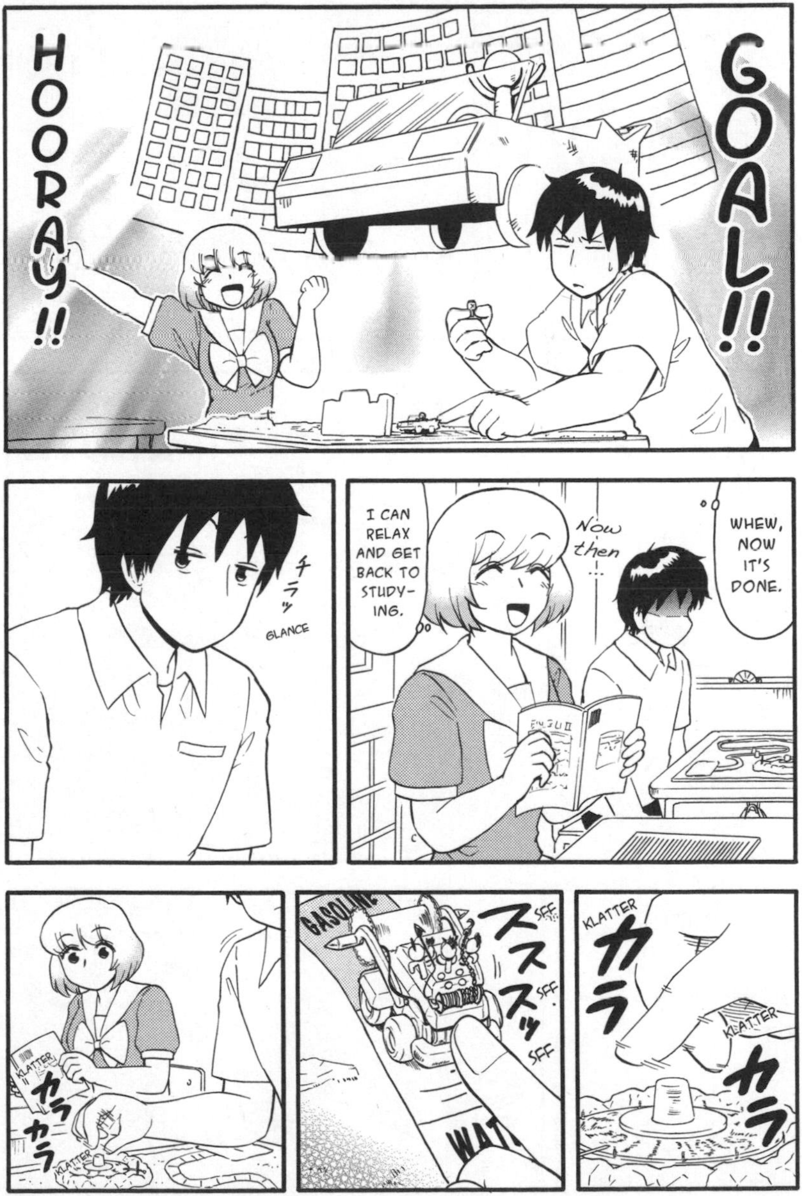
GOAL!!
HOORAY!!
WHEW, NOW IT'S DONE.
Now then...
I CAN RELAX AND GET BACK TO STUDY-ING.
チラッ
GLANCE
KLATTER
カラ
KLATTER
カラ
ススッ
SFF
SFF
SFF
KLATTER
カラカラ
KLATTER

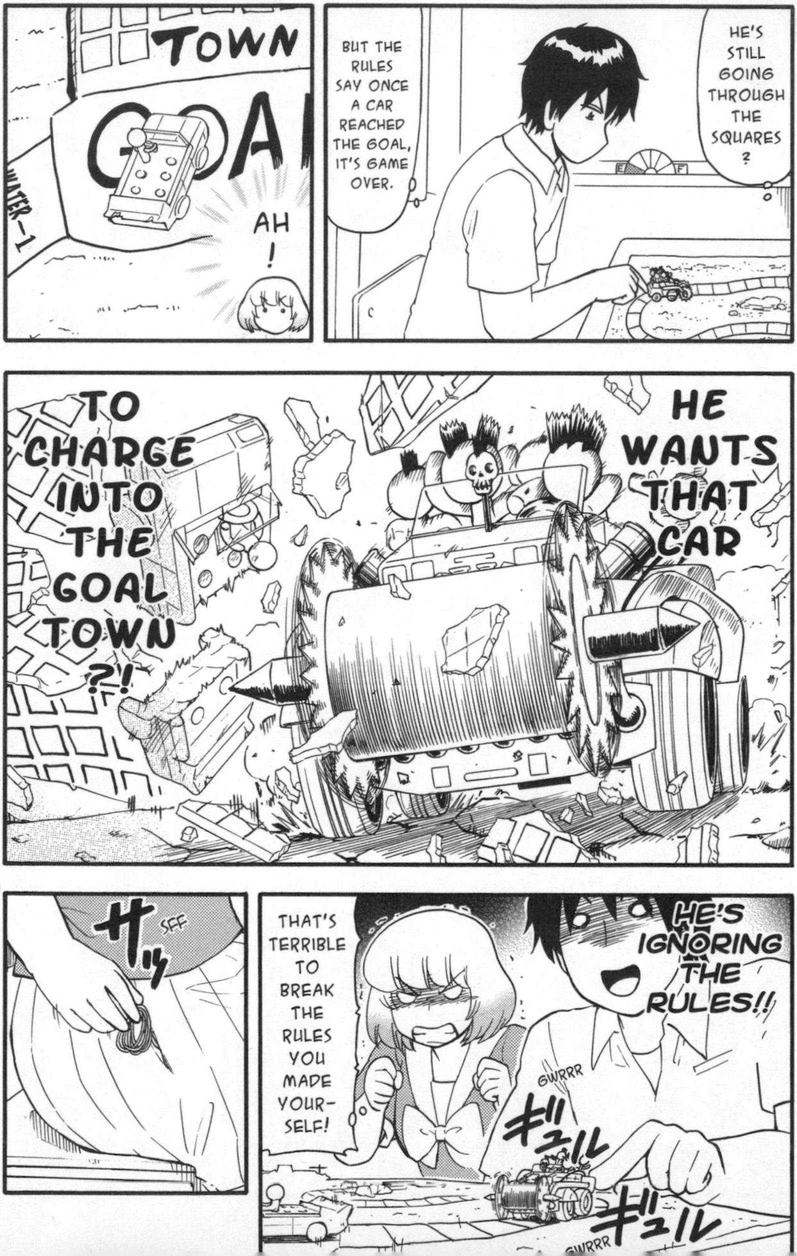
TOWN
GOAL
WATER-1
AH!
BUT THE RULES SAY ONCE A CAR REACHED THE GOAL, IT'S GAME OVER.
HE'S STILL GOING THROUGH THE SQUARES?
HE WANTS THAT CAR
TO CHARGE INTO THE GOAL TOWN?!
サッ
SFF
HE'S IGNORING THE RULES!!
THAT'S TERRIBLE TO BREAK THE RULES YOU MADE YOURSELF!
ギュル
GWRRR
ギュル
GWRRR

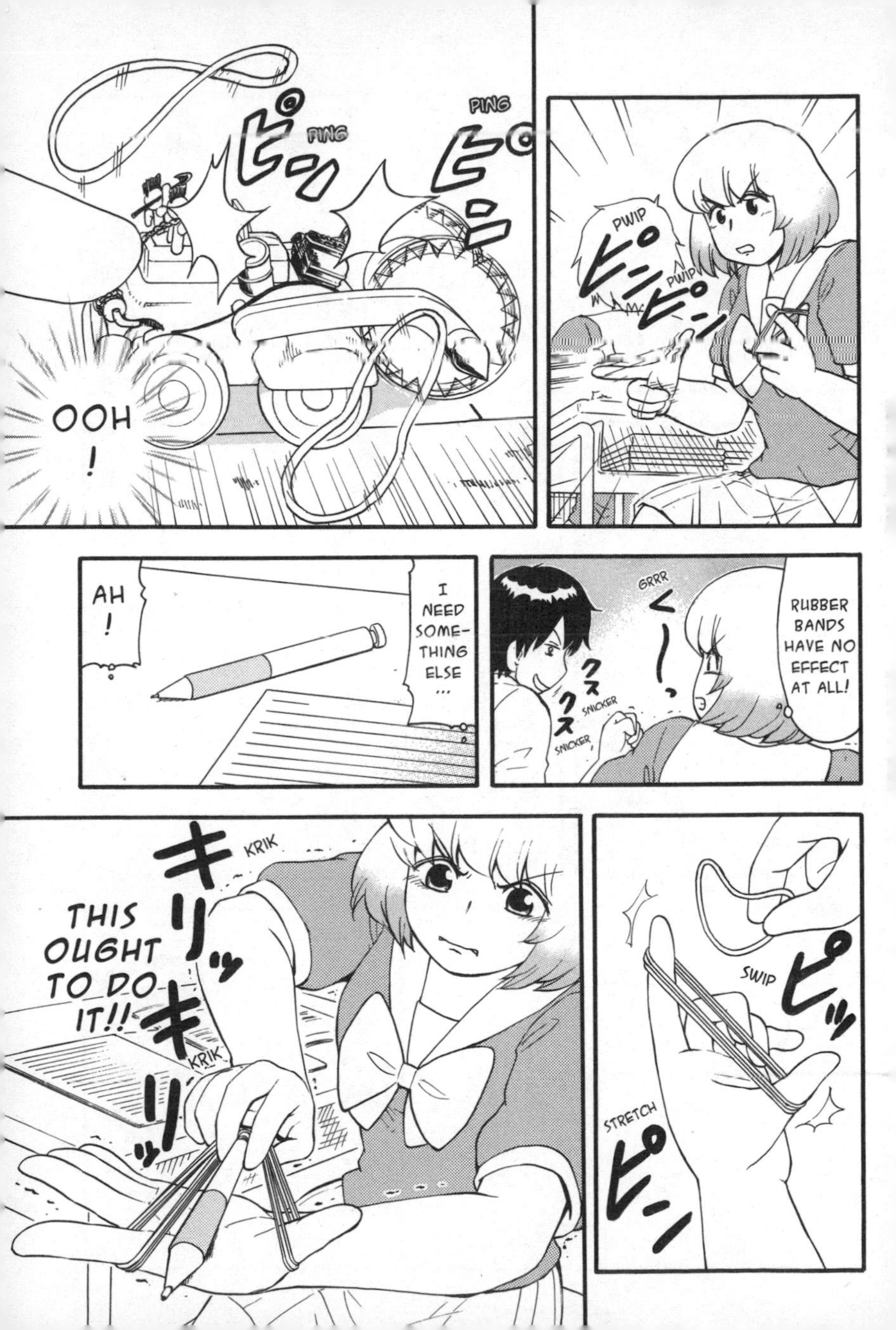

PWIP
PWIP
PING
PING
OOH!
RUBBER BANDS HAVE NO EFFECT AT ALL!
GRRR
SNICKER
SNICKER
I NEED SOMETHING ELSE...
AH!
SWIP
STRETCH
KRIK
KRIK
THIS OUGHT TO DO IT!!

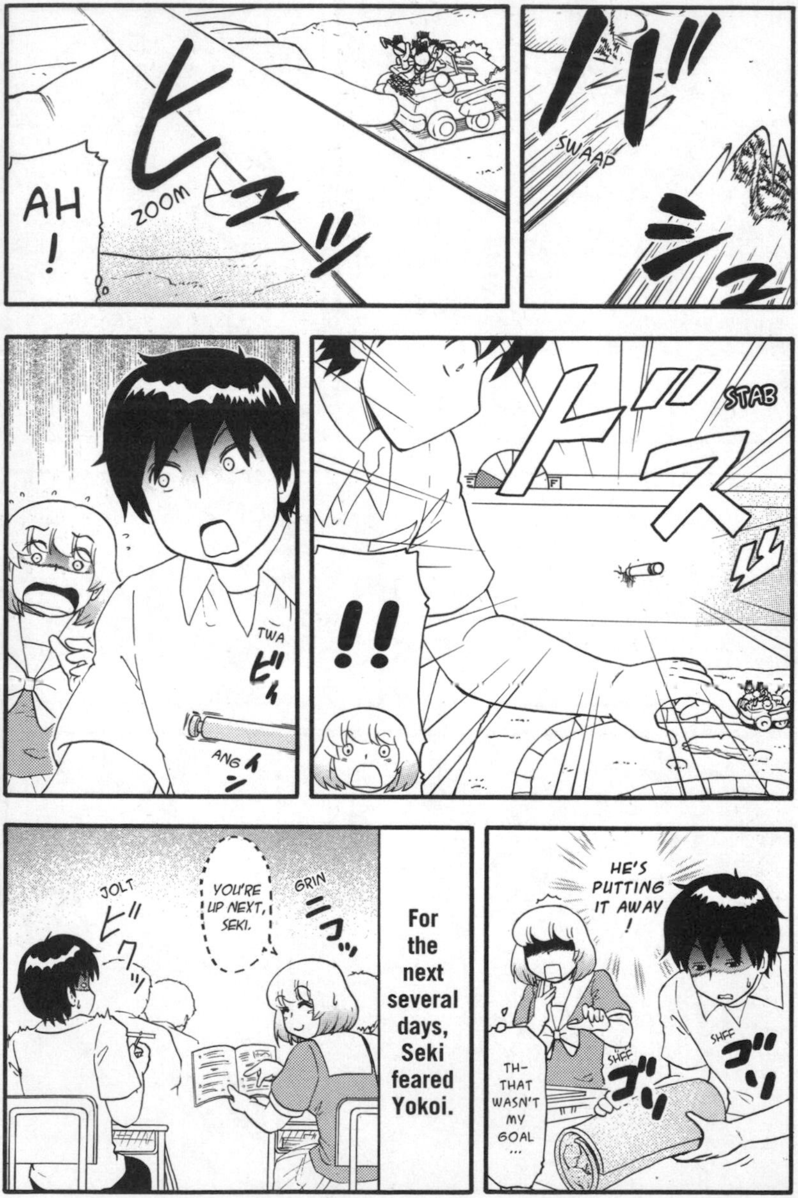
SWAAP
AH!
ZOOM
STAB
!!
TWA
ANG
HE'S PUTTING IT AWAY!
SHFF
SHFF
TH-THAT WASN'T MY GOAL...
For the next several days, Seki feared Yokoi.
GRIN
YOU'RE UP NEXT, SEKI.
JOLT

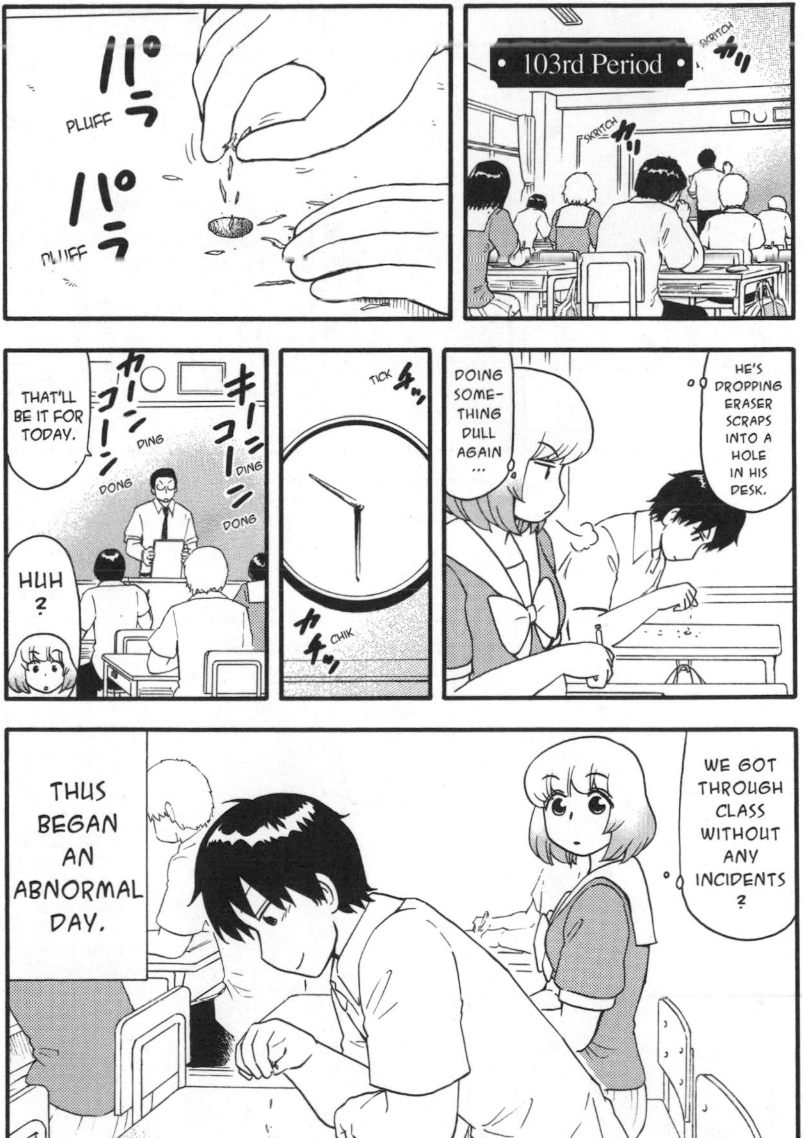
• 103rd Period •
SKRITCH
ガリ
SKRITCH
ガリ
パラ
PLUFF
パラ
PLUFF
HE'S DROPPING ERASER SCRAPS INTO A HOLE IN HIS DESK.
DOING SOME-THING DULL AGAIN ...
TICK
チッ
カチッ
CHIK
キーンコーン
DING
DONG
カーンコーン
DING
DONG
THAT'LL BE IT FOR TODAY.
HUH ?
WE GOT THROUGH CLASS WITHOUT ANY INCIDENTS ?
THUS BEGAN AN ABNORMAL DAY.

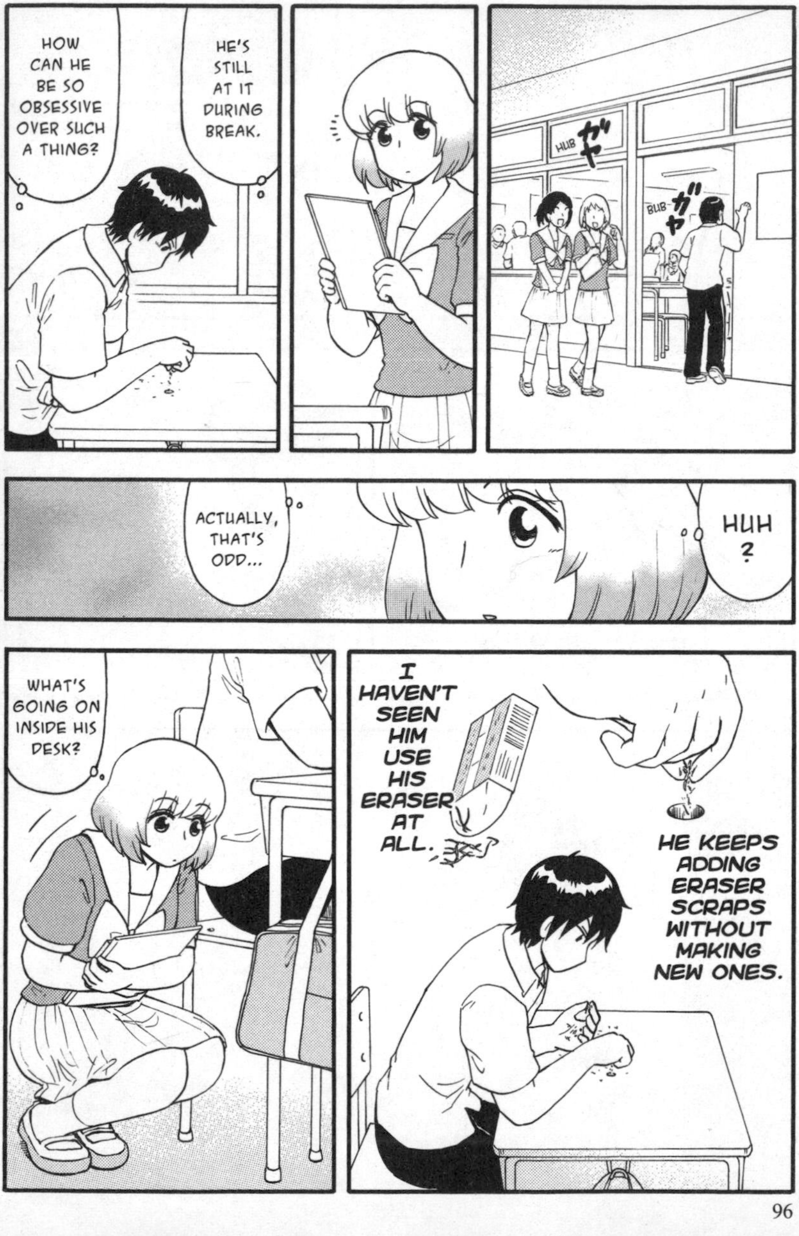
HUB ガヤ
BUB- ガヤ
HE'S STILL AT IT DURING BREAK.
HOW CAN HE BE SO OBSESSIVE OVER SUCH A THING?
HUH?
ACTUALLY, THAT'S ODD...
I HAVEN'T SEEN HIM USE HIS ERASER AT ALL.
HE KEEPS ADDING ERASER SCRAPS WITHOUT MAKING NEW ONES.
WHAT'S GOING ON INSIDE HIS DESK?

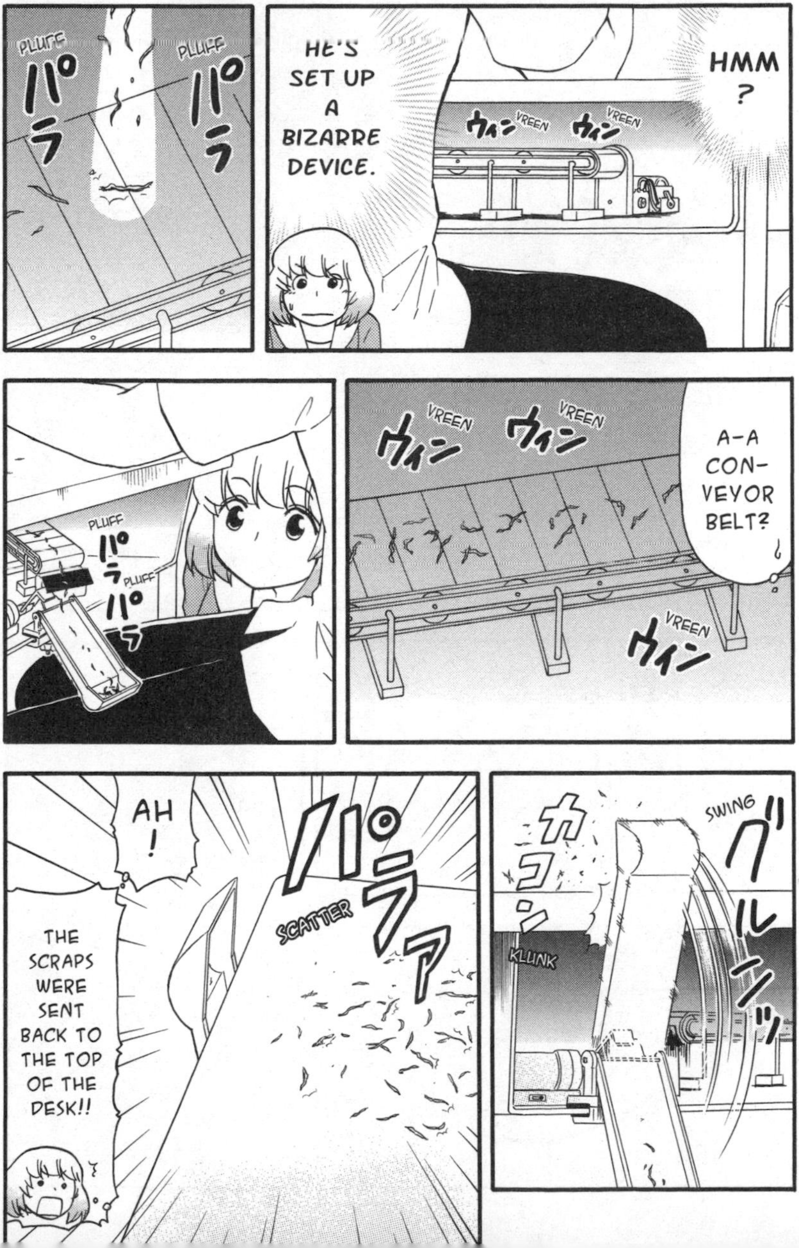
HMM
?
VREEN
ウィン
VREEN
ウィン
HE'S SET UP A BIZARRE DEVICE.
PLUFF
パラ
PLUFF
パラ
VREEN
ウィン
VREEN
ウィン
A-A CON-VEYOR BELT?
VREEN
ウィン
PLUFF
パラ
PLUFF
パラ
SWING
グルンッ
カコン
KLUNK
AH
!
パラァ
SCATTER
THE SCRAPS WERE SENT BACK TO THE TOP OF THE DESK!!

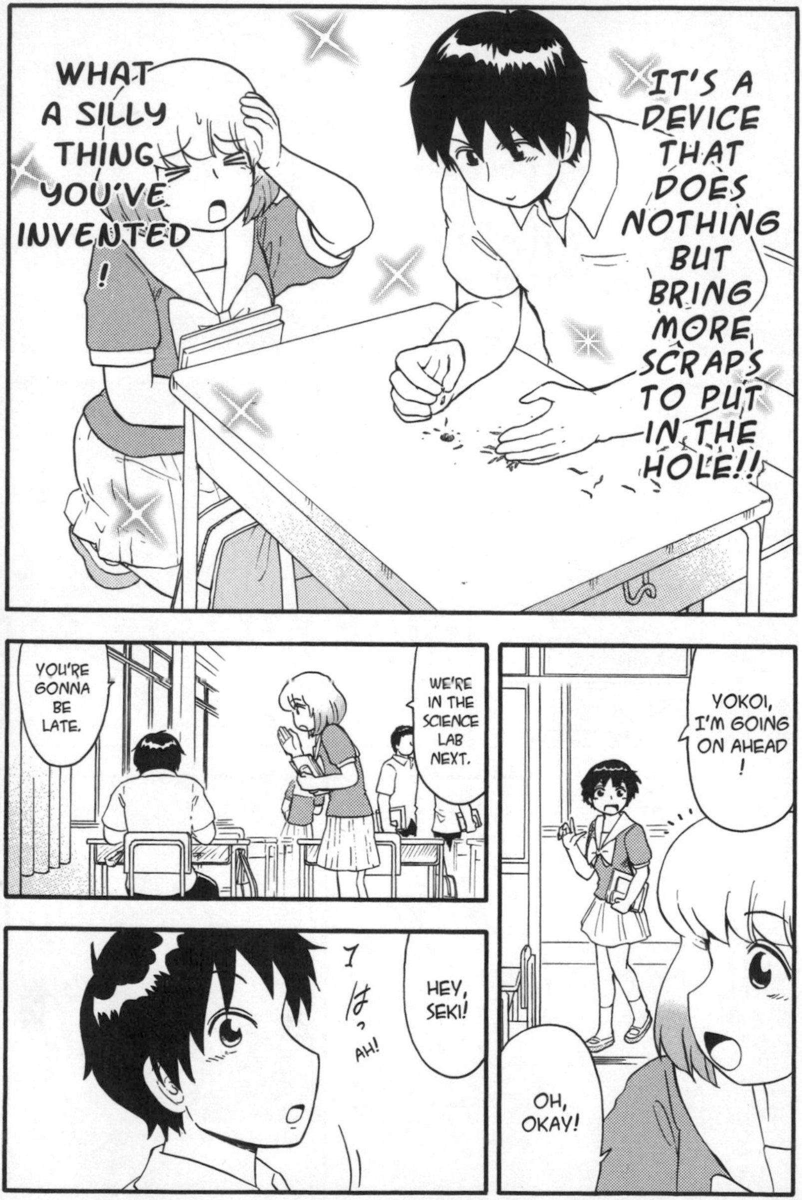
IT'S A DEVICE THAT DOES NOTHING BUT BRING MORE SCRAPS TO PUT IN THE HOLE!!
WHAT A SILLY THING YOU'VE INVENTED!
YOKOI, I'M GOING ON AHEAD!
OH, OKAY!
WE'RE IN THE SCIENCE LAB NEXT.
YOU'RE GONNA BE LATE.
HEY, SEKI!
AH!

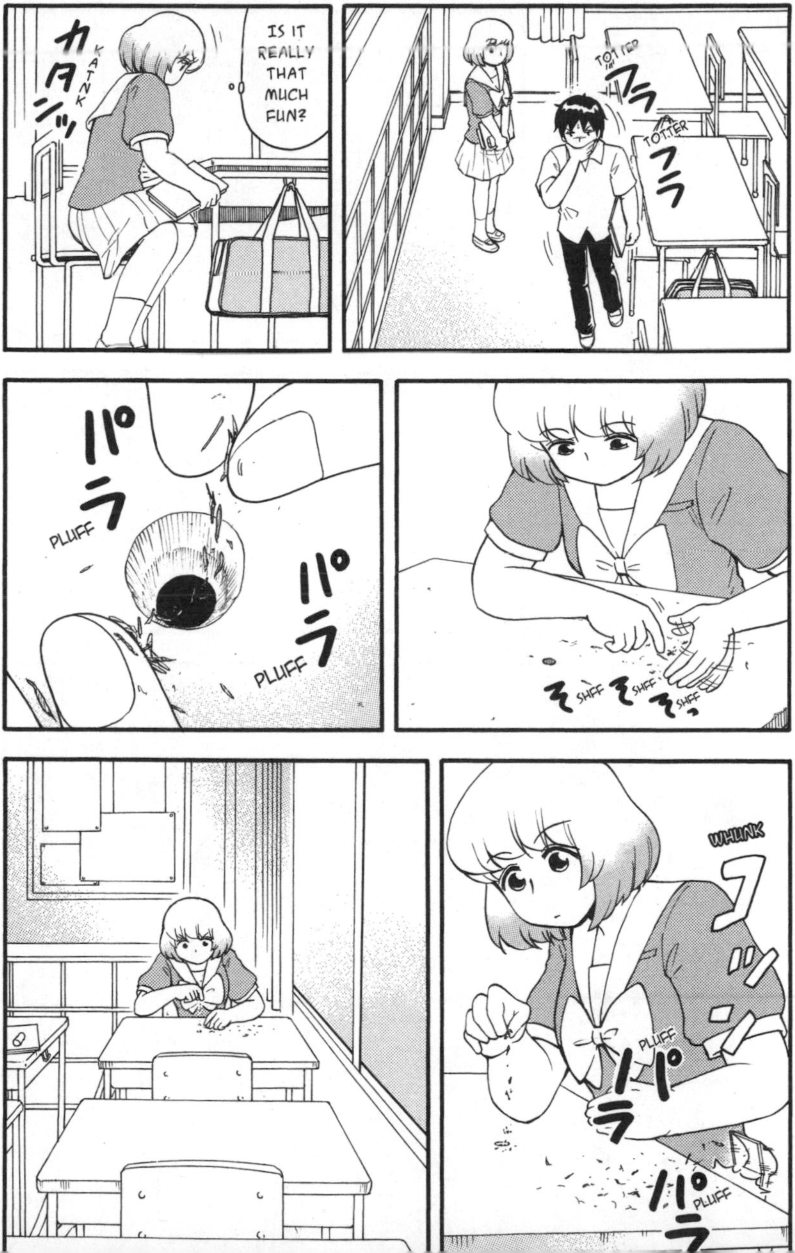
TOTTER
フラ
TOTTER
フラ
カタンッ
KATNK
IS IT REALLY THAT MUCH FUN?
SHFF
SHFF
SHFF
パラ
PLUFF
パラ
PLUFF
WHUNK
PLUFF
パラ
PLUFF
パラ

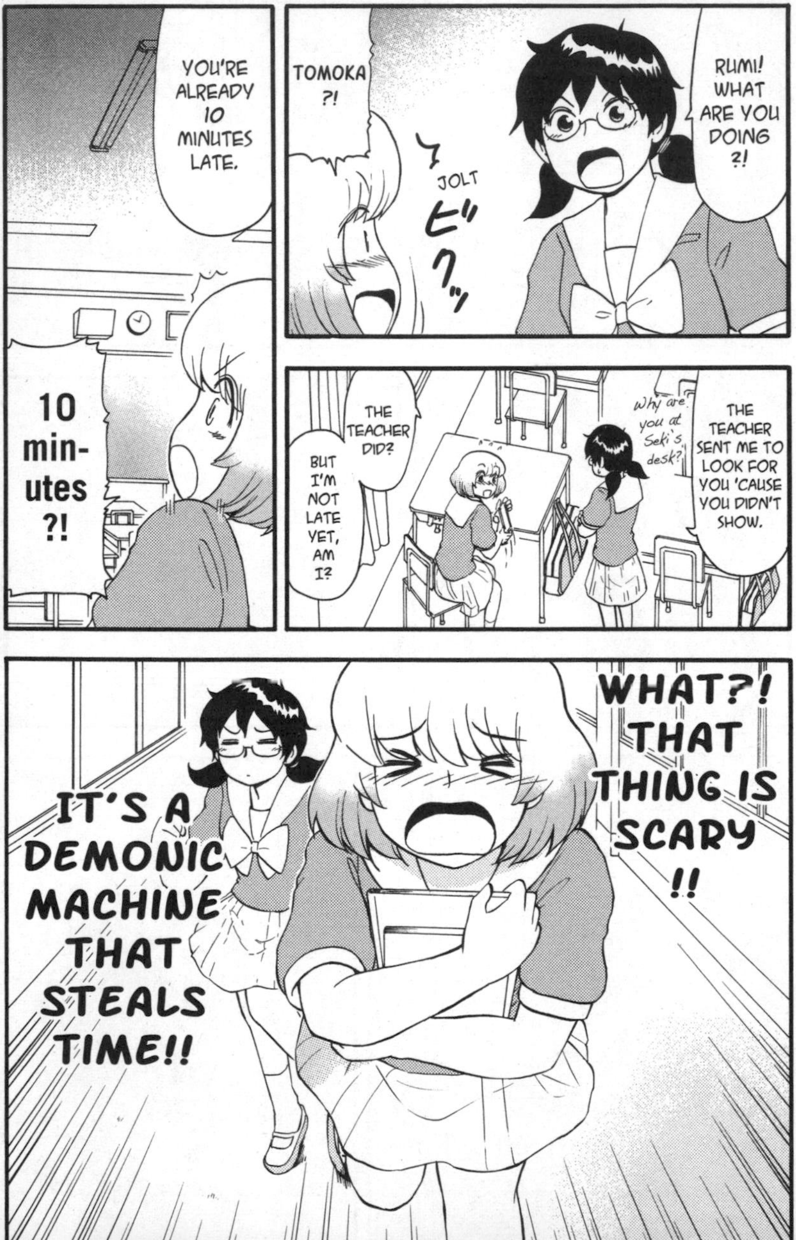
RUMI! WHAT ARE YOU DOING ?!
TOMOKA ?!
JOLT
ビクッ
Why are you at Seki's desk?
THE TEACHER SENT ME TO LOOK FOR YOU 'CAUSE YOU DIDN'T SHOW.
THE TEACHER DID?
BUT I'M NOT LATE YET, AM I?
YOU'RE ALREADY 10 MINUTES LATE.
10 min-utes ?!
WHAT?! THAT THING IS SCARY !!
IT'S A DEMONIC MACHINE THAT STEALS TIME!!

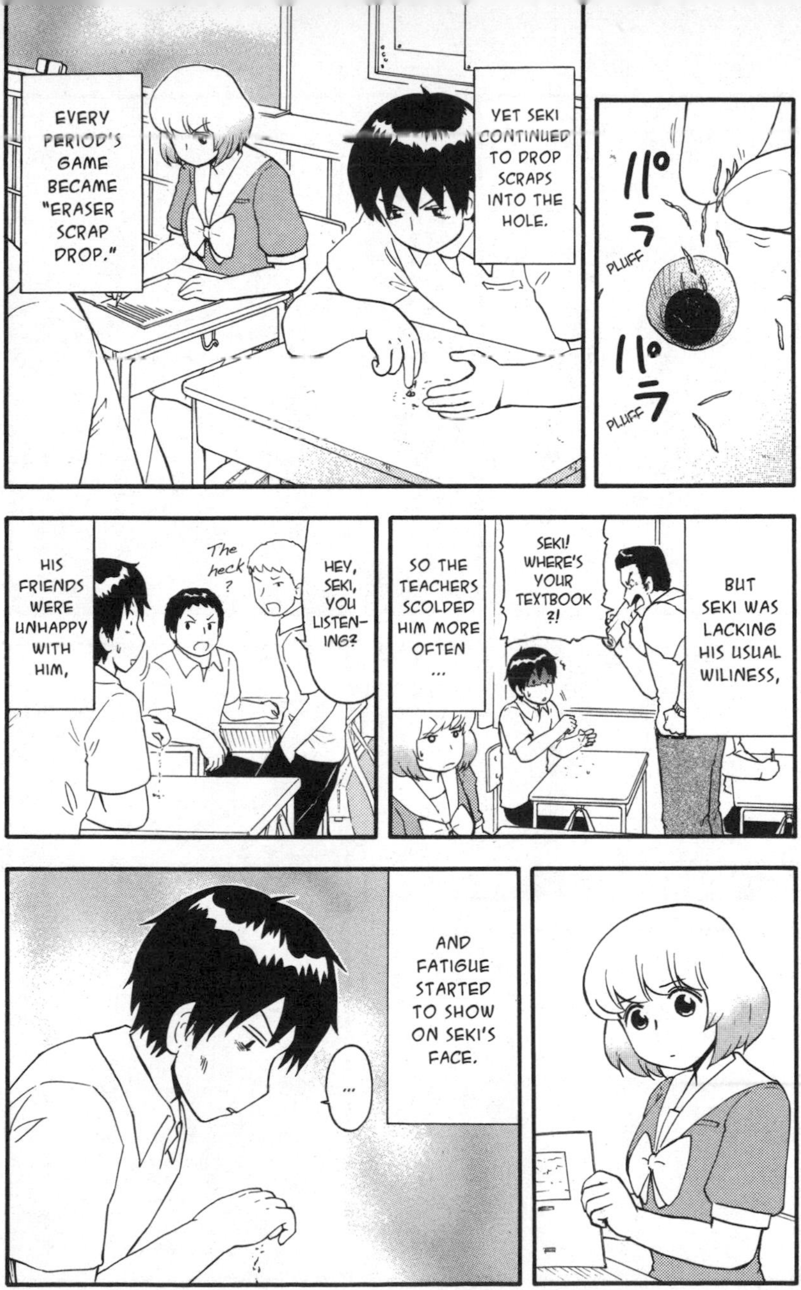
パラ
PLUFF
パラ
PLUFF
YET SEKI CONTINUED TO DROP SCRAPS INTO THE HOLE.
EVERY PERIOD'S GAME BECAME "ERASER SCRAP DROP."
BUT SEKI WAS LACKING HIS USUAL WILINESS,
SEKI! WHERE'S YOUR TEXTBOOK?!
SO THE TEACHERS SCOLDED HIM MORE OFTEN...
HEY, SEKI, YOU LISTENING?
The heck?
HIS FRIENDS WERE UNHAPPY WITH HIM,
AND FATIGUE STARTED TO SHOW ON SEKI'S FACE.
...

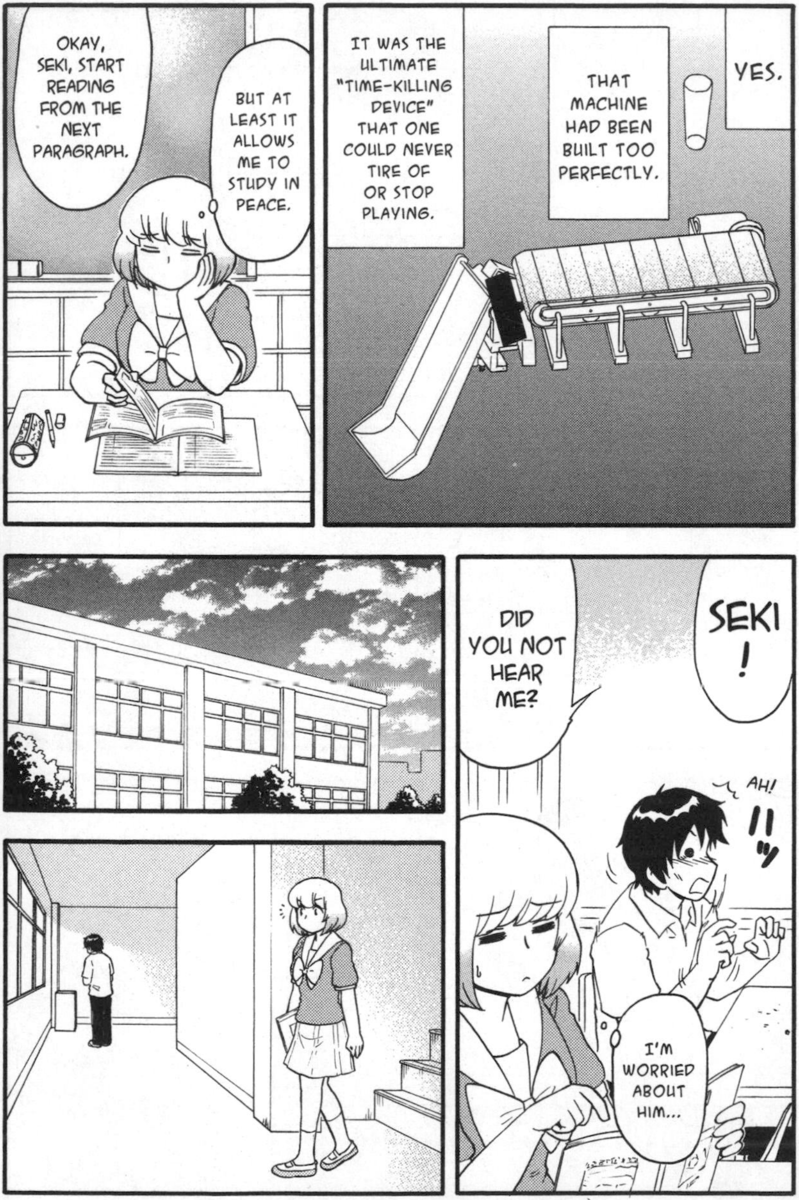
YES.
THAT MACHINE HAD BEEN BUILT TOO PERFECTLY.
IT WAS THE ULTIMATE "TIME-KILLING DEVICE" THAT ONE COULD NEVER TIRE OF OR STOP PLAYING.
BUT AT LEAST IT ALLOWS ME TO STUDY IN PEACE.
OKAY, SEKI, START READING FROM THE NEXT PARAGRAPH.
SEKI!
DID YOU NOT HEAR ME?
AH!
ハッ
I'M WORRIED ABOUT HIM...

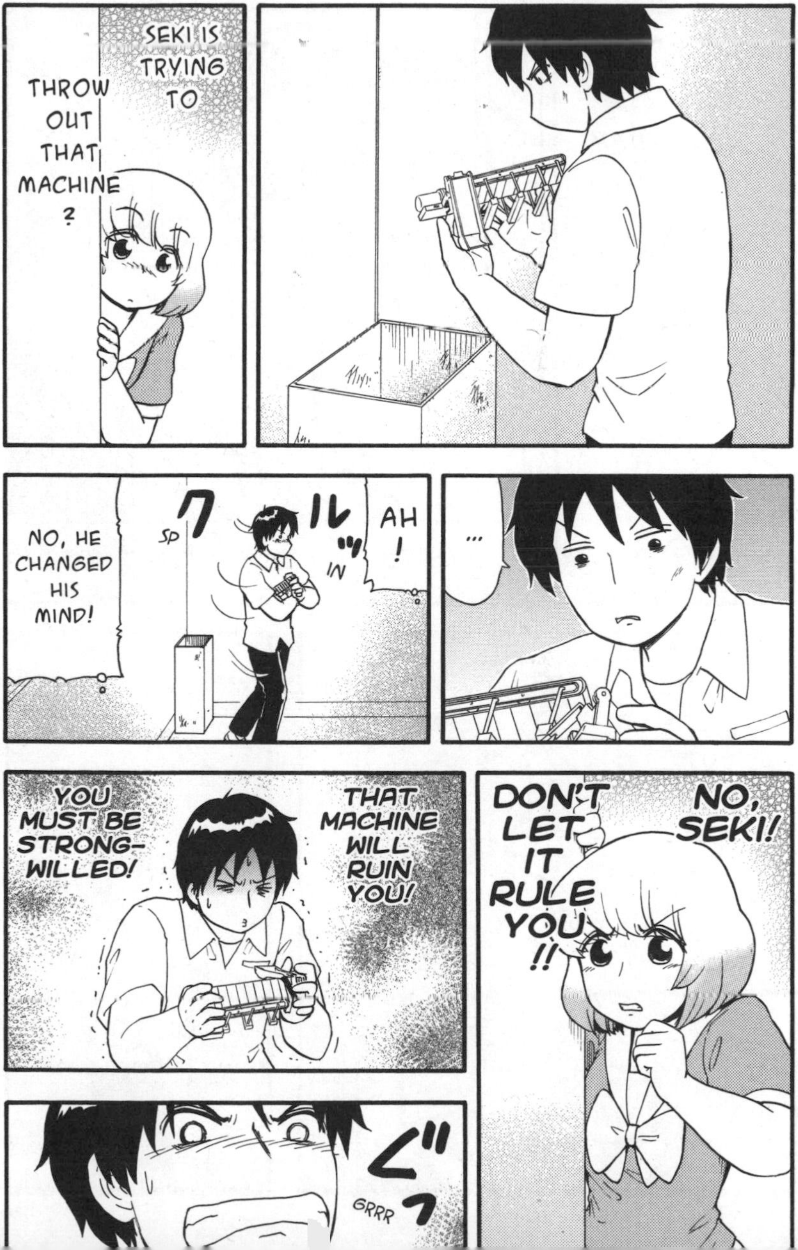
SEKI IS TRYING TO
THROW OUT THAT MACHINE ?
...
AH !
NO, HE CHANGED HIS MIND!
SP
IN
NO, SEKI!
DON'T LET IT RULE YOU !!
THAT MACHINE WILL RUIN YOU!
YOU MUST BE STRONG-WILLED!
GRRR

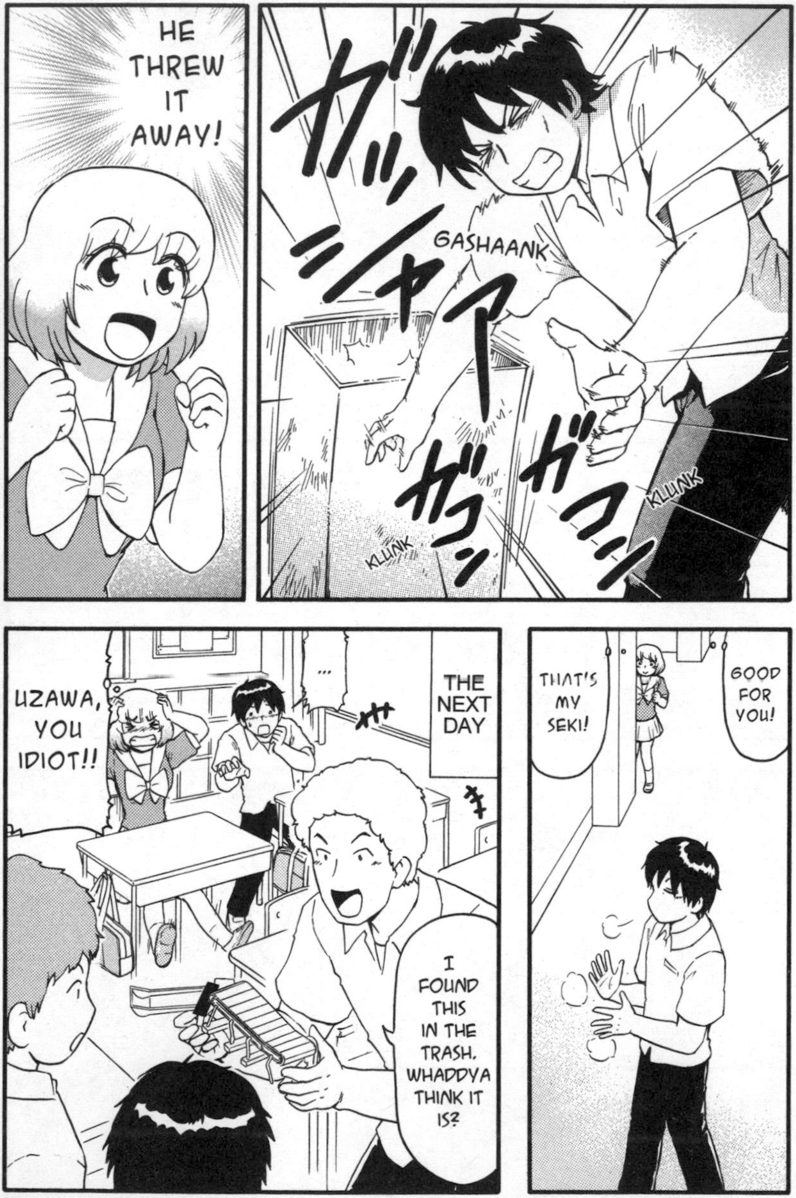
GASHAANK
KLUNK
KLUNK
HE THREW IT AWAY!
GOOD FOR YOU!
THAT'S MY SEKI!
THE NEXT DAY
...
UZAWA, YOU IDIOT!!
I FOUND THIS IN THE TRASH. WHADDYA THINK IT IS?

My Neighbor Seki

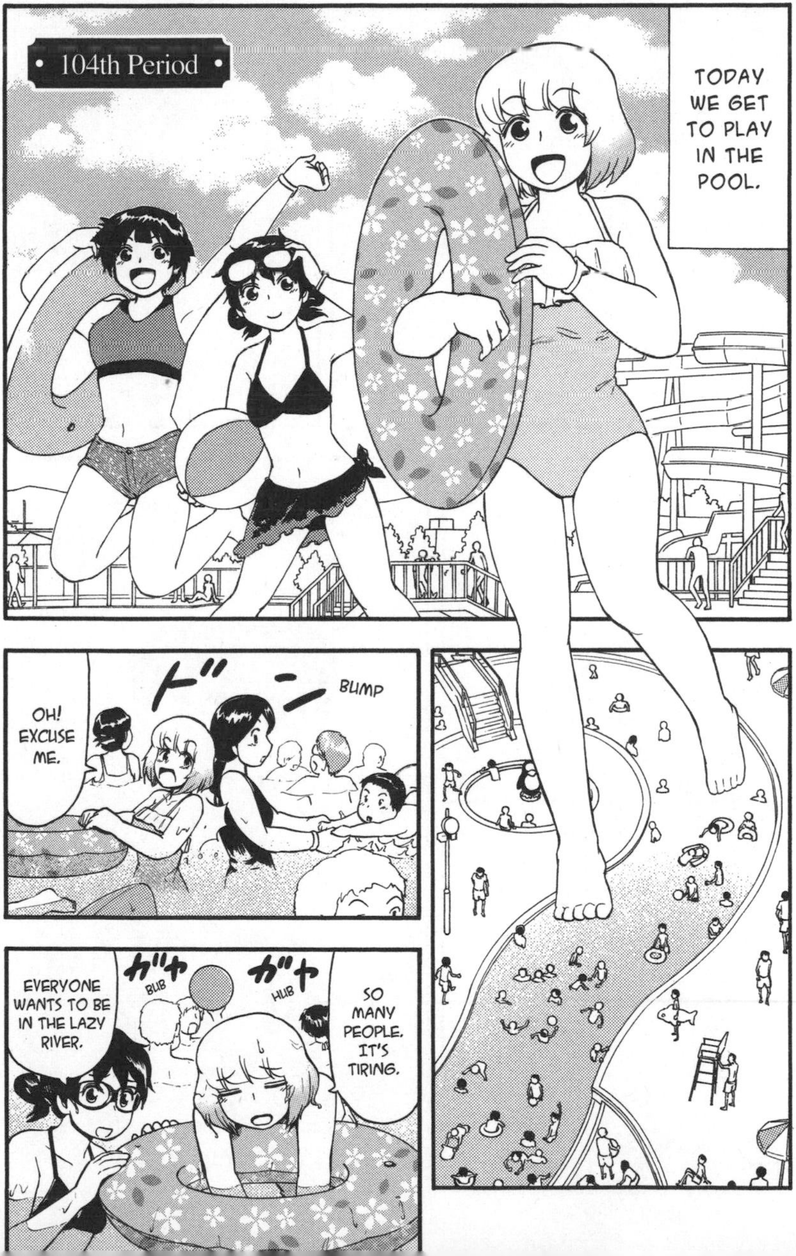
104th Period
TODAY WE GET TO PLAY IN THE POOL.
ドーン
BUMP
OH! EXCUSE ME.
ガヤ
BUB
ガヤ
HUB
SO MANY PEOPLE. IT'S TIRING.
EVERYONE WANTS TO BE IN THE LAZY RIVER.

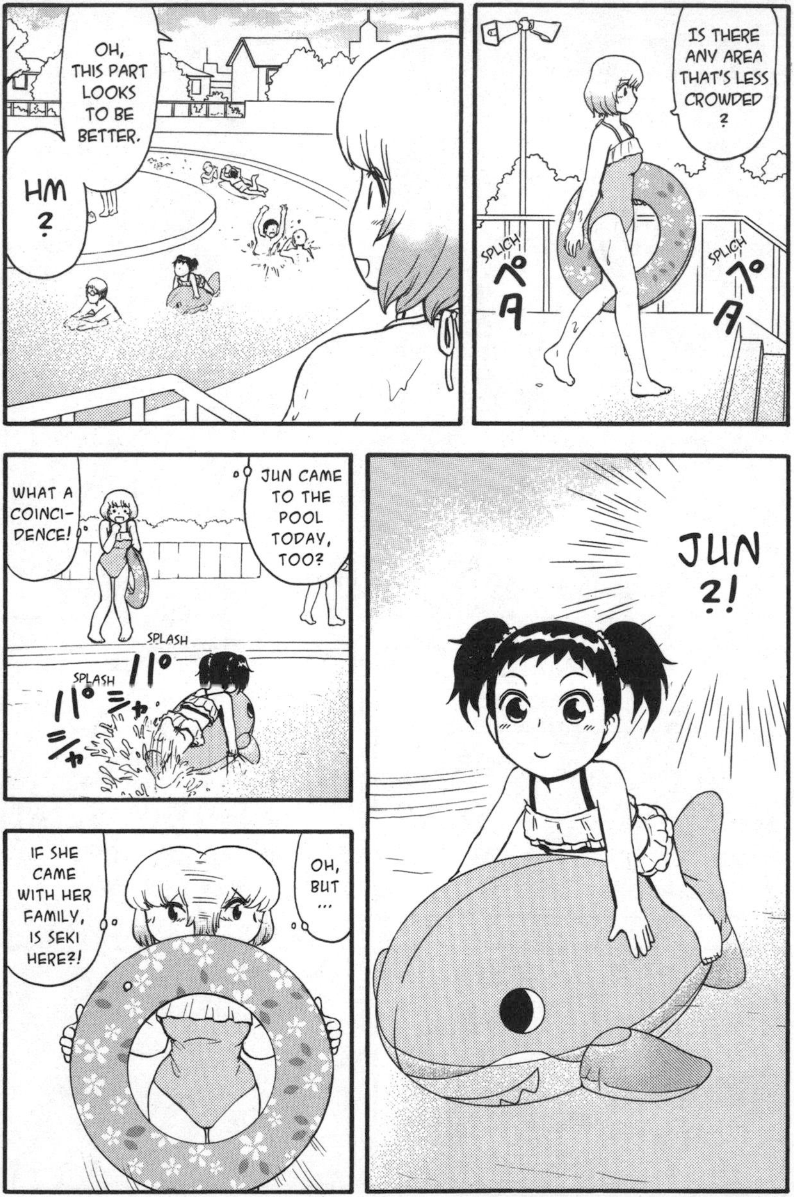

IS THERE ANY AREA THAT'S LESS CROWDED?
SPLICH
ペタ
SPLICH
ペタ
OH, THIS PART LOOKS TO BE BETTER.
HM?
JUN?!
JUN CAME TO THE POOL TODAY, TOO?
WHAT A COINCIDENCE!
SPLASH
パ
SPLASH
パシャ
シャ
OH, BUT...
IF SHE CAME WITH HER FAMILY, IS SEKI HERE?!

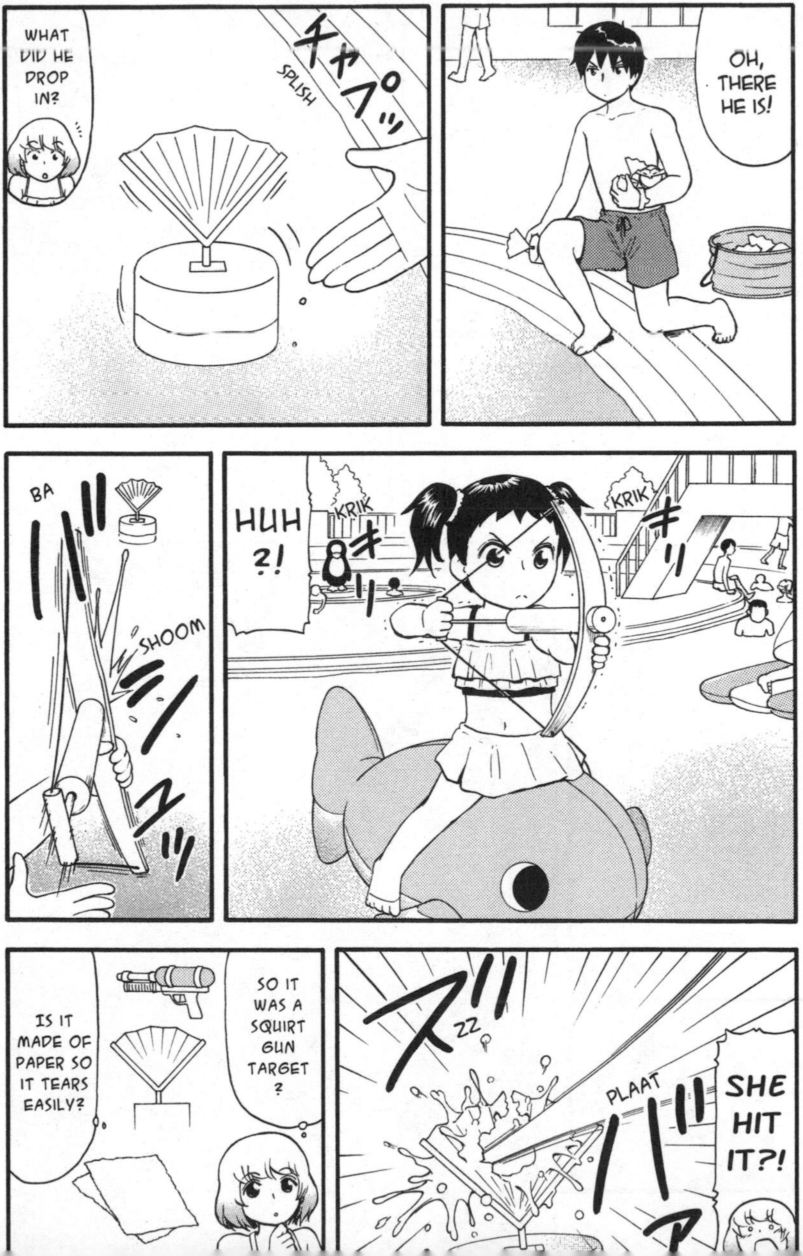
OH, THERE HE IS!
WHAT DID HE DROP IN?
チャプッ
SPLISH
HUH ?!
キリ
KRIK
キリ
KRIK
バ
BA
シュッ
SHOOM
ズ
ZZ
パァ
PLAAT
SHE HIT IT?!
SO IT WAS A SQUIRT GUN TARGET?
IS IT MADE OF PAPER SO IT TEARS EASILY?

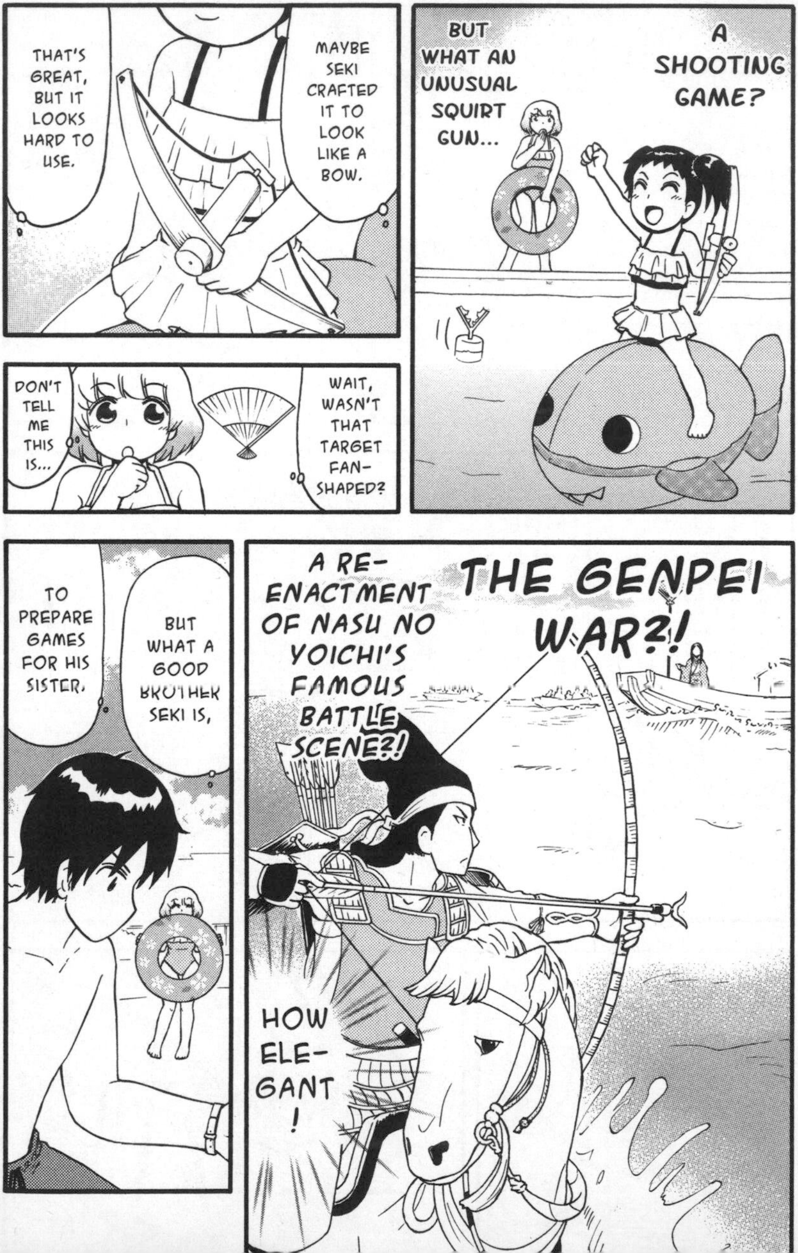
A SHOOTING GAME?
BUT WHAT AN UNUSUAL SQUIRT GUN...
MAYBE SEKI CRAFTED IT TO LOOK LIKE A BOW.
THAT'S GREAT, BUT IT LOOKS HARD TO USE.
WAIT, WASN'T THAT TARGET FAN-SHAPED?
DON'T TELL ME THIS IS...
THE GENPEI WAR?!
A RE-ENACTMENT OF NASU NO YOICHI'S FAMOUS BATTLE SCENE?!
HOW ELEGANT!
BUT WHAT A GOOD BROTHER SEKI IS,
TO PREPARE GAMES FOR HIS SISTER.

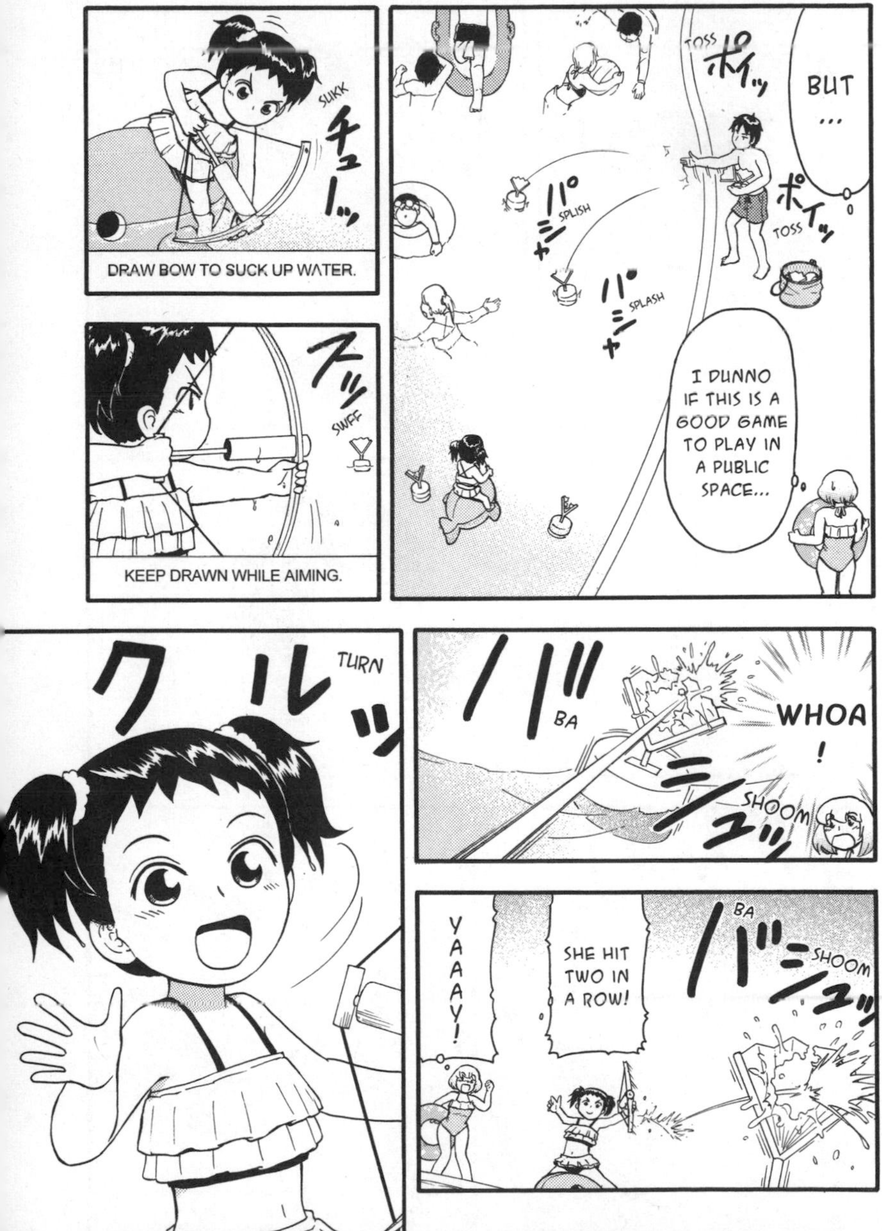

BUT ...
TOSS ポイッ
TOSS ポイッ
SPLISH パシャ
SPLASH パシャ
I DUNNO IF THIS IS A GOOD GAME TO PLAY IN A PUBLIC SPACE...
SUKK チューッ
DRAW BOW TO SUCK UP WATER.
SWFF スッ
KEEP DRAWN WHILE AIMING.
BA バ
WHOA!
SHOOM シュッ
BA バ
SHOOM シュッ
YAAAAY!
SHE HIT TWO IN A ROW!
TURN クルッ

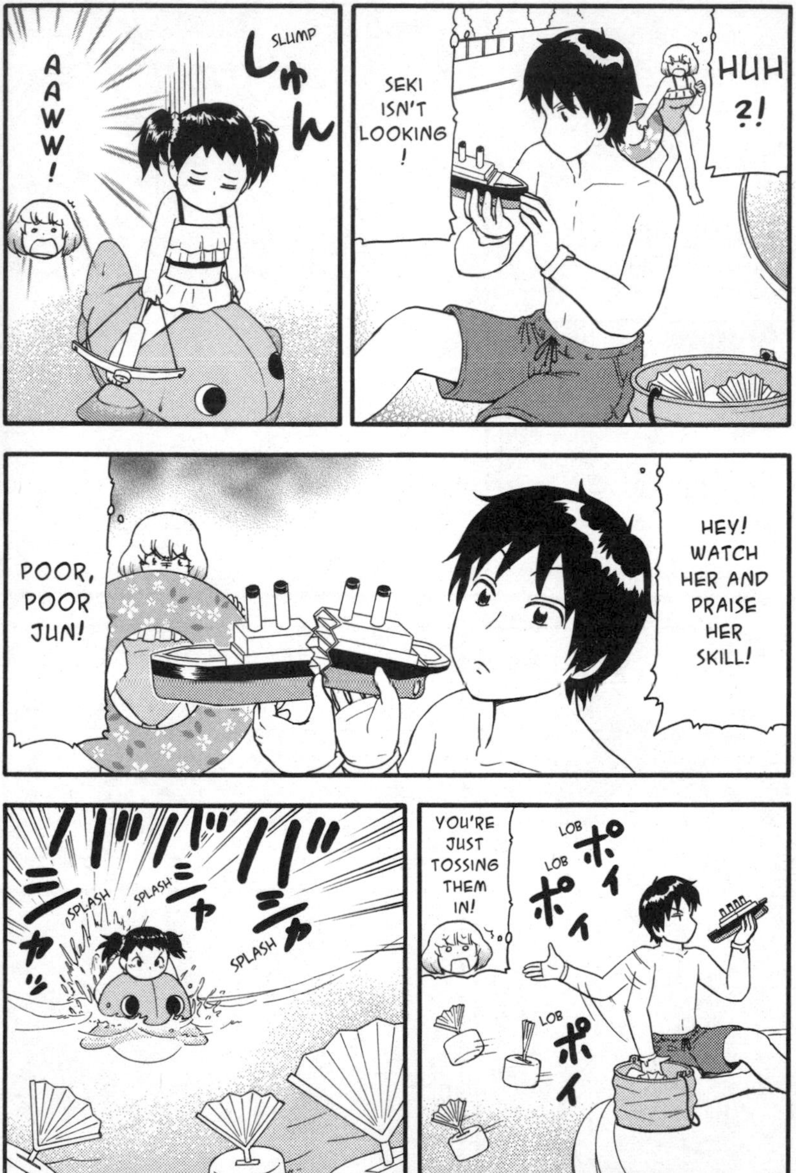
HUH ?!
SEKI ISN'T LOOKING !
SLUMP
しゅん
AAWW!
HEY! WATCH HER AND PRAISE HER SKILL!
POOR, POOR JUN!
YOU'RE JUST TOSSING THEM IN!
LOB
ポイ
LOB
ポイ
LOB
ポイ
バババ
SPLASH
シャ
SPLASH
シャ
SPLASH
シャ
SPLASH
シャカッ

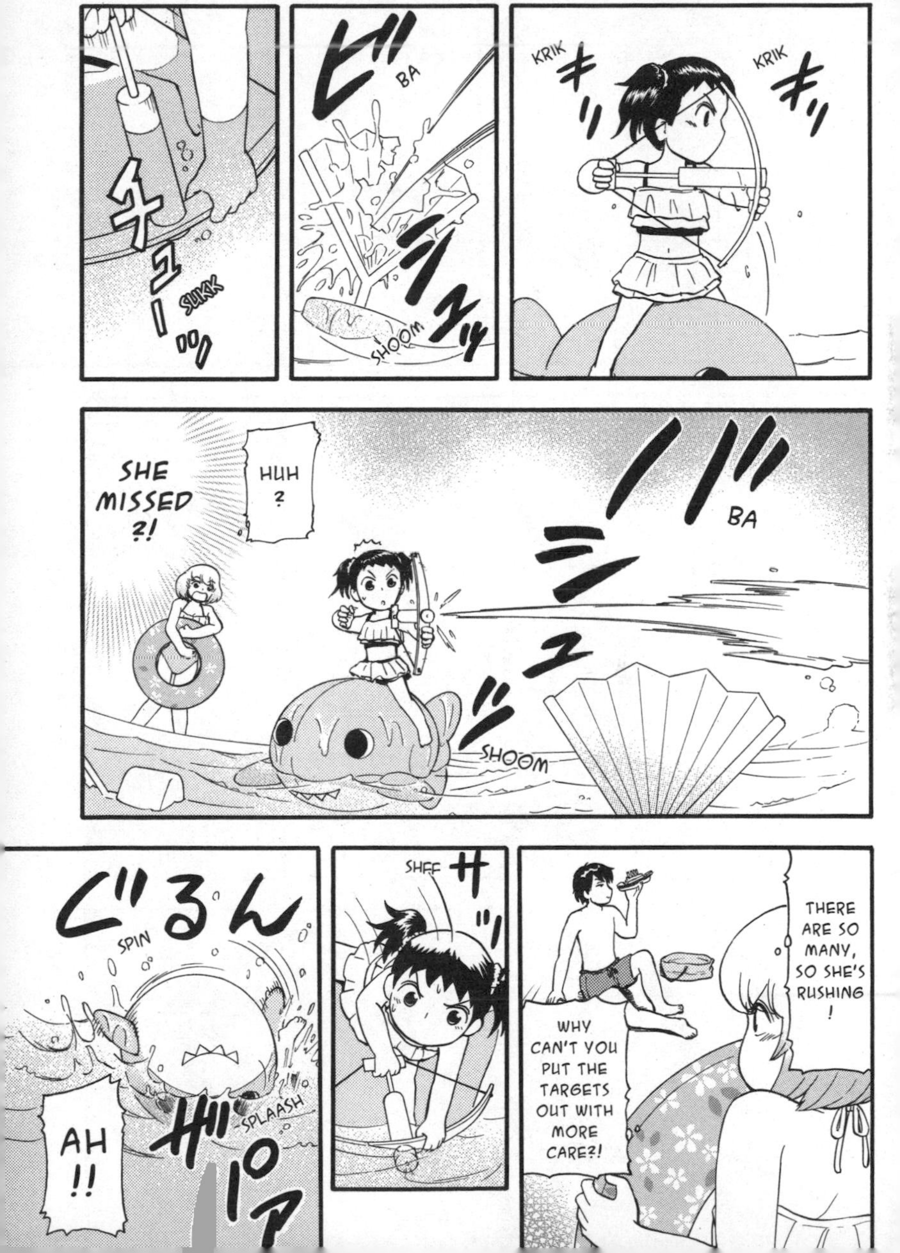

KRIK
KRIK
BA
SHOOM
SUKK
BA
SHOOM
HUH?
SHE MISSED?!
THERE ARE SO MANY, SO SHE'S RUSHING!
WHY CAN'T YOU PUT THE TARGETS OUT WITH MORE CARE?!
SHFF
SPIN
SPLAASH
AH!!

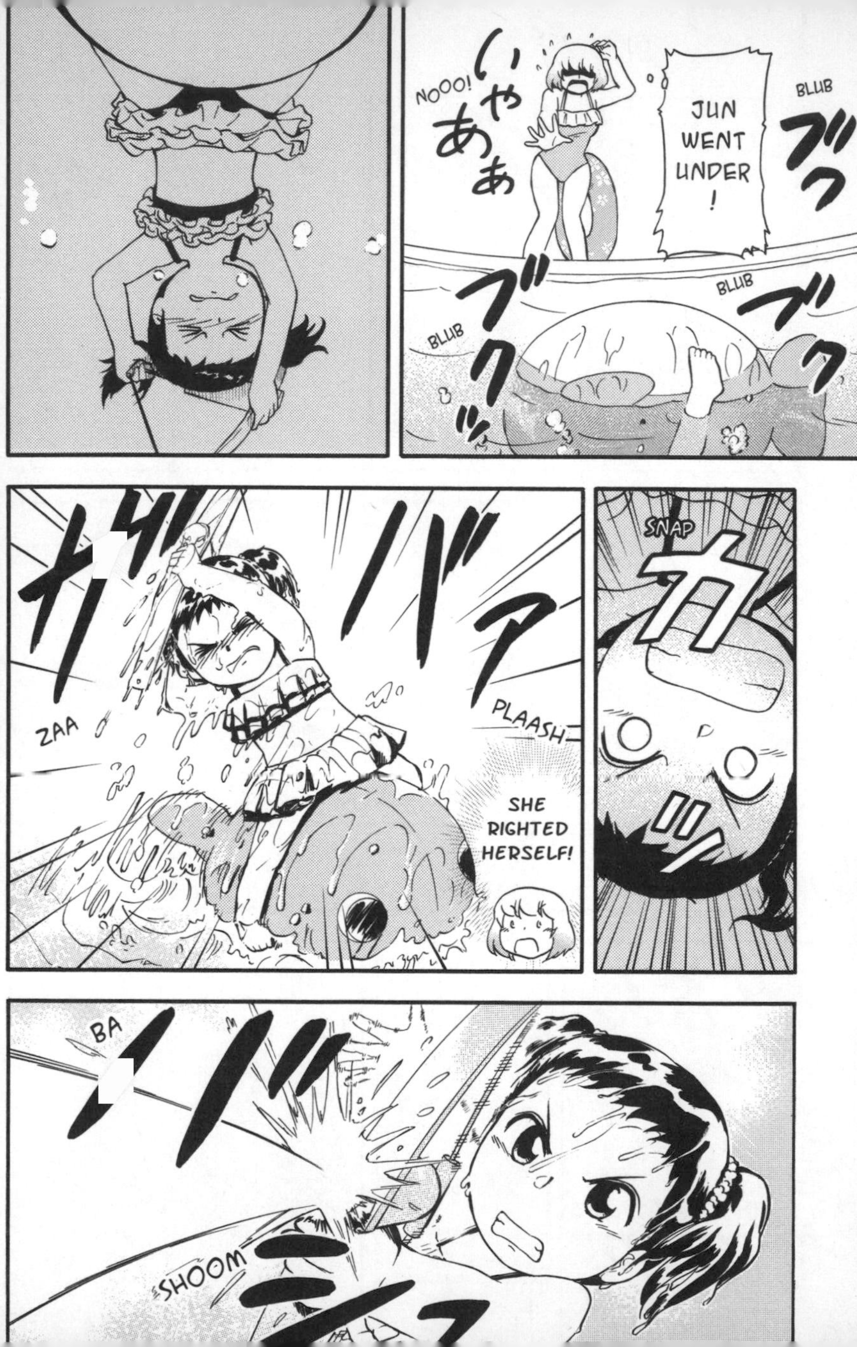
JUN WENT UNDER!
NOOO!
BLUB
BLUB
BLUB
SNAP
PLAASH
ZAA
SHE RIGHTED HERSELF!
BA
SHOOM

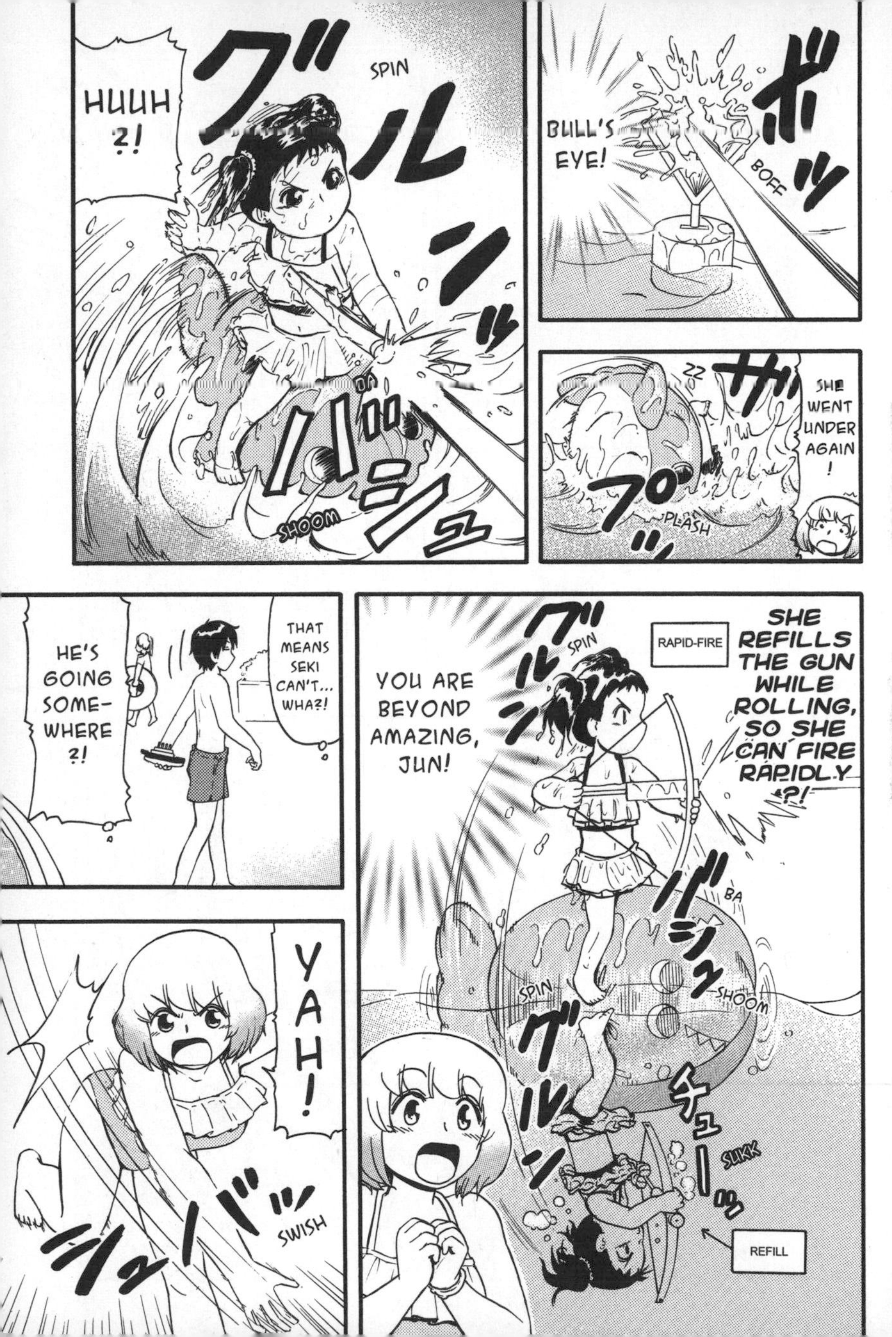
BULL'S EYE!
BOFF
ZZ
SHE WENT UNDER AGAIN!
PLASH
SPIN
HUUH?!
BA
SHOOM
RAPID-FIRE
SHE REFILLS THE GUN WHILE ROLLING, SO SHE CAN FIRE RAPIDLY?!
SPIN
YOU ARE BEYOND AMAZING, JUN!
BA
SPIN
SHOOM
SUKK
REFILL
THAT MEANS SEKI CAN'T... WHA?!
HE'S GOING SOME-WHERE?!
YAH!
SWISH

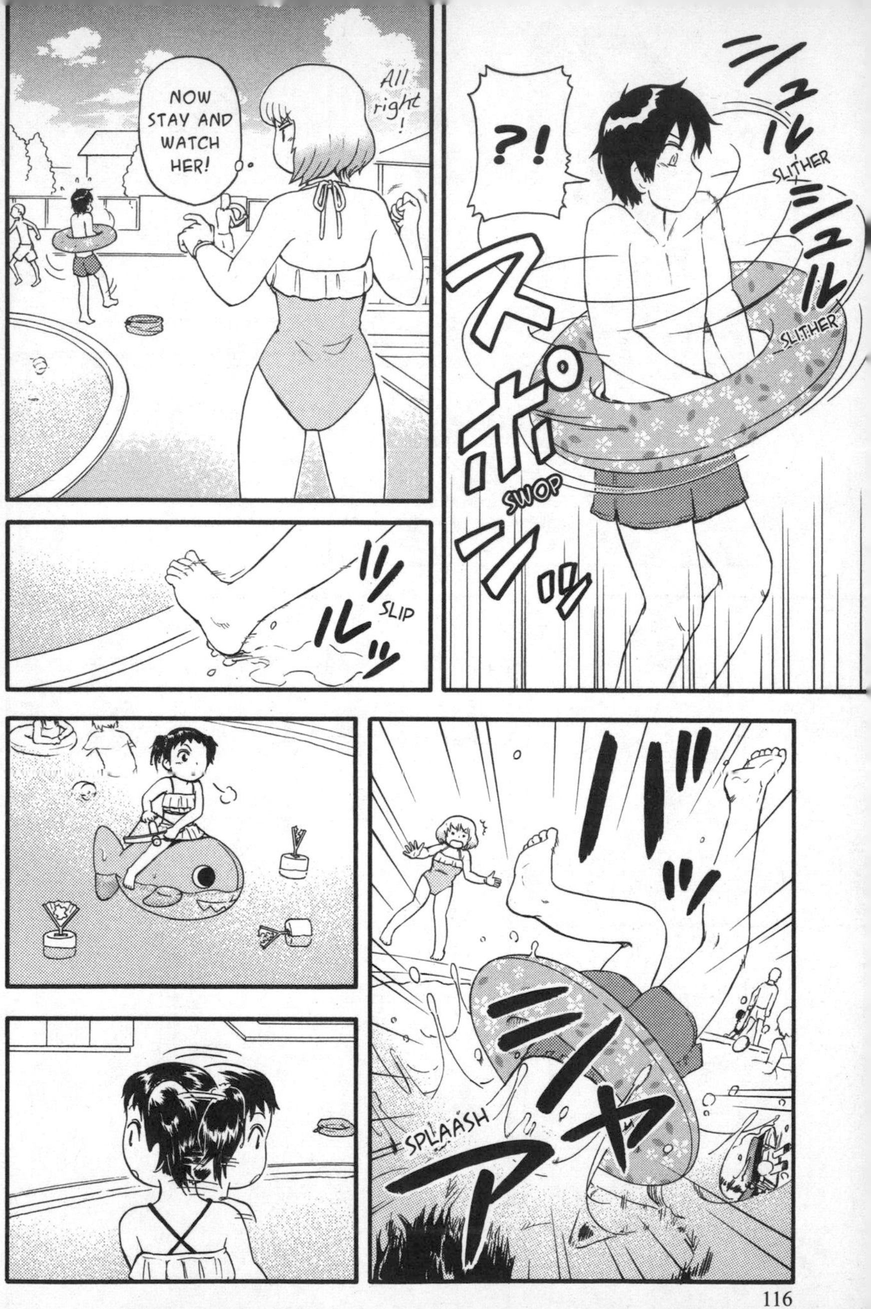

?!
シュル
SLITHER
シュル
SLITHER
スポンッ
SWOP
NOW STAY AND WATCH HER!
All right!
ツルッ
SLIP
バッ
シャア
SPLAASH

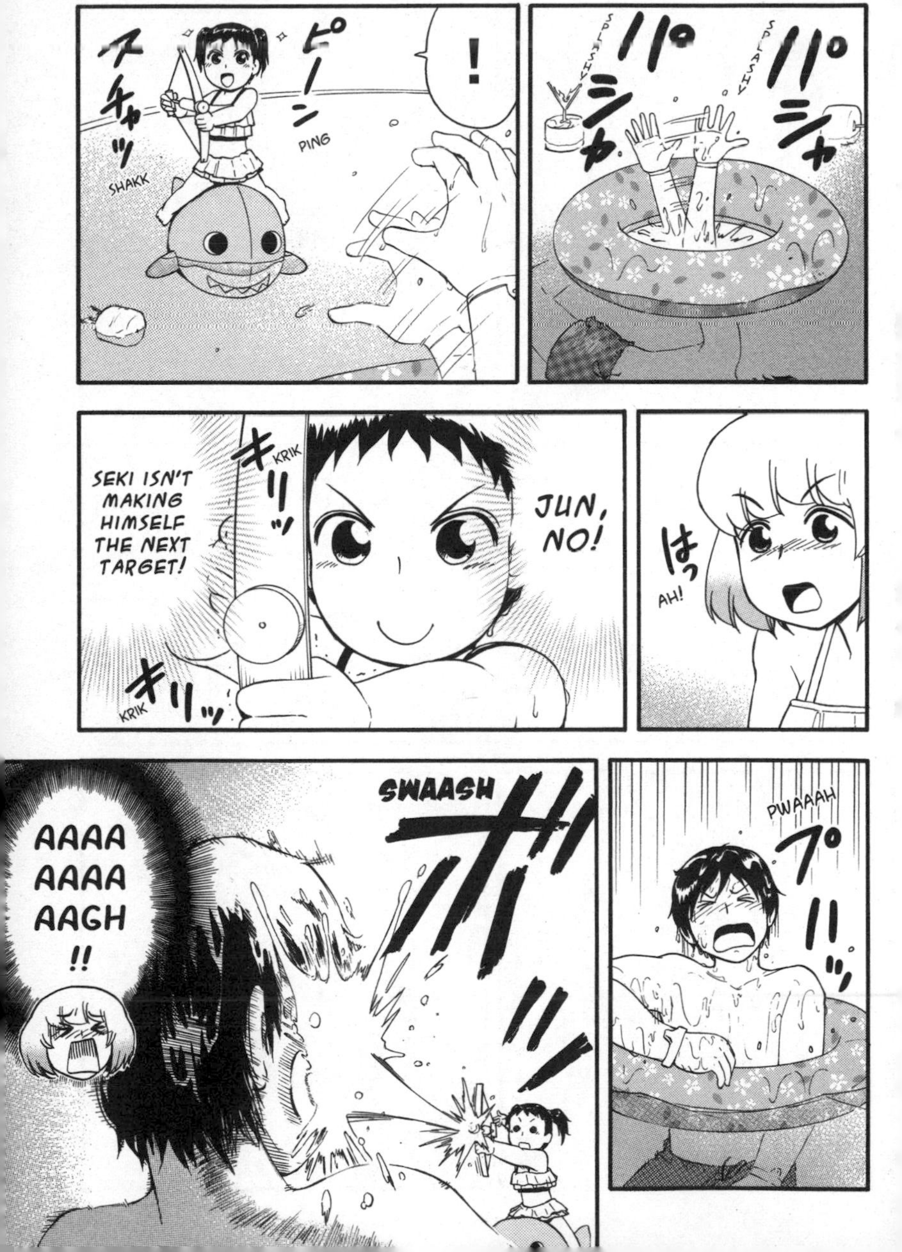
!
ピーン
PING
スチャッ
SHAKK
パシャ
SPLASH
パシャ
SPLASH
はっ
AH!
JUN, NO!
SEKI ISN'T MAKING HIMSELF THE NEXT TARGET!
キリッ
KRIK
キリッ
KRIK
プハッ
PWAAAH
SWAASH
ザバッ
AAAA AAAA AAGH !!

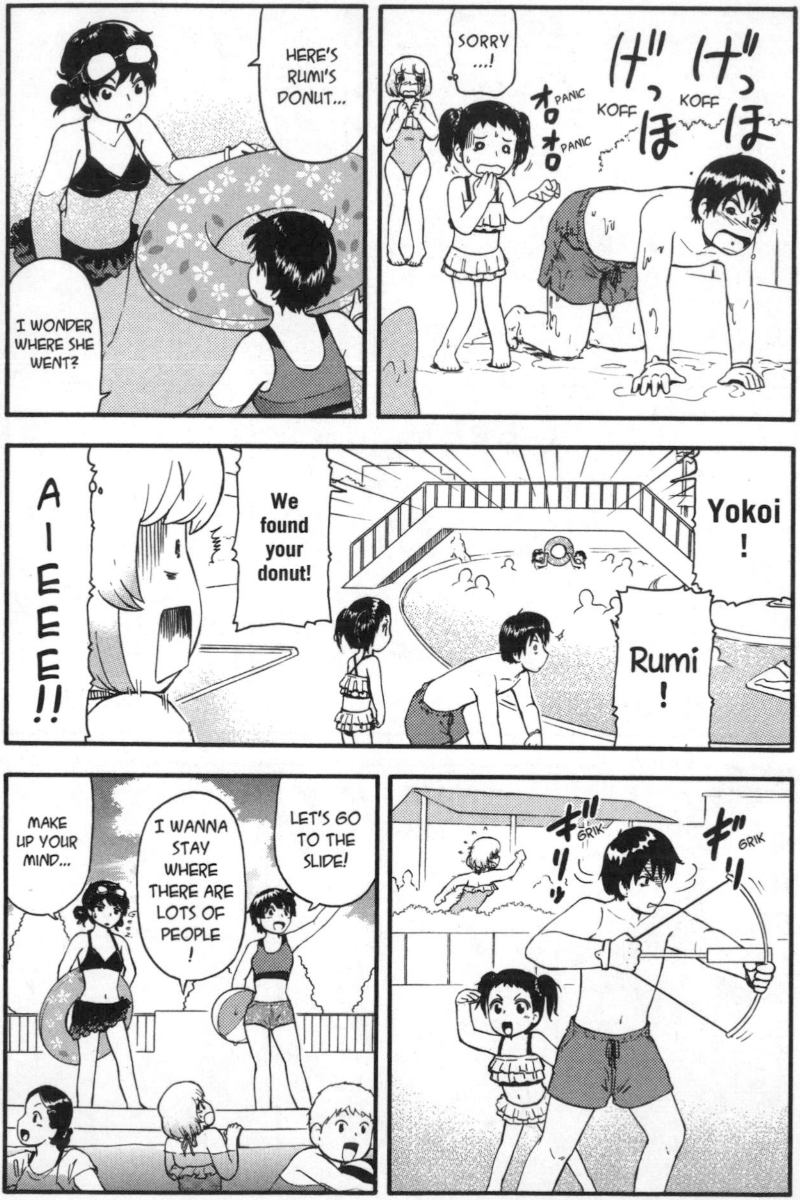
HERE'S RUMI'S DONUT...
I WONDER WHERE SHE WENT?
SORRY ...!
げっほ げっほ
KOFF KOFF
オロオロ
PANIC PANIC
AIEEE!!
We found your donut!
Yokoi!
Rumi!
MAKE UP YOUR MIND...
I WANNA STAY WHERE THERE ARE LOTS OF PEOPLE!
LET'S GO TO THE SLIDE!
ギリッ ギリッ
GRIK GRIK

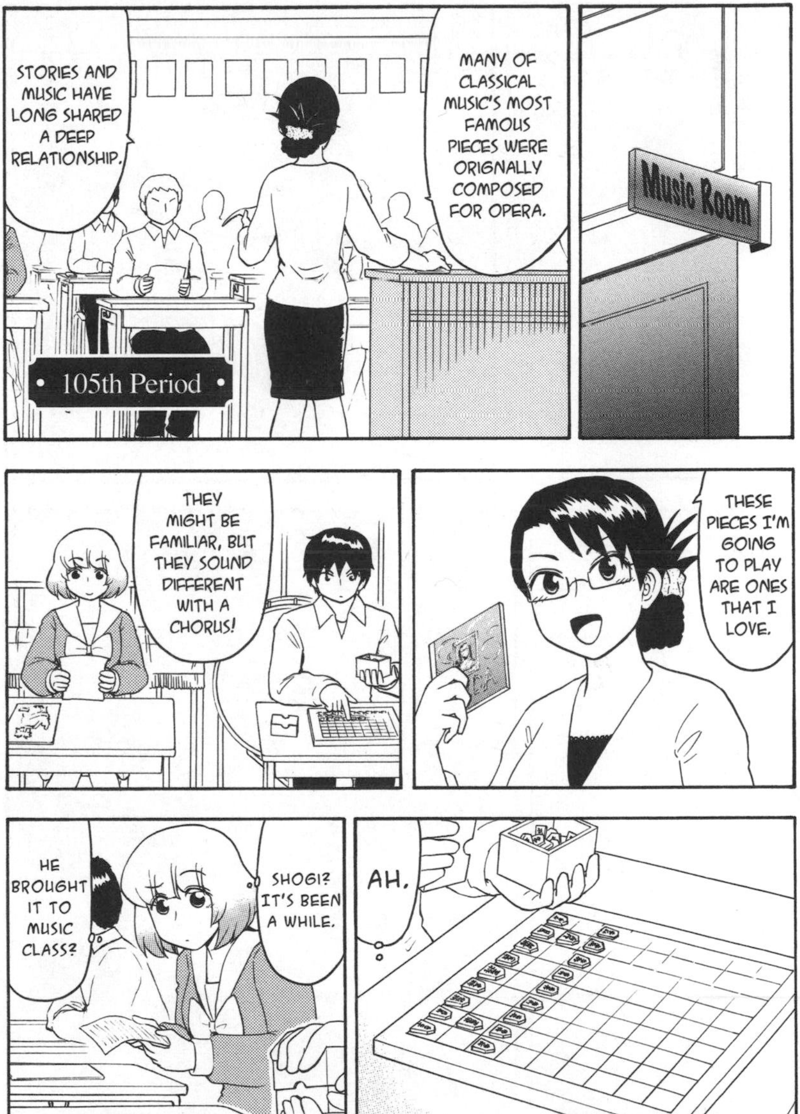
Music Room
MANY OF CLASSICAL MUSIC'S MOST FAMOUS PIECES WERE ORIGNALLY COMPOSED FOR OPERA.
STORIES AND MUSIC HAVE LONG SHARED A DEEP RELATIONSHIP.
• 105th Period •
THESE PIECES I'M GOING TO PLAY ARE ONES THAT I LOVE.
THEY MIGHT BE FAMILIAR, BUT THEY SOUND DIFFERENT WITH A CHORUS!
AH.
SHOGI? IT'S BEEN A WHILE.
HE BROUGHT IT TO MUSIC CLASS?

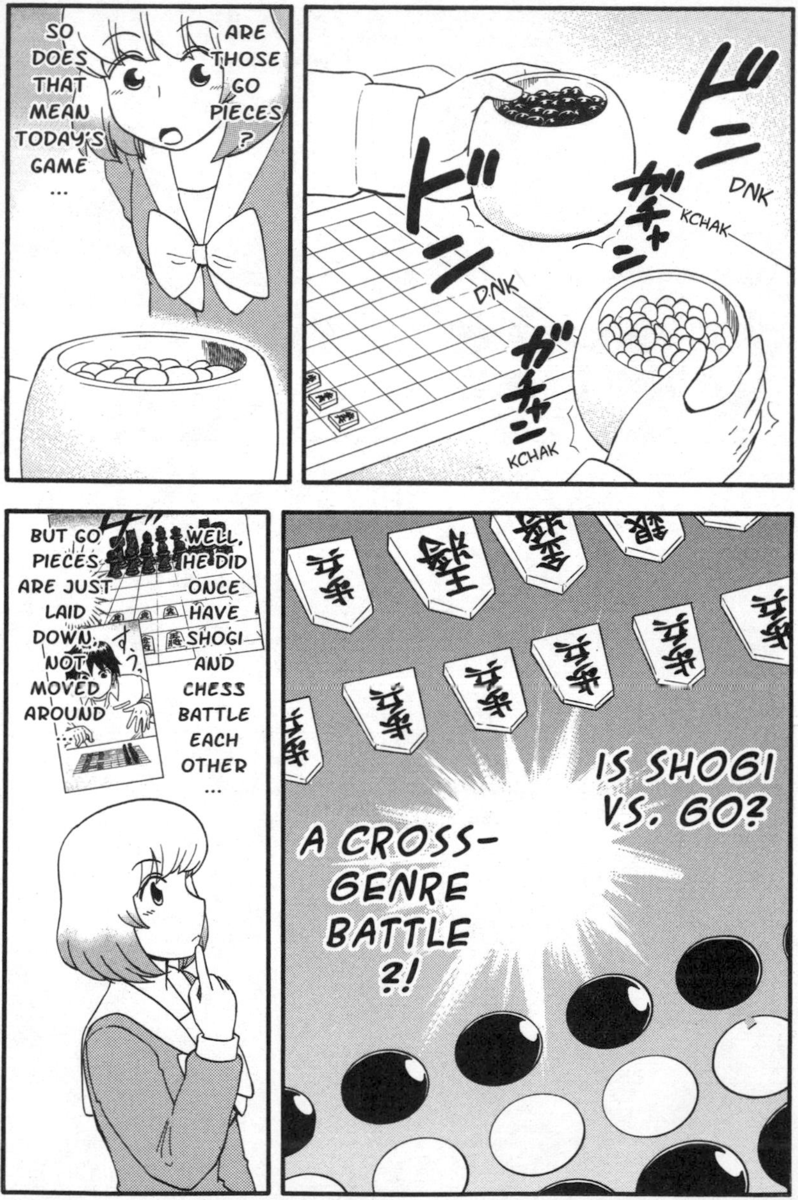
DNK
KCHAK
DNK
KCHAK
ARE THOSE GO PIECES?
SO DOES THAT MEAN TODAY'S GAME...
IS SHOGI VS. GO?
A CROSS-GENRE BATTLE?!
WELL, HE DID ONCE HAVE SHOGI AND CHESS BATTLE EACH OTHER...
BUT GO PIECES ARE JUST LAID DOWN, NOT MOVED AROUND

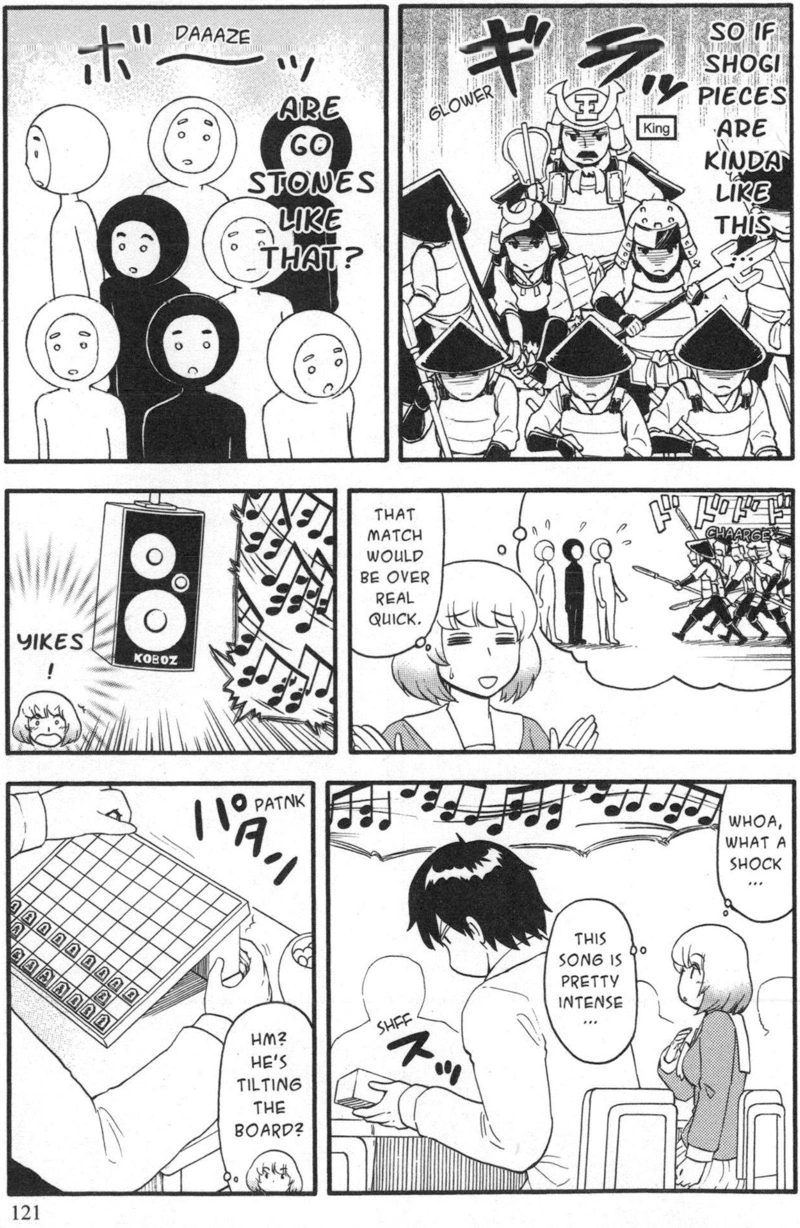
ギラッ
GLOWER
King
SO IF SHOGI PIECES ARE KINDA LIKE THIS
ボーッ
DAAAZE
ARE GO STONES LIKE THAT?
THAT MATCH WOULD BE OVER REAL QUICK.
ドドドド
CHAARGE
KOBOZ
YIKES!
WHOA, WHAT A SHOCK...
THIS SONG IS PRETTY INTENSE...
スッ
SHFF
パタッ
PATNK
HM? HE'S TILTING THE BOARD?

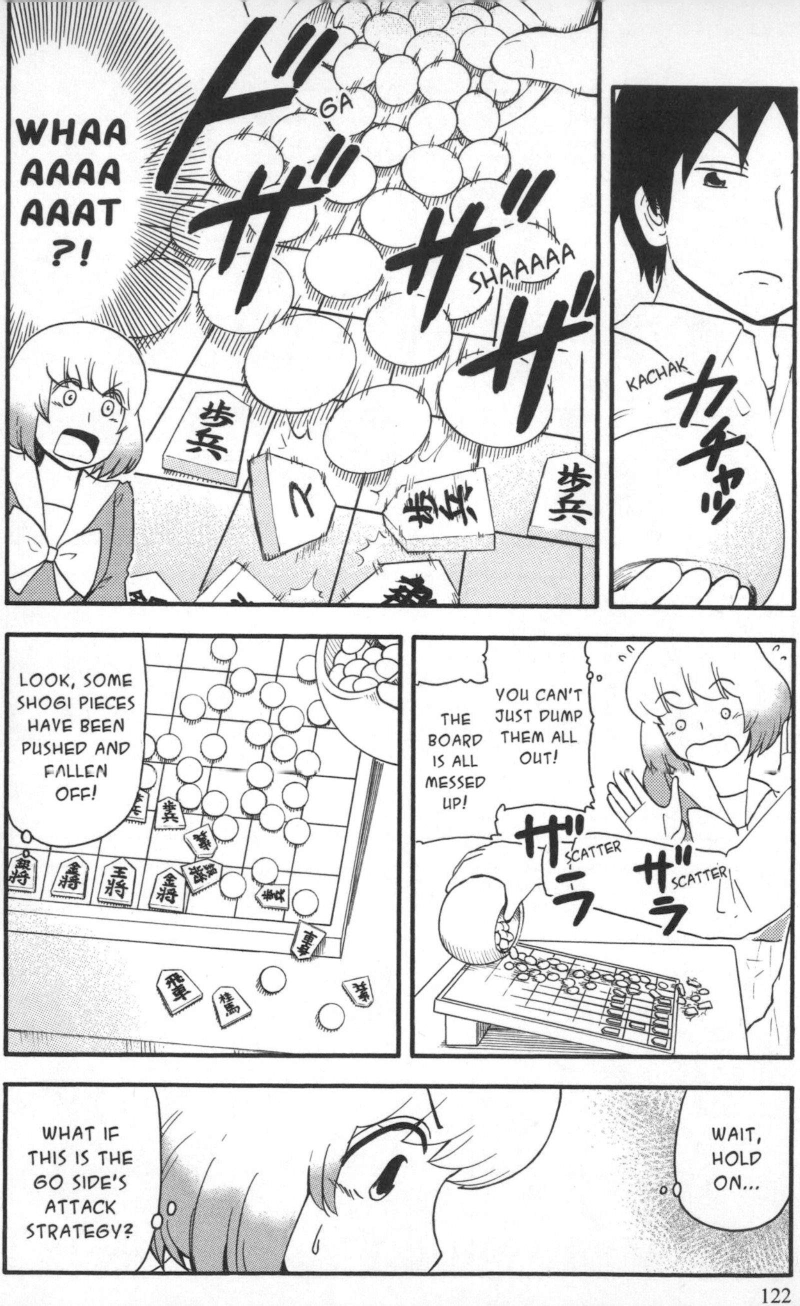

GA
WHAA AAAA AAAT ?!
SHAAAAA
KACHAK
LOOK, SOME SHOGI PIECES HAVE BEEN PUSHED AND FALLEN OFF!
YOU CAN'T JUST DUMP THEM ALL OUT!
THE BOARD IS ALL MESSED UP!
SCATTER
SCATTER
WAIT, HOLD ON...
WHAT IF THIS IS THE GO SIDE'S ATTACK STRATEGY?

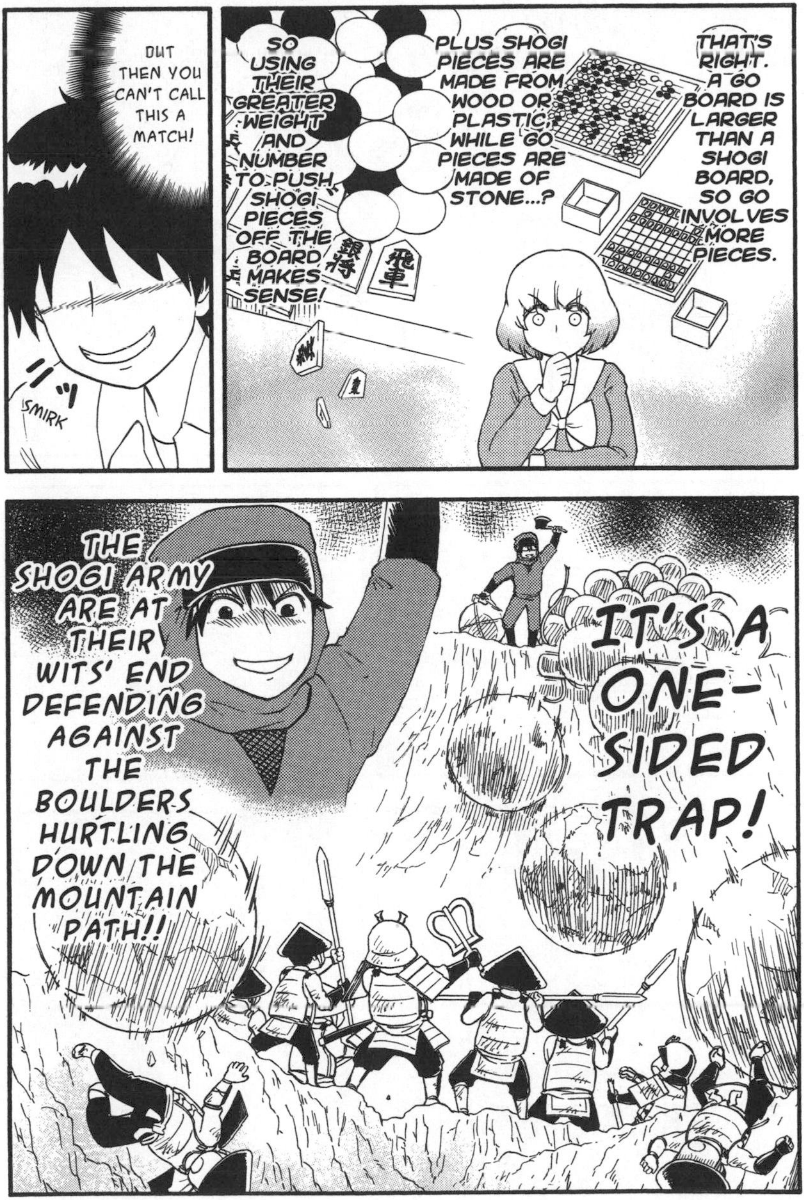
THAT'S RIGHT. A GO BOARD IS LARGER THAN A SHOGI BOARD, SO GO INVOLVES MORE PIECES.
PLUS SHOGI PIECES ARE MADE FROM WOOD OR PLASTIC, WHILE GO PIECES ARE MADE OF STONE...?
SO USING THEIR GREATER WEIGHT AND NUMBER TO PUSH SHOGI PIECES OFF THE BOARD MAKES SENSE!
BUT THEN YOU CAN'T CALL THIS A MATCH!
ニッ
SMIRK
IT'S A ONE-SIDED TRAP!
THE SHOGI ARMY ARE AT THEIR WITS' END DEFENDING AGAINST THE BOULDERS HURTLING DOWN THE MOUNTAIN PATH!!

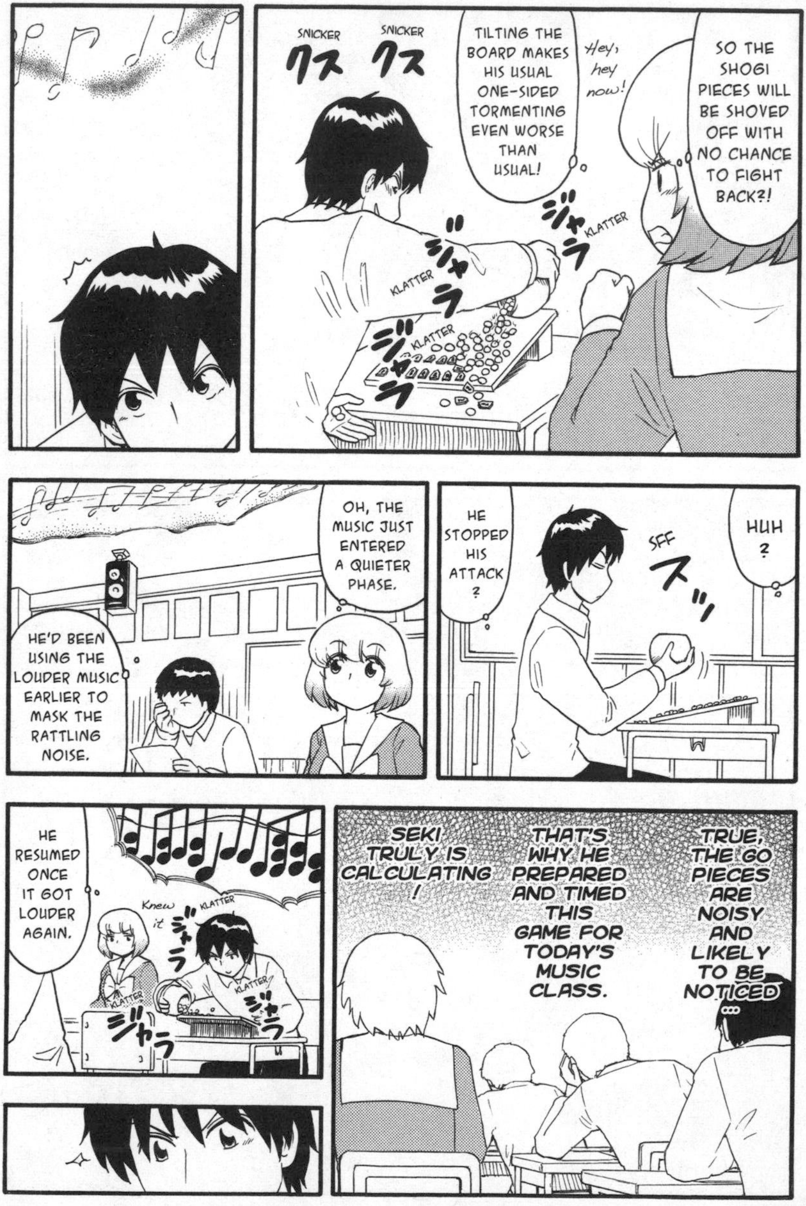
SO THE SHOGI PIECES WILL BE SHOVED OFF WITH NO CHANCE TO FIGHT BACK?!
Hey, hey now!
TILTING THE BOARD MAKES HIS USUAL ONE-SIDED TORMENTING EVEN WORSE THAN USUAL!
SNICKER クス
SNICKER クス
KLATTER ジャラ
KLATTER ジャラ
KLATTER ジャラ
HUH?
SFF スッ
HE STOPPED HIS ATTACK?
OH, THE MUSIC JUST ENTERED A QUIETER PHASE.
HE'D BEEN USING THE LOUDER MUSIC EARLIER TO MASK THE RATTLING NOISE.
TRUE, THE GO PIECES ARE NOISY AND LIKELY TO BE NOTICED...
THAT'S WHY HE PREPARED AND TIMED THIS GAME FOR TODAY'S MUSIC CLASS.
SEKI TRULY IS CALCULATING!
HE RESUMED ONCE IT GOT LOUDER AGAIN.
Knew it
KLATTER ジャラ
KLATTER ジャラ
KLATTER ジャラ

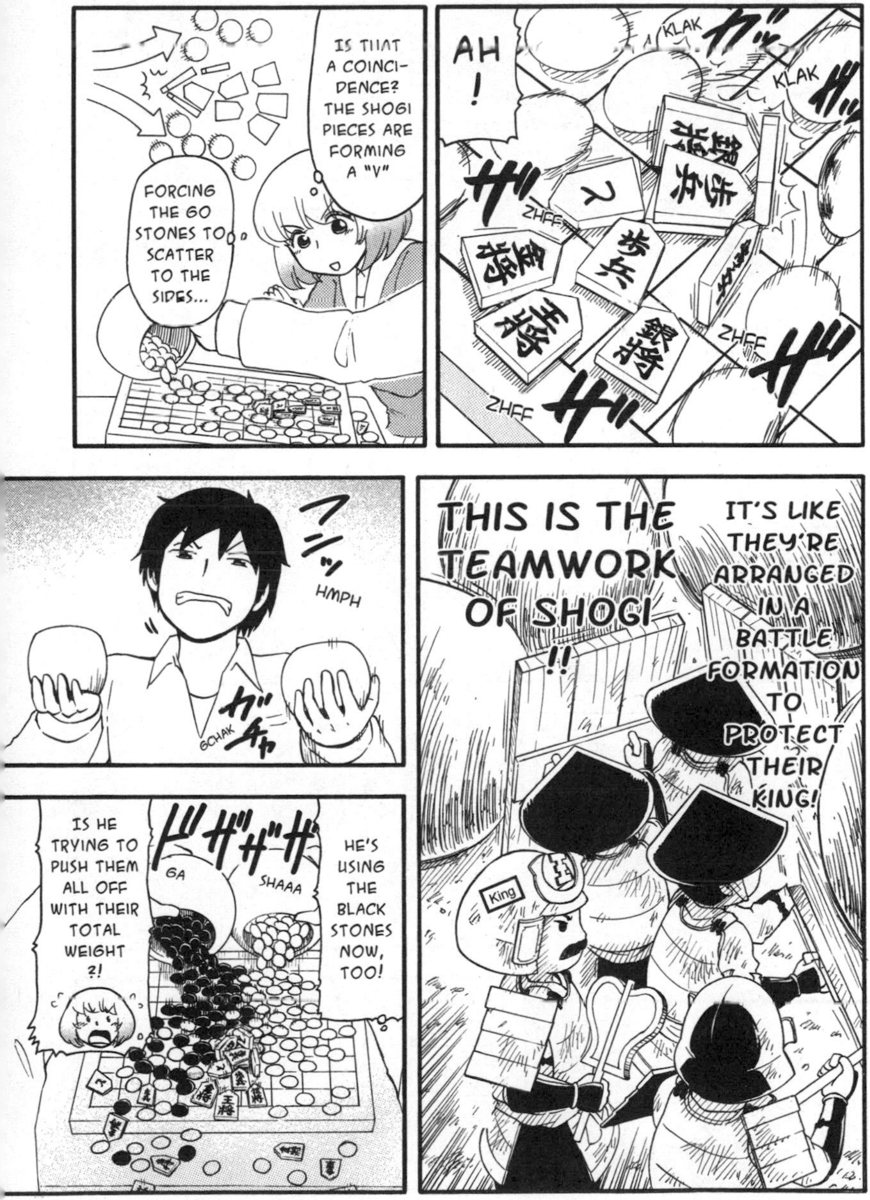
AH!
KLAK
KLAK
ZHFF
ZHFF
ZHFF
Is that a coincidence? The shogi pieces are forming a "V"
Forcing the go stones to scatter to the sides...
This is the teamwork of shogi!!
It's like they're arranged in a battle formation to protect their king!
King
HMPH
GCHAK
He's using the black stones now, too!
Is he trying to push them all off with their total weight?!
GA
SHAAA

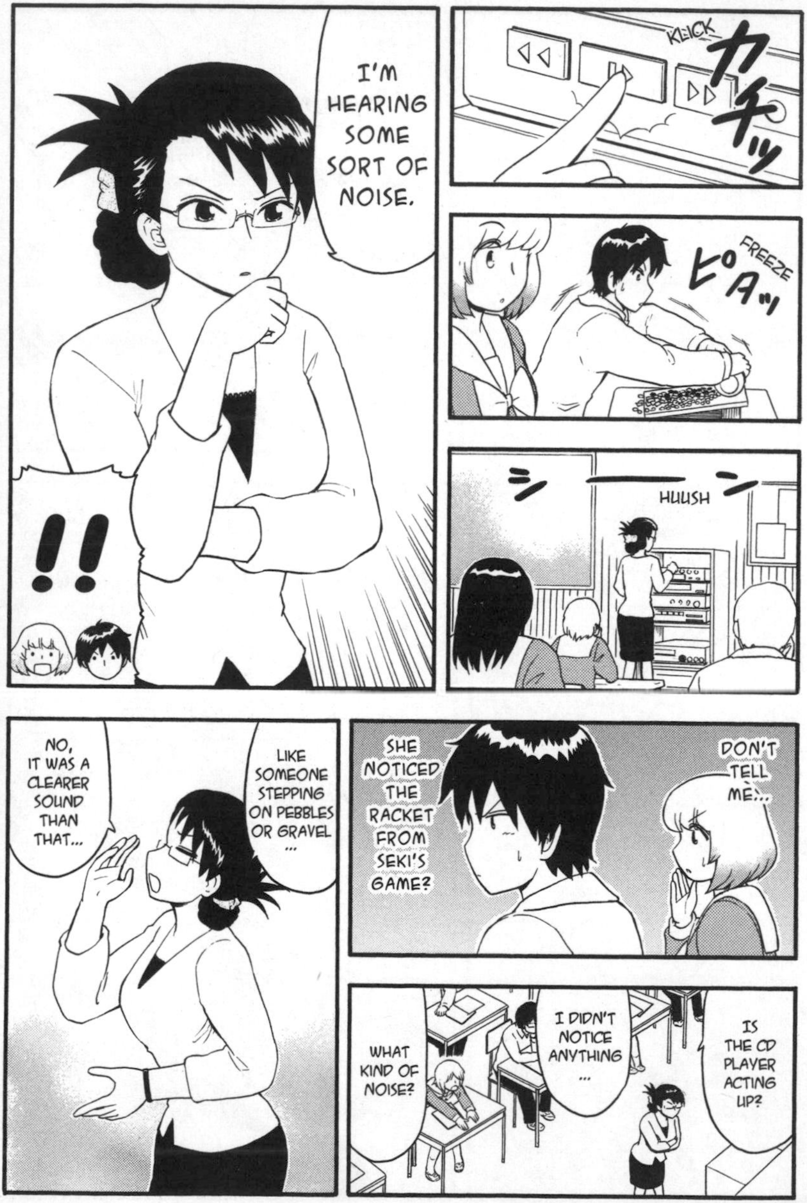
KLICK
カチッ
FREEZE
ピタッ
シーーーン
HUUSH
I'M HEARING SOME SORT OF NOISE.
!!
DON'T TELL ME...
SHE NOTICED THE RACKET FROM SEKI'S GAME?
IS THE CD PLAYER ACTING UP?
I DIDN'T NOTICE ANYTHING ...
WHAT KIND OF NOISE?
LIKE SOMEONE STEPPING ON PEBBLES OR GRAVEL ...
NO, IT WAS A CLEARER SOUND THAN THAT...

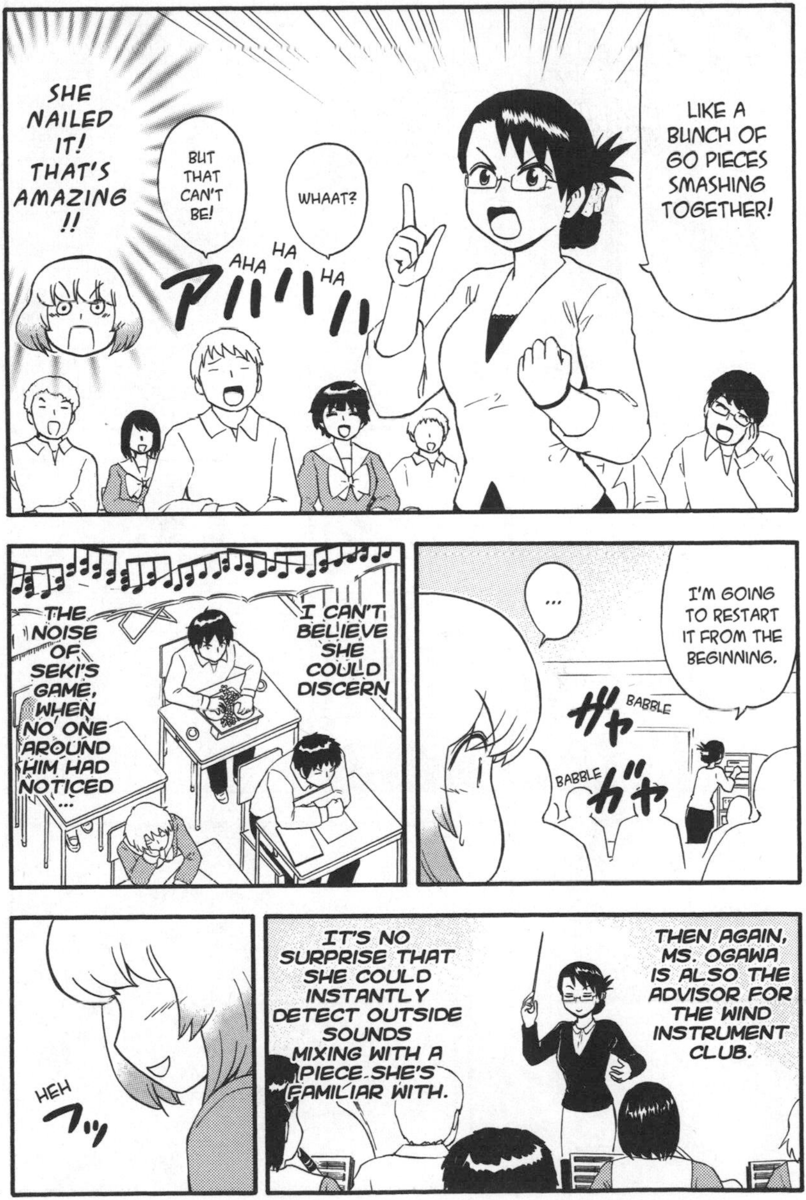
LIKE A BUNCH OF GO PIECES SMASHING TOGETHER!
WHAAT?
BUT THAT CAN'T BE!
SHE NAILED IT! THAT'S AMAZING!!
アハハハ
AHA HA HA
...
I'M GOING TO RESTART IT FROM THE BEGINNING.
ザワ
BABBLE
ガヤ
BABBLE
I CAN'T BELIEVE SHE COULD DISCERN
THE NOISE OF SEKI'S GAME, WHEN NO ONE AROUND HIM HAD NOTICED...
THEN AGAIN, MS. OGAWA IS ALSO THE ADVISOR FOR THE WIND INSTRUMENT CLUB.
IT'S NO SURPRISE THAT SHE COULD INSTANTLY DETECT OUTSIDE SOUNDS MIXING WITH A PIECE SHE'S FAMILIAR WITH.
HEH
フッ

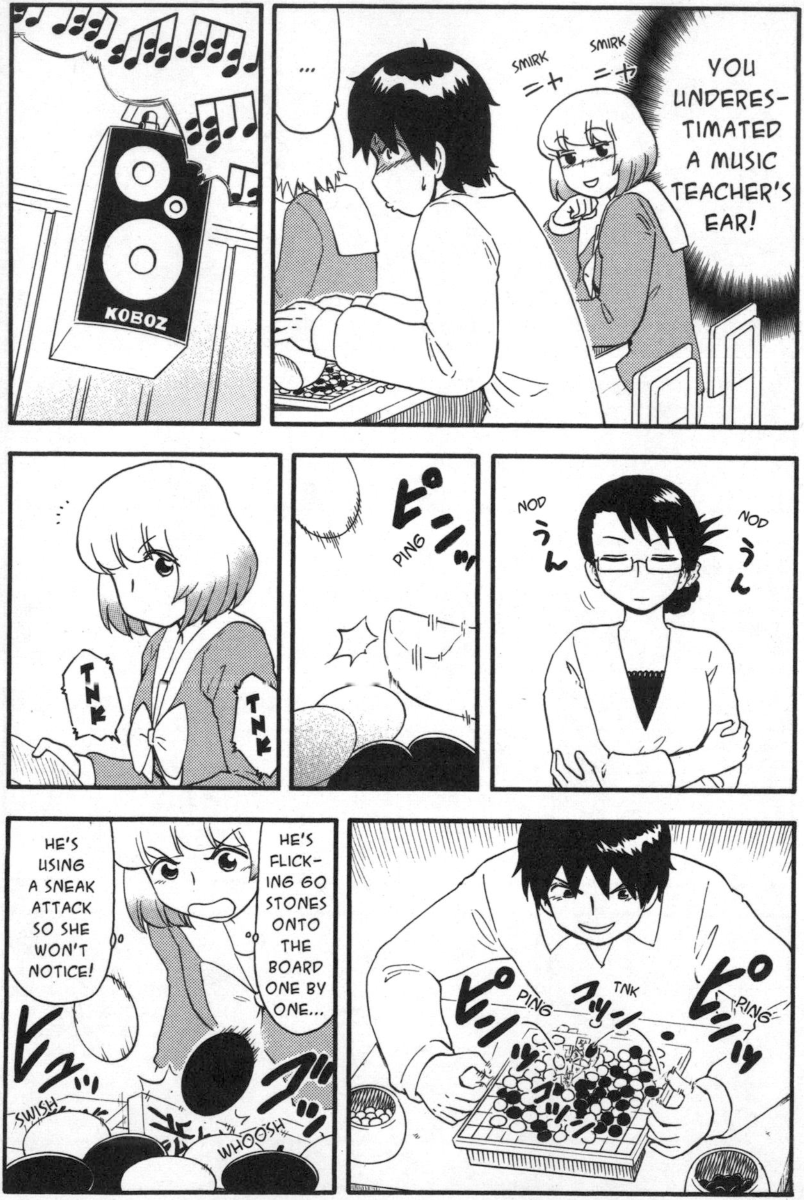
YOU UNDERES-TIMATED A MUSIC TEACHER'S EAR!
SMIRK
ニヤ
SMIRK
ニヤ
...
KOBOZ
NOD
うん
NOD
うん
PING
ピンッ
...
TNK
TNK
PING
PING
TNK
HE'S FLICKING GO STONES ONTO THE BOARD ONE BY ONE...
HE'S USING A SNEAK ATTACK SO SHE WON'T NOTICE!
SWISH
WHOOSH

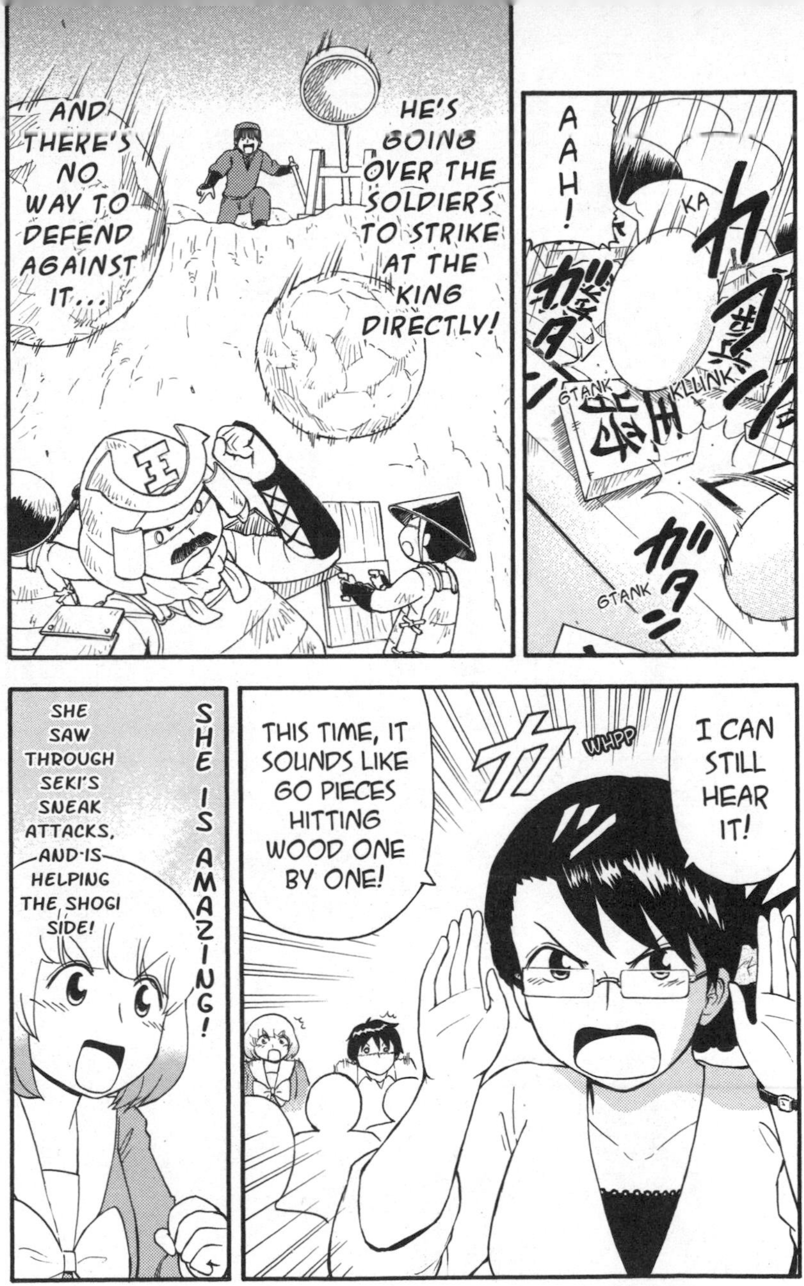
HE'S GOING OVER THE SOLDIERS TO STRIKE AT THE KING DIRECTLY!
AND THERE'S NO WAY TO DEFEND AGAINST IT...
AAH!
KA
KLUNK
GTANK
GTANK
I CAN STILL HEAR IT!
WHPP
THIS TIME, IT SOUNDS LIKE GO PIECES HITTING WOOD ONE BY ONE!
SHE IS AMAZING!
SHE SAW THROUGH SEKI'S SNEAK ATTACKS, AND IS HELPING THE SHOGI SIDE!

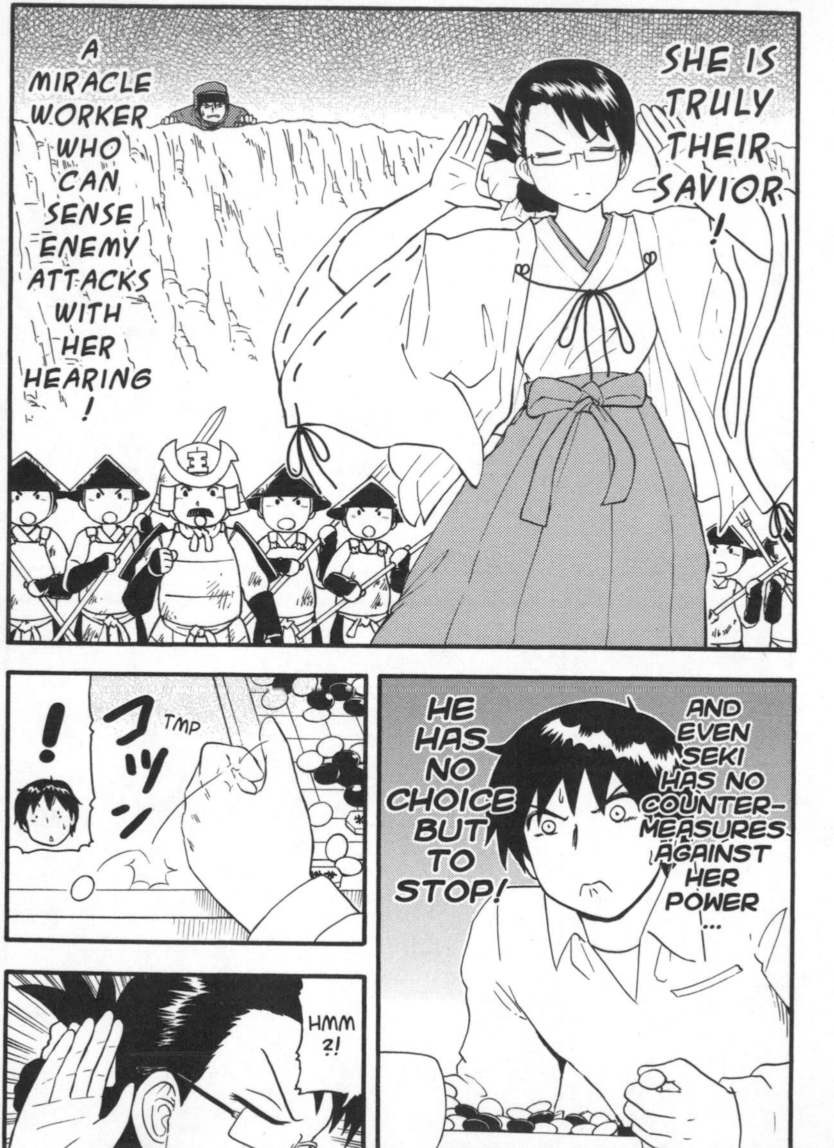
SHE IS TRULY THEIR SAVIOR!
A MIRACLE WORKER WHO CAN SENSE ENEMY ATTACKS WITH HER HEARING!
AND EVEN SEKI HAS NO COUNTER-MEASURES AGAINST HER POWER...
HE HAS NO CHOICE BUT TO STOP!
!
コツン
TMP
HMM?!

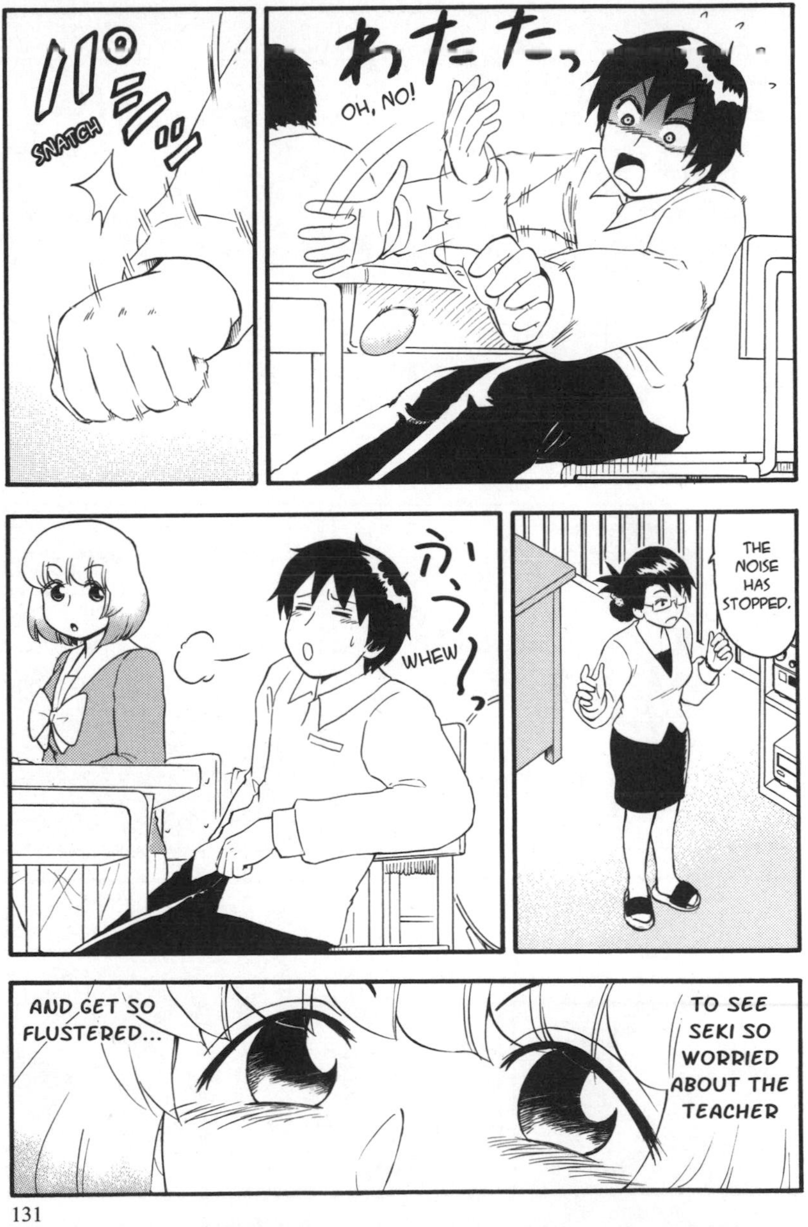

わたたっ
OH, NO!
SNATCH
THE NOISE HAS STOPPED.
WHEW
TO SEE SEKI SO WORRIED ABOUT THE TEACHER
AND GET SO FLUSTERED...

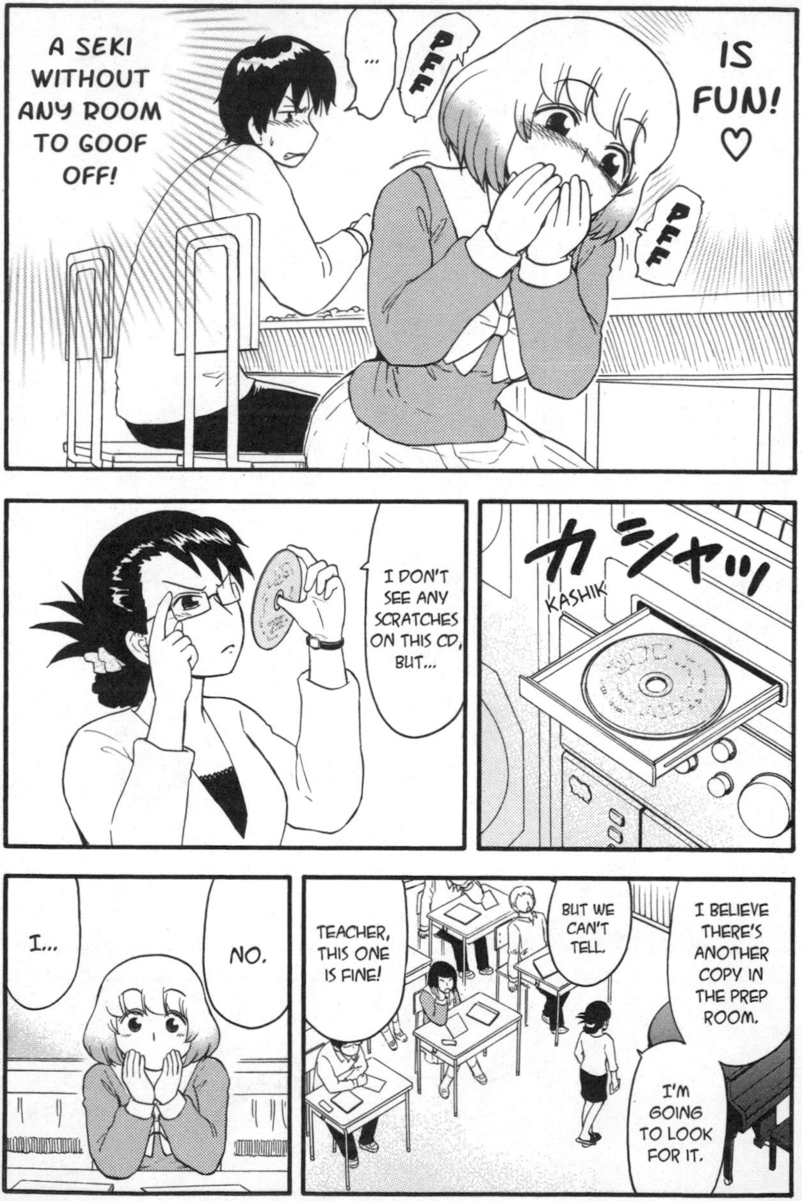
A SEKI WITHOUT ANY ROOM TO GOOF OFF!
IS FUN! ♡
PFF
...
PFF
カシャッ
KASHIK
I DON'T SEE ANY SCRATCHES ON THIS CD, BUT...
BUT WE CAN'T TELL.
I BELIEVE THERE'S ANOTHER COPY IN THE PREP ROOM.
I'M GOING TO LOOK FOR IT.
TEACHER, THIS ONE IS FINE!
NO.
I...

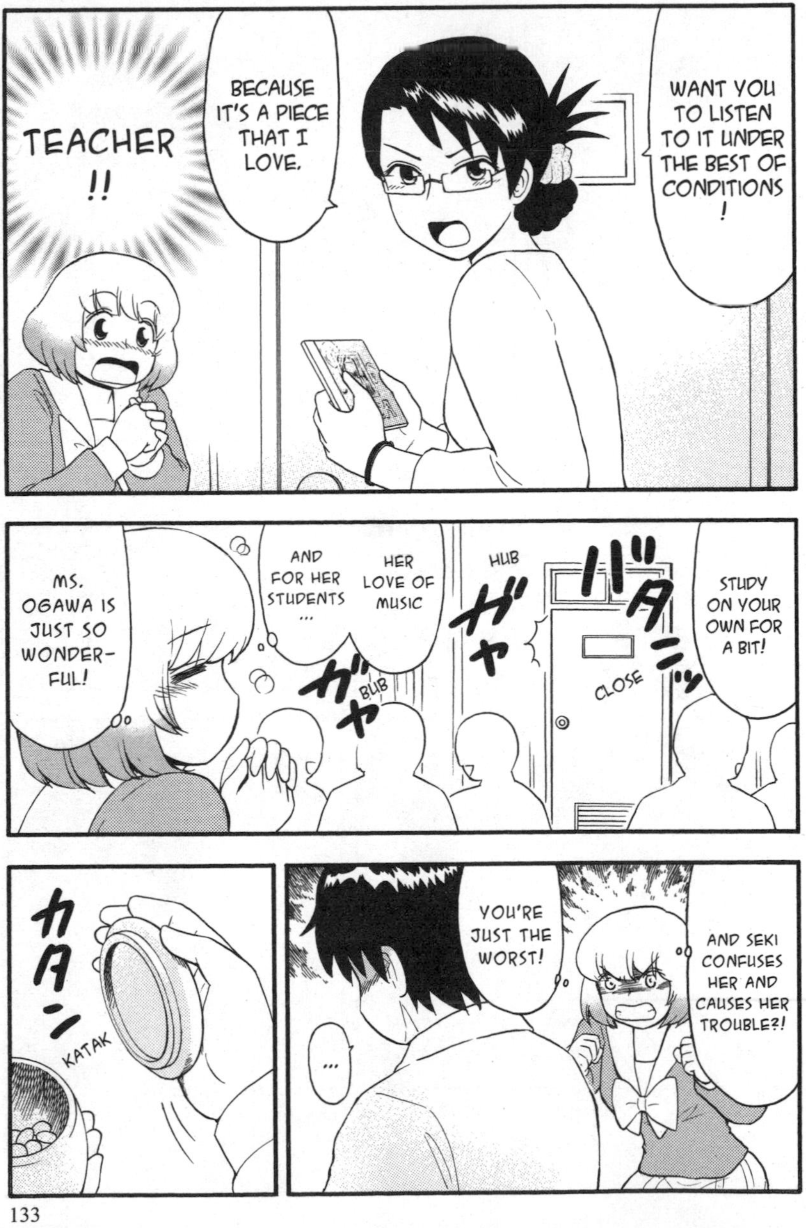
WANT YOU TO LISTEN TO IT UNDER THE BEST OF CONDITIONS!
BECAUSE IT'S A PIECE THAT I LOVE.
TEACHER!!
STUDY ON YOUR OWN FOR A BIT!
CLOSE
HUB
BUB
HER LOVE OF MUSIC
AND FOR HER STUDENTS...
MS. OGAWA IS JUST SO WONDER-FUL!
AND SEKI CONFUSES HER AND CAUSES HER TROUBLE?!
YOU'RE JUST THE WORST!
...
KATAK

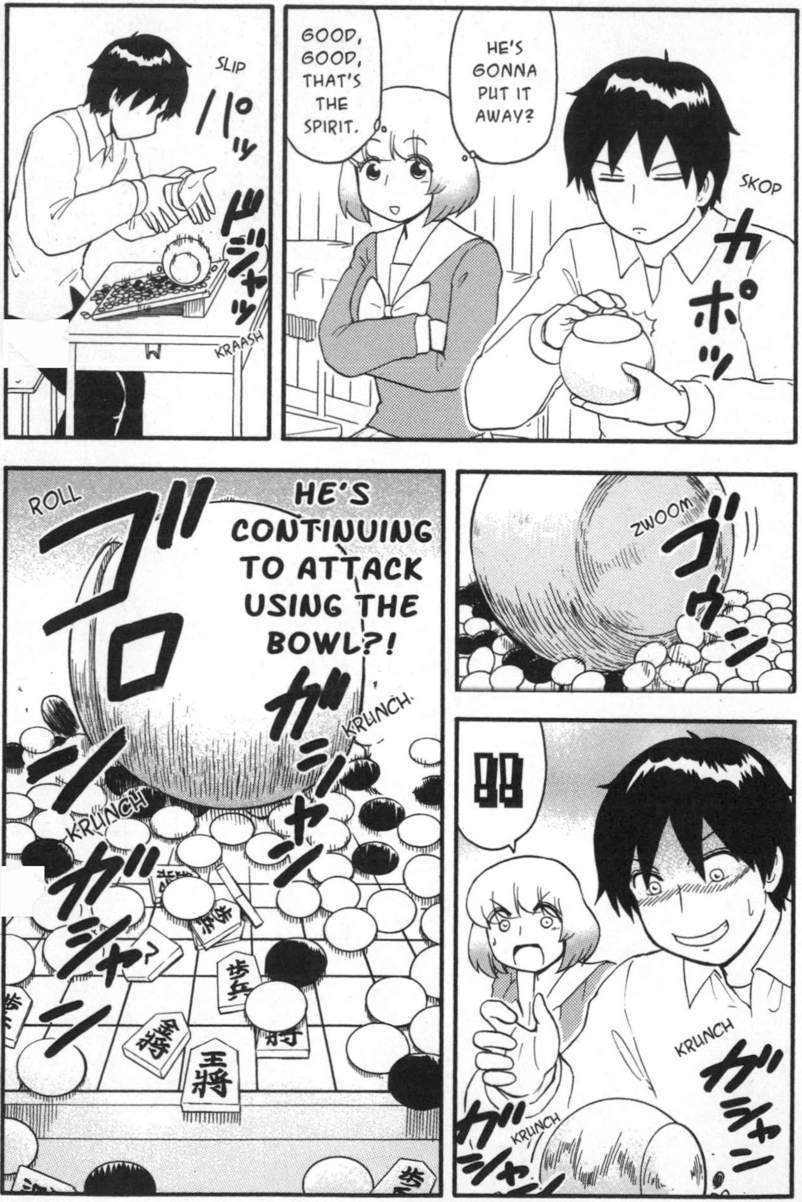
HE'S GONNA PUT IT AWAY?
SKOP
GOOD, GOOD, THAT'S THE SPIRIT.
SLIP
KRAASH
ZWOOM
ROLL
HE'S CONTINUING TO ATTACK USING THE BOWL?!
KRUNCH
KRUNCH
!!
KRUNCH
KRUNCH

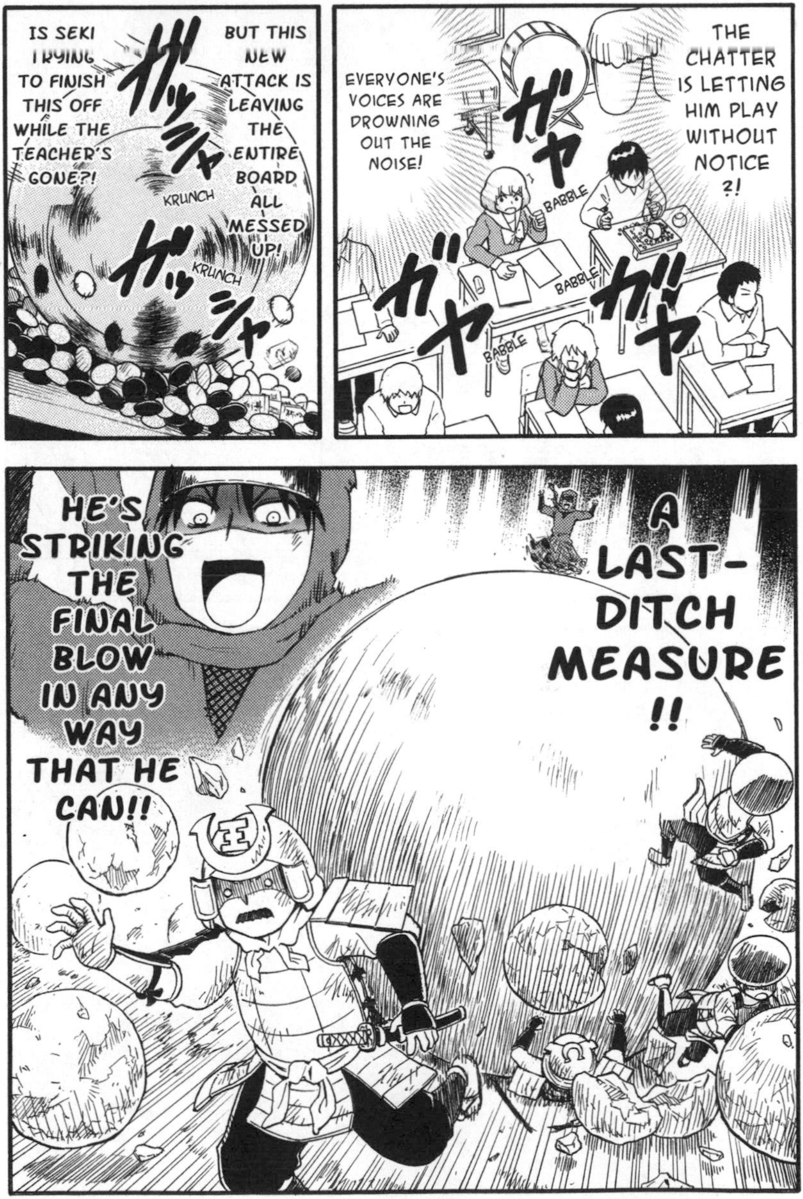
THE CHATTER IS LETTING HIM PLAY WITHOUT NOTICE ?!
EVERYONE'S VOICES ARE DROWNING OUT THE NOISE!
ガヤ
BABBLE
ガヤ
BABBLE
ガヤ
BABBLE
BUT THIS NEW ATTACK IS LEAVING THE ENTIRE BOARD ALL MESSED UP!
IS SEKI TRYING TO FINISH THIS OFF WHILE THE TEACHER'S GONE?!
ガッシャ
KRUNCH
ガッシャ
KRUNCH
A LAST-DITCH MEASURE !!
HE'S STRIKING THE FINAL BLOW IN ANY WAY THAT HE CAN!!

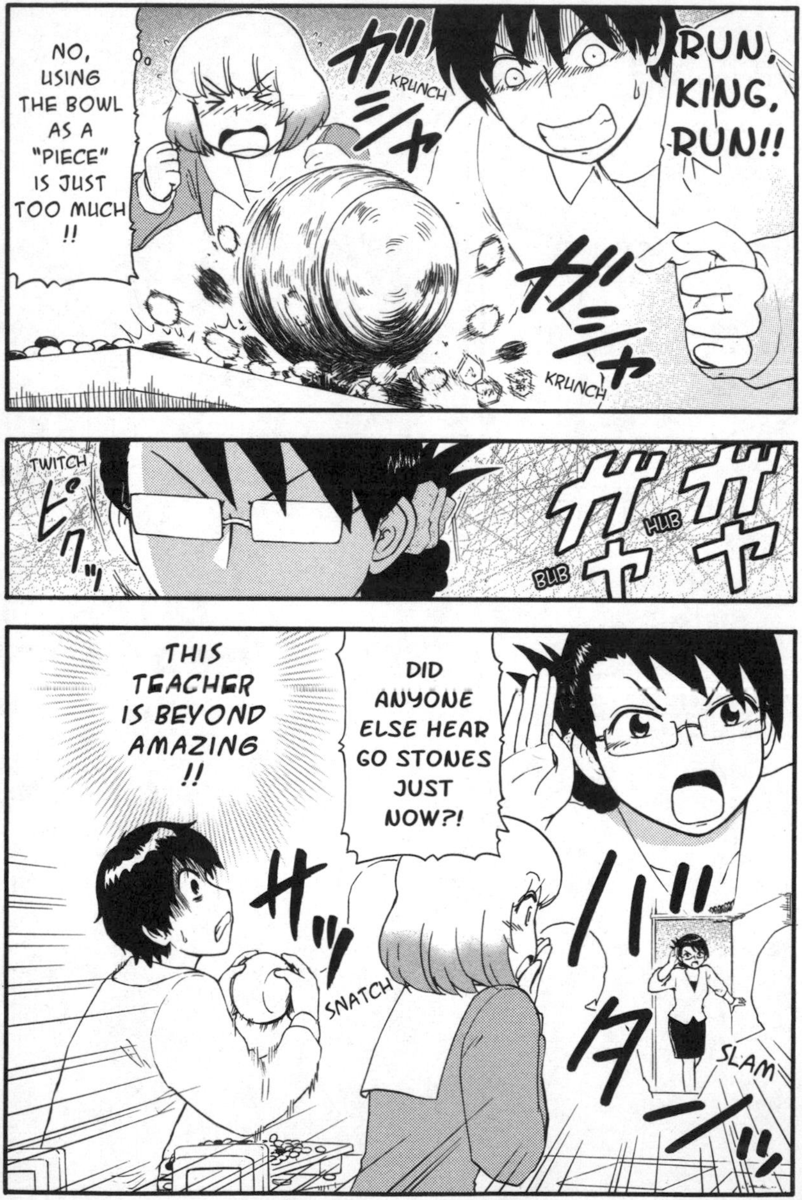
RUN, KING, RUN!!
ガシャ
KRUNCH
ガシャ
KRUNCH
NO, USING THE BOWL AS A "PIECE" IS JUST TOO MUCH!!
ガヤ
HUB
ガヤ
BUB
ピクッ
TWITCH
DID ANYONE ELSE HEAR GO STONES JUST NOW?!
バタン
SLAM
サッ
SNATCH
THIS TEACHER IS BEYOND AMAZING!!

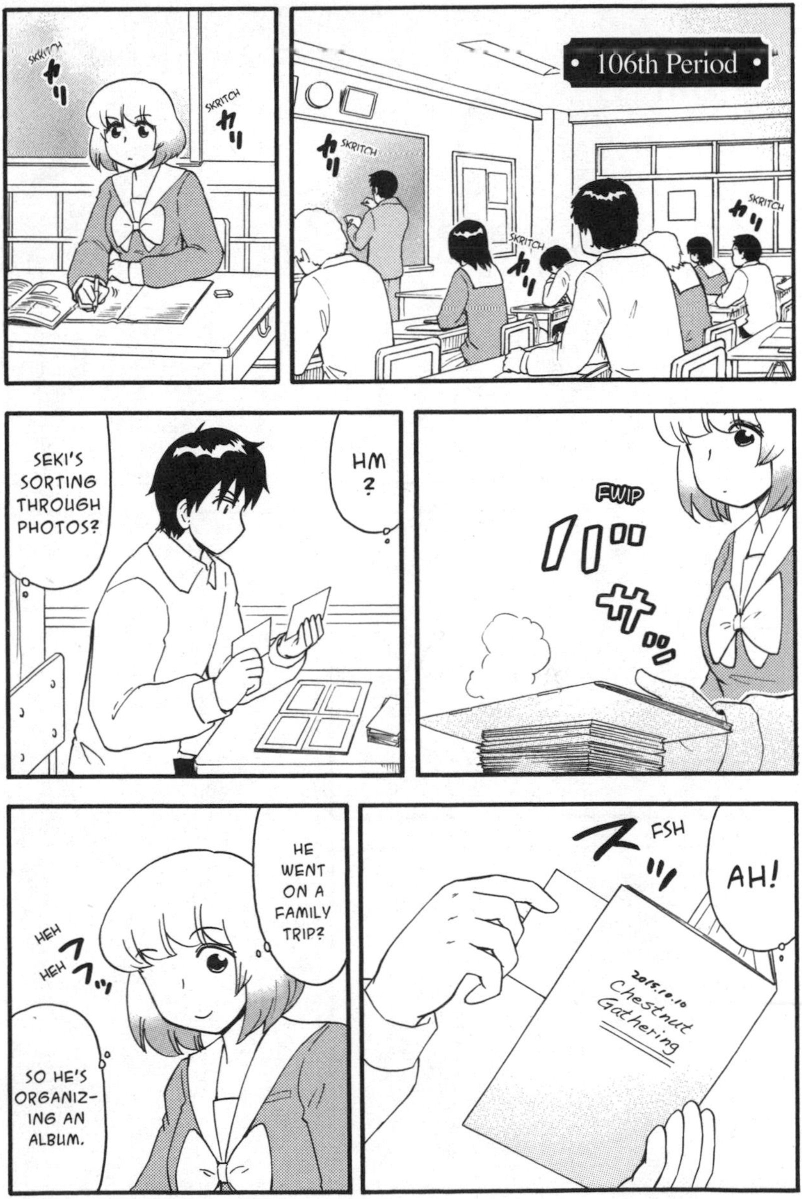
• 106th Period •
SKRITCH
SKRITCH
SKRITCH
SKRITCH
SKRITCH
FWIP
HM?
SEKI'S SORTING THROUGH PHOTOS?
FSH
AH!
2015.10.10 Chestnut Gathering
HE WENT ON A FAMILY TRIP?
HEH HEH
SO HE'S ORGANIZING AN ALBUM.

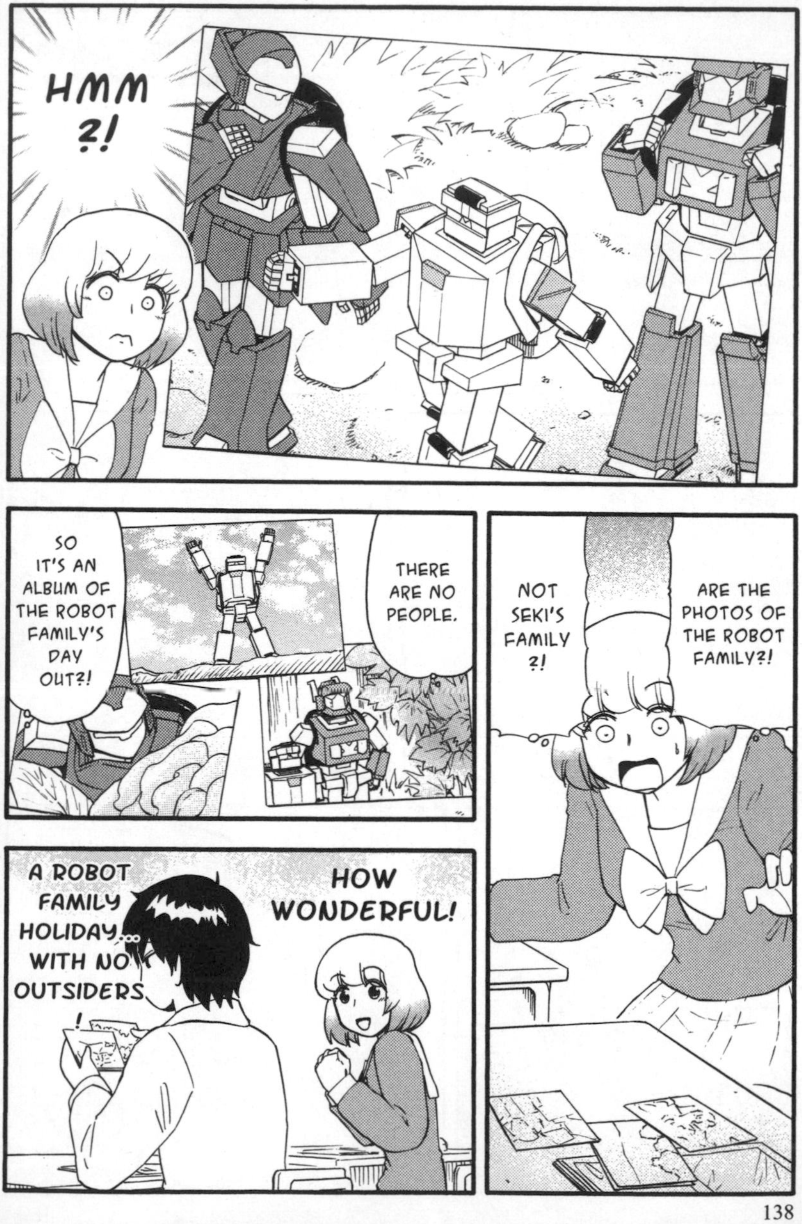
HMM ?!
ARE THE PHOTOS OF THE ROBOT FAMILY?!
NOT SEKI'S FAMILY ?!
THERE ARE NO PEOPLE.
SO IT'S AN ALBUM OF THE ROBOT FAMILY'S DAY OUT?!
HOW WONDERFUL!
A ROBOT FAMILY HOLIDAY... WITH NO OUTSIDERS
!

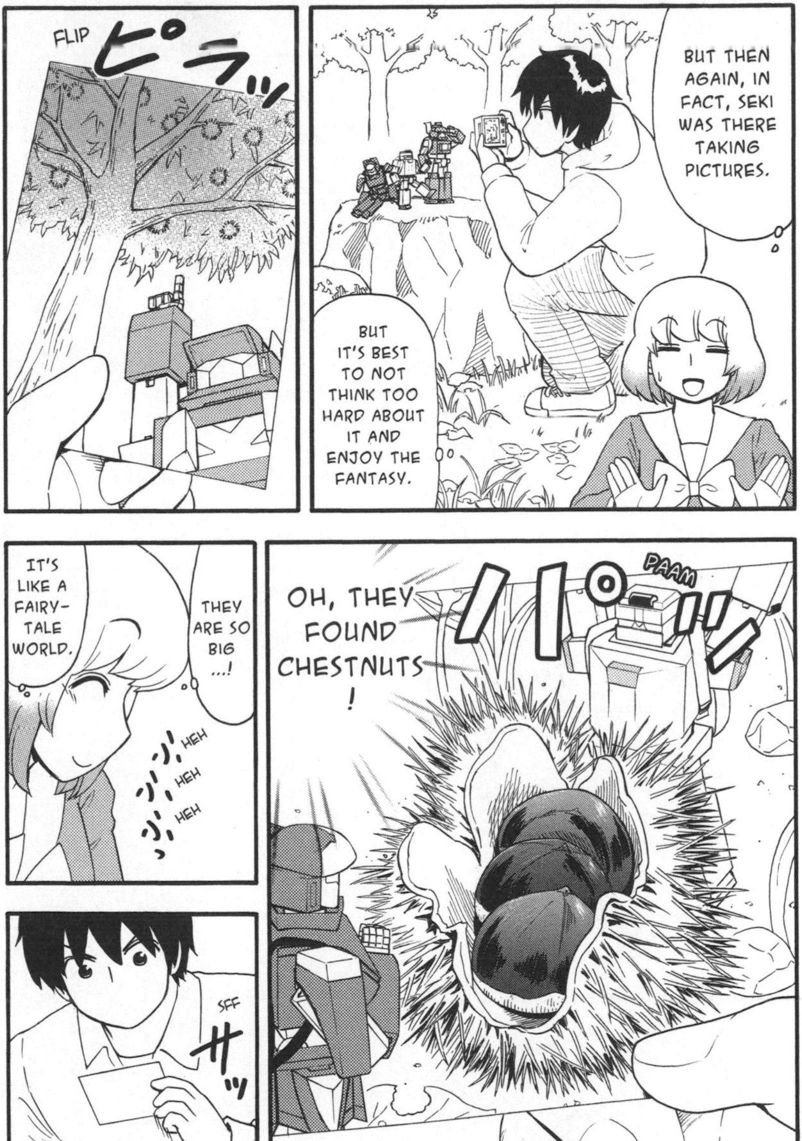

BUT THEN AGAIN, IN FACT, SEKI WAS THERE TAKING PICTURES.
BUT IT'S BEST TO NOT THINK TOO HARD ABOUT IT AND ENJOY THE FANTASY.
FLIP ピラッ
PAAM パーン
OH, THEY FOUND CHESTNUTS!
THEY ARE SO BIG...!
IT'S LIKE A FAIRY-TALE WORLD.
HEH HEH HEH ふふふ
SFF サッ

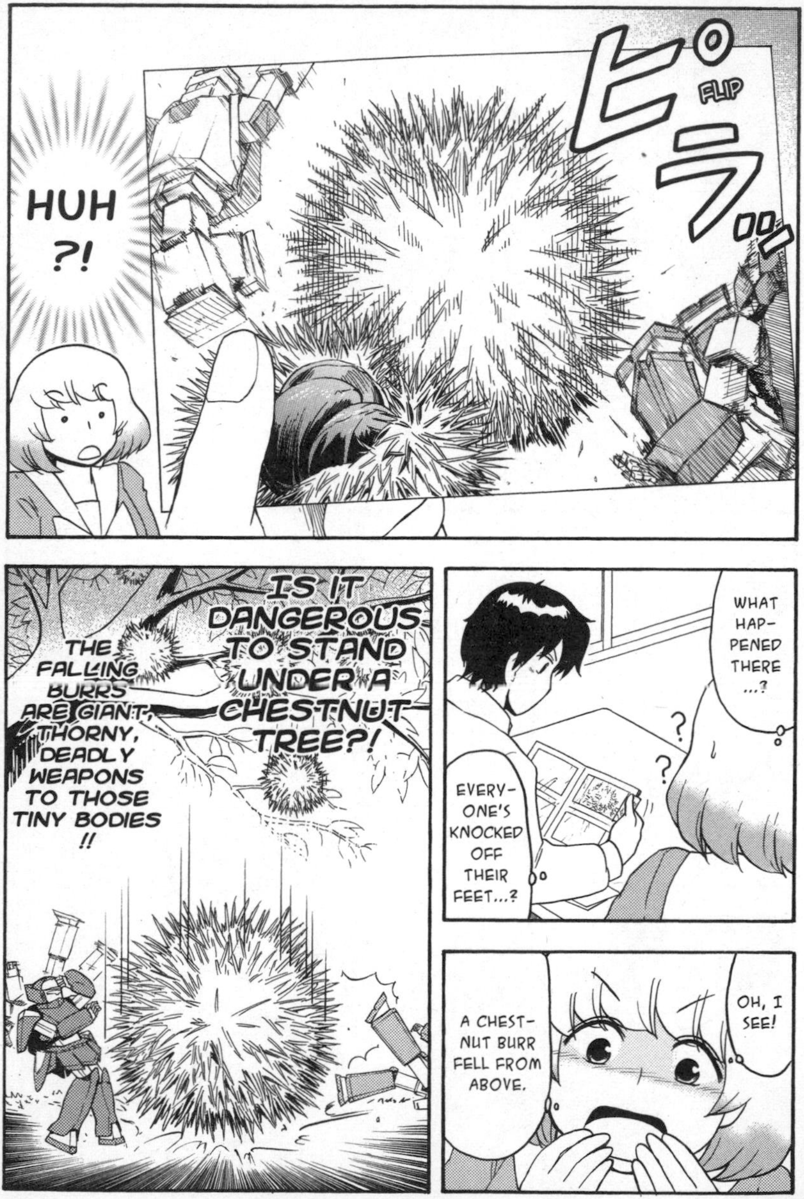

ピラ
FLIP
HUH ?!
WHAT HAP-PENED THERE ...?
EVERY-ONE'S KNOCKED OFF THEIR FEET...?
OH, I SEE!
A CHEST-NUT BURR FELL FROM ABOVE.
IS IT DANGEROUS TO STAND UNDER A CHESTNUT TREE?!
THE FALLING BURRS ARE GIANT, THORNY, DEADLY WEAPONS TO THOSE TINY BODIES !!

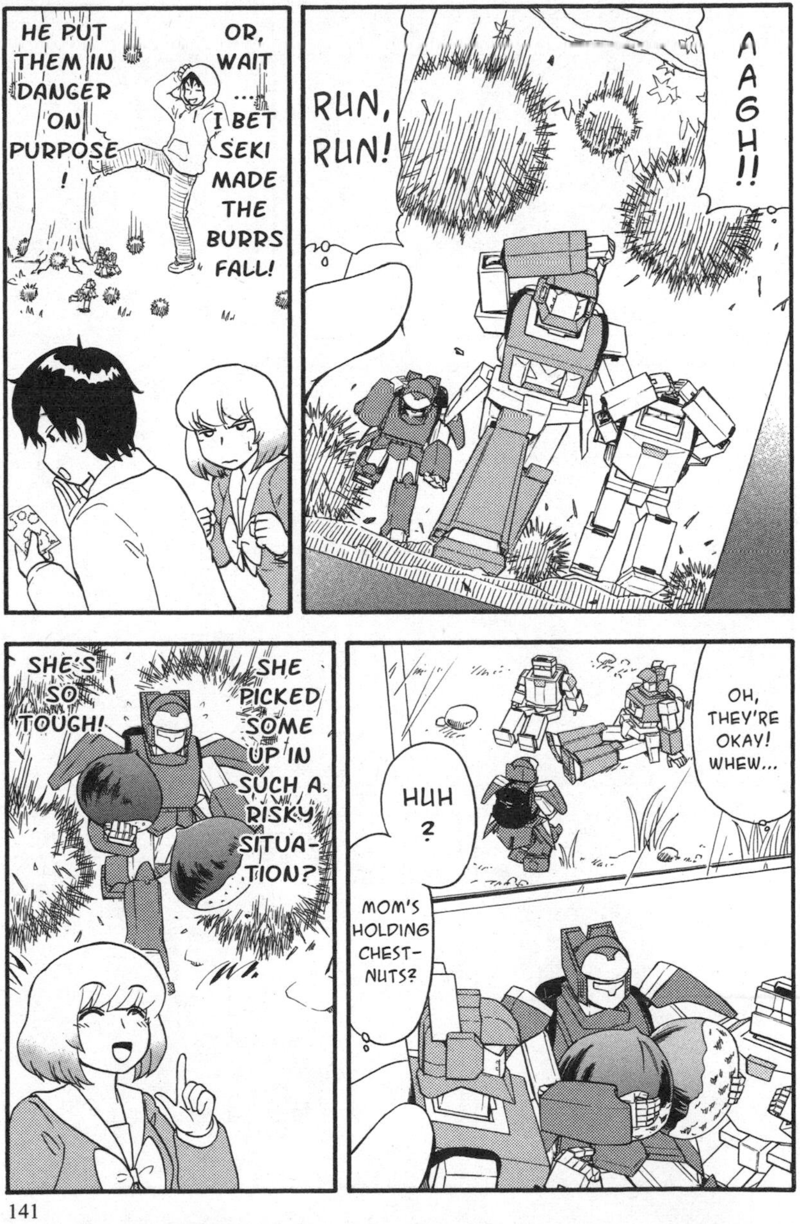
AAGH!!
RUN, RUN!
OR, WAIT ... I BET SEKI MADE THE BURRS FALL!
HE PUT THEM IN DANGER ON PURPOSE!
OH, THEY'RE OKAY! WHEW...
HUH?
MOM'S HOLDING CHESTNUTS?
SHE PICKED SOME UP IN SUCH A RISKY SITUATION?
SHE'S SO TOUGH!

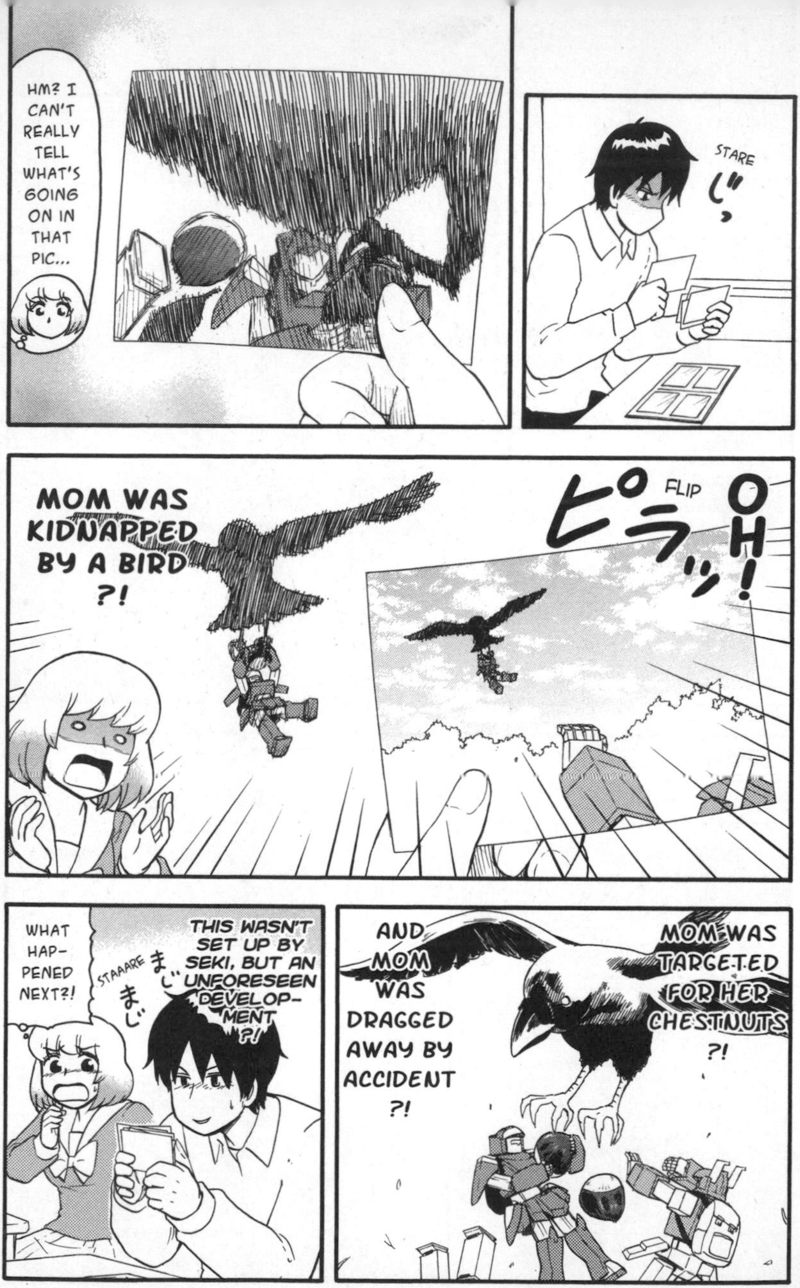
STARE
じっ
HM? I CAN'T REALLY TELL WHAT'S GOING ON IN THAT PIC...
FLIP
ピラッ
OH!
MOM WAS KIDNAPPED BY A BIRD ?!
MOM WAS TARGETED FOR HER CHESTNUTS ?!
AND MOM WAS DRAGGED AWAY BY ACCIDENT ?!
THIS WASN'T SET UP BY SEKI, BUT AN UNFORESEEN DEVELOPMENT ?!
STAAARE
まじ まじ
WHAT HAPPENED NEXT?!

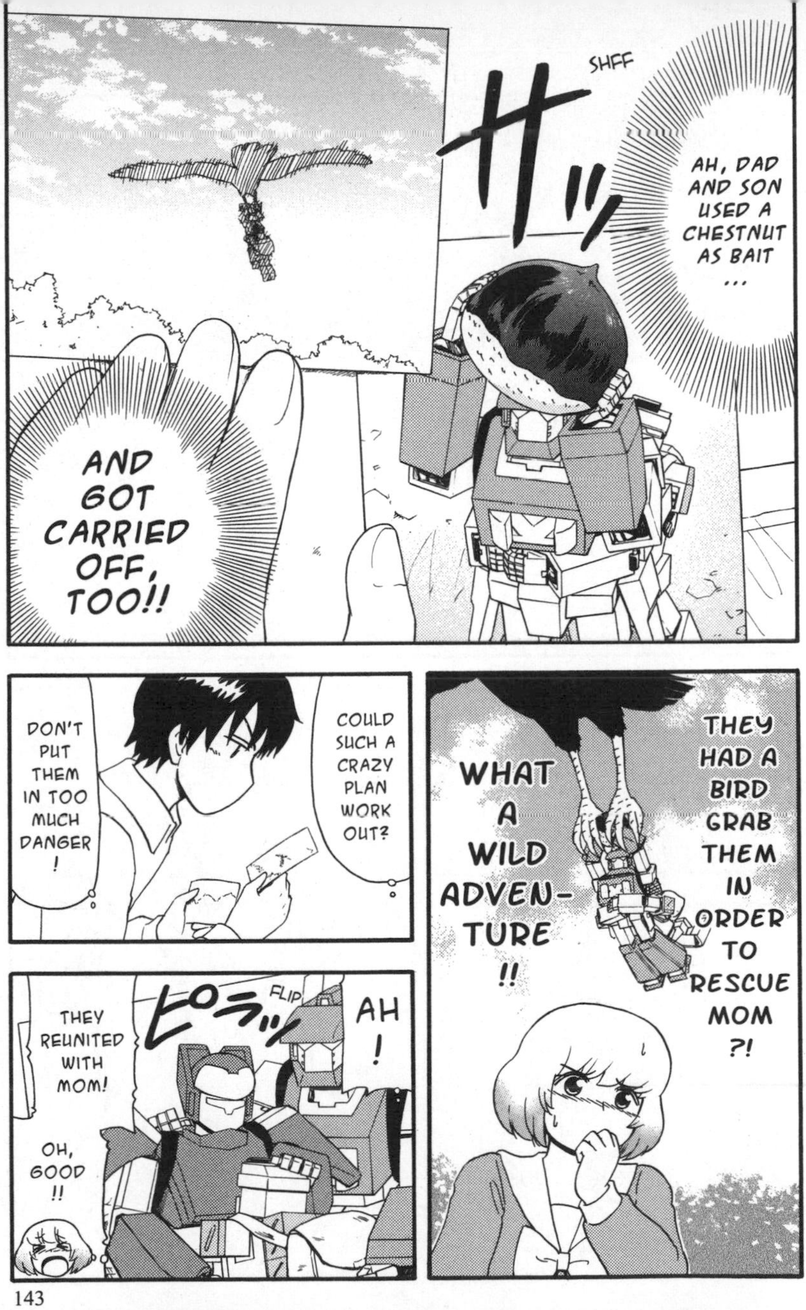
SHFF
AH, DAD AND SON USED A CHESTNUT AS BAIT ...
AND GOT CARRIED OFF, TOO!!
THEY HAD A BIRD GRAB THEM IN ORDER TO RESCUE MOM ?!
WHAT A WILD ADVEN-TURE !!
COULD SUCH A CRAZY PLAN WORK OUT?
DON'T PUT THEM IN TOO MUCH DANGER !
FLIP
AH !
THEY REUNITED WITH MOM!
OH, GOOD !!

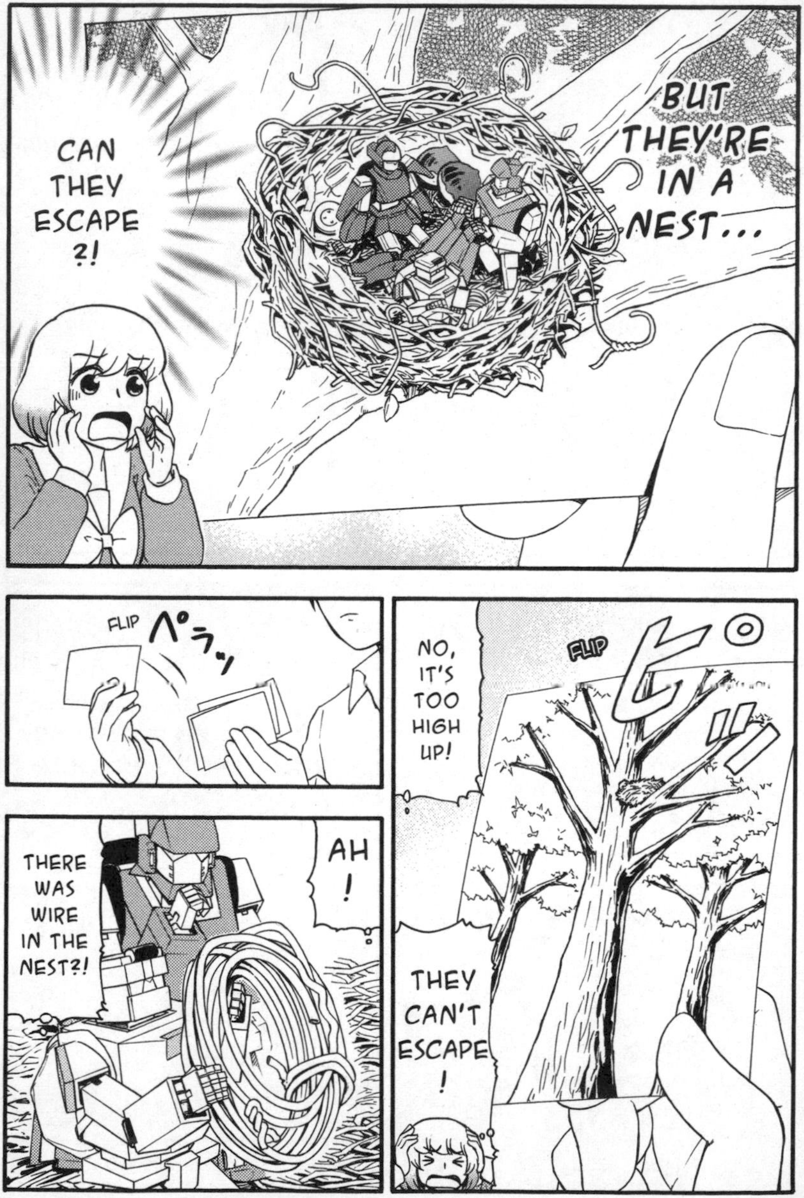
BUT THEY'RE IN A NEST...
CAN THEY ESCAPE?!
FLIP ピッ
NO, IT'S TOO HIGH UP!
THEY CAN'T ESCAPE!
FLIP ペラッ
AH!
THERE WAS WIRE IN THE NEST?!

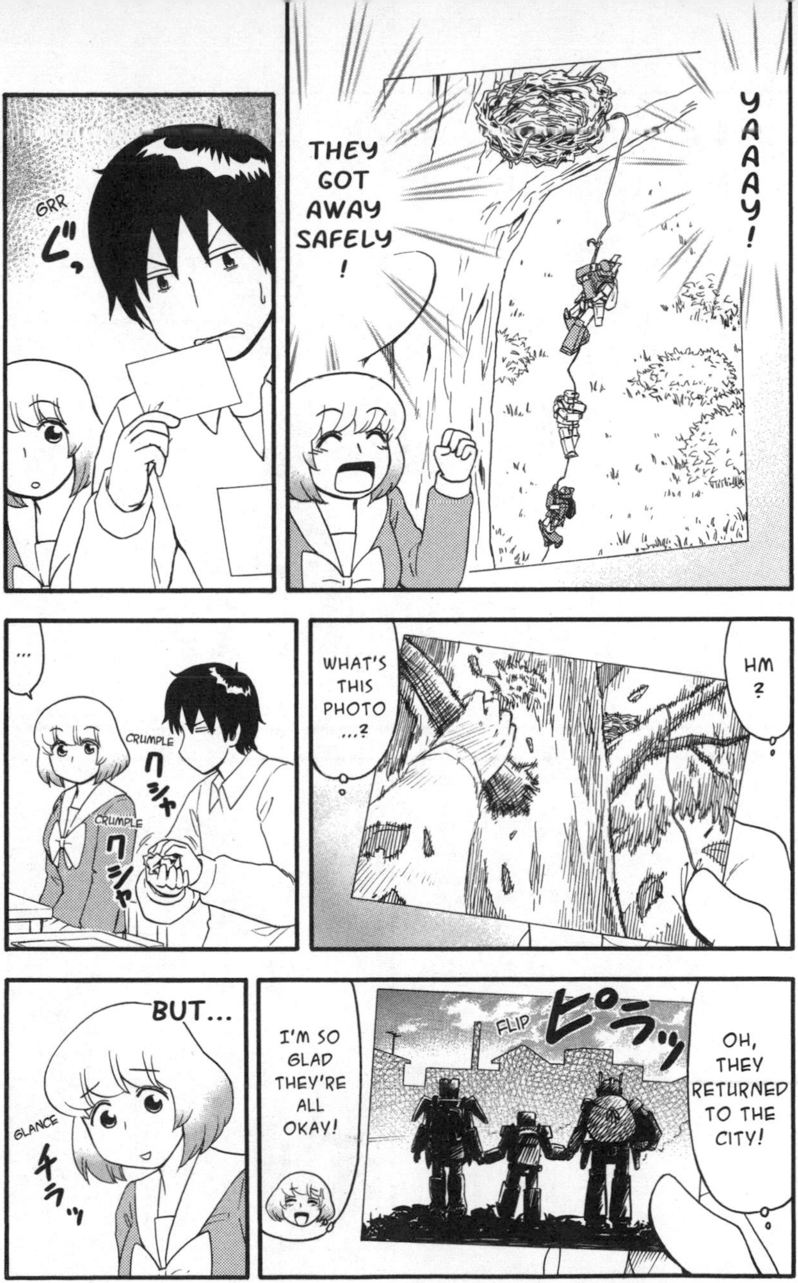
YAAAAY!
THEY GOT AWAY SAFELY!
GRR
ぐっ
HM?
WHAT'S THIS PHOTO...?
...
CRUMPLE
クシャ
CRUMPLE
クシャ
OH, THEY RETURNED TO THE CITY!
FLIP
ピラッ
I'M SO GLAD THEY'RE ALL OKAY!
BUT...
GLANCE
チラッ

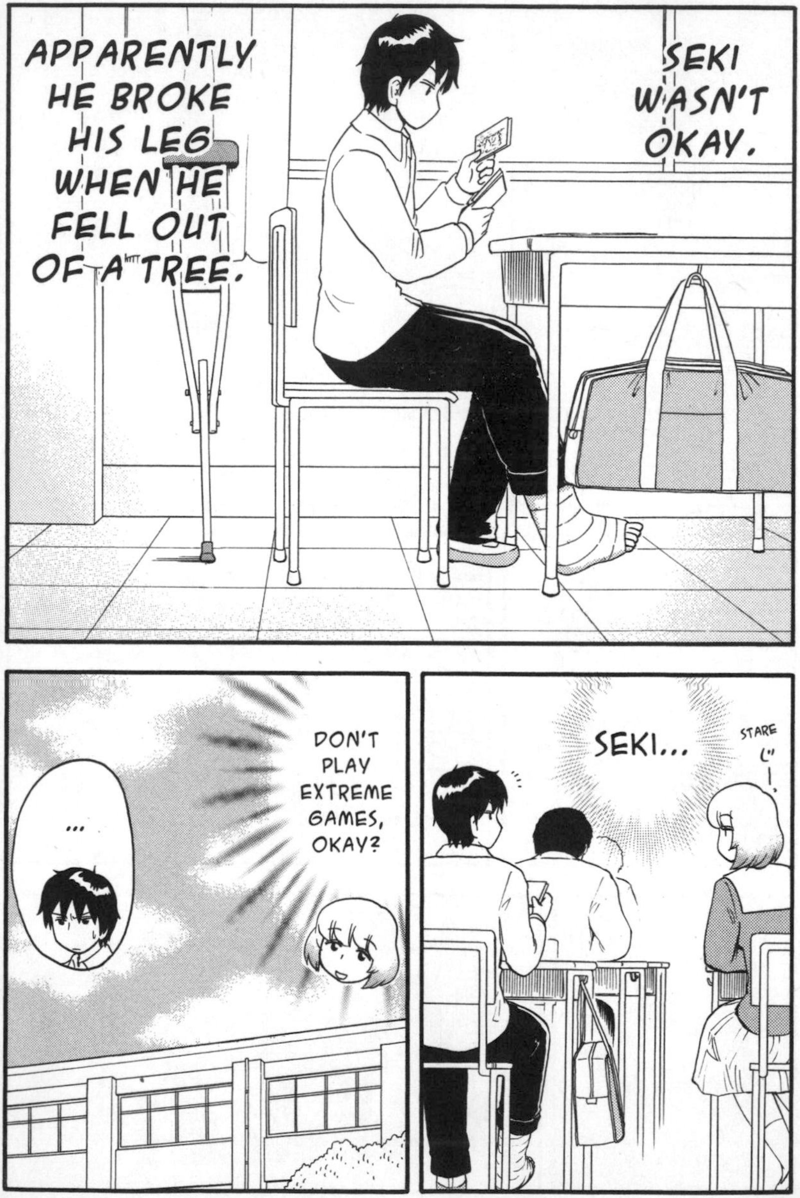
SEKI WASN'T OKAY.
APPARENTLY HE BROKE HIS LEG WHEN HE FELL OUT OF A TREE.
SEKI...
STARE
DON'T PLAY EXTREME GAMES, OKAY?
...

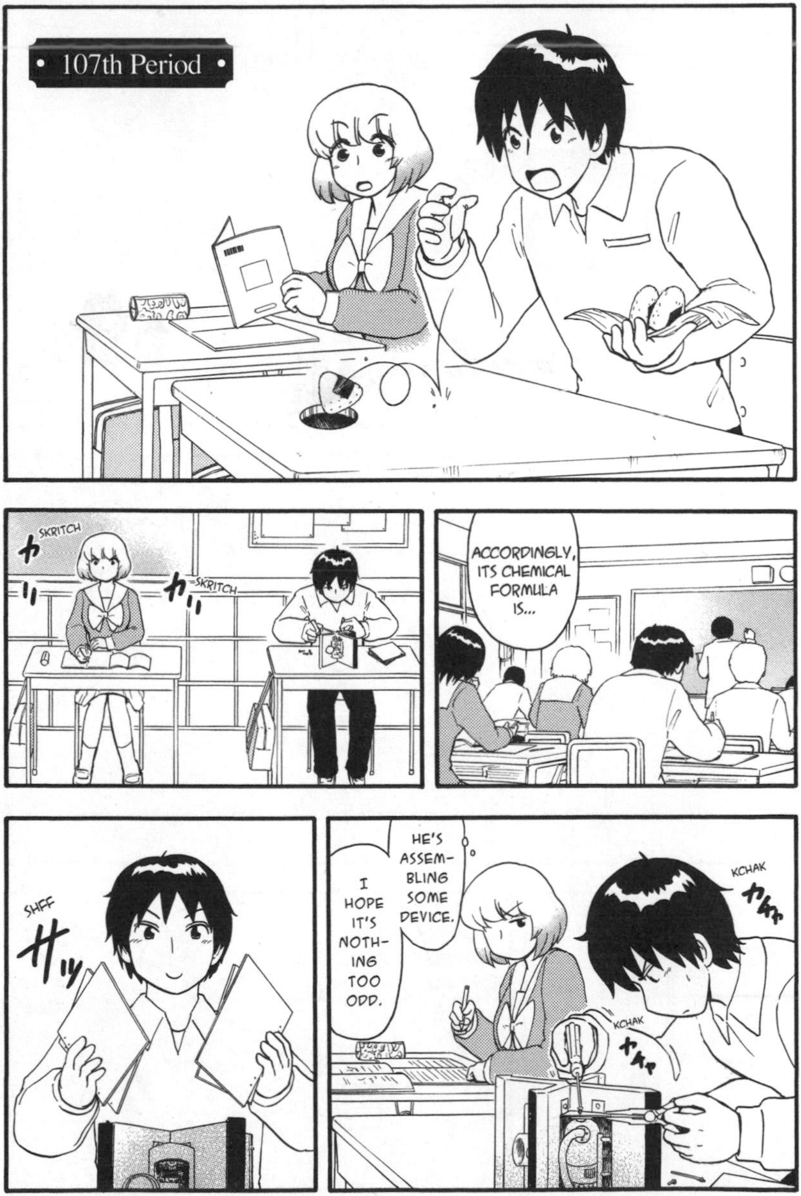
107th Period
ACCORDINGLY, ITS CHEMICAL FORMULA IS...
SKRITCH
SKRITCH
HE'S ASSEM-BLING SOME DEVICE.
I HOPE IT'S NOTH-ING TOO ODD.
KCHAK
KCHAK
SHFF

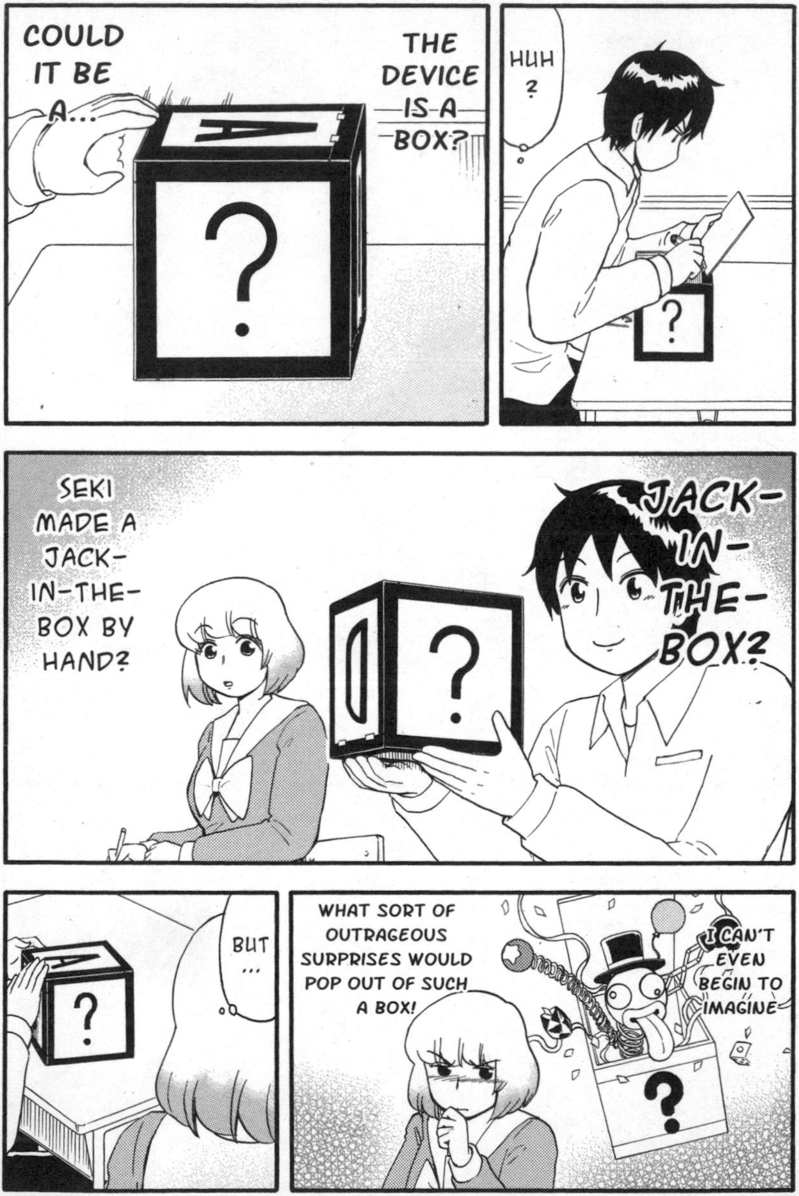
HUH?
THE DEVICE IS A BOX?
COULD IT BE A...
JACK-IN-THE-BOX?
SEKI MADE A JACK-IN-THE-BOX BY HAND?
I CAN'T EVEN BEGIN TO IMAGINE
WHAT SORT OF OUTRAGEOUS SURPRISES WOULD POP OUT OF SUCH A BOX!
BUT...

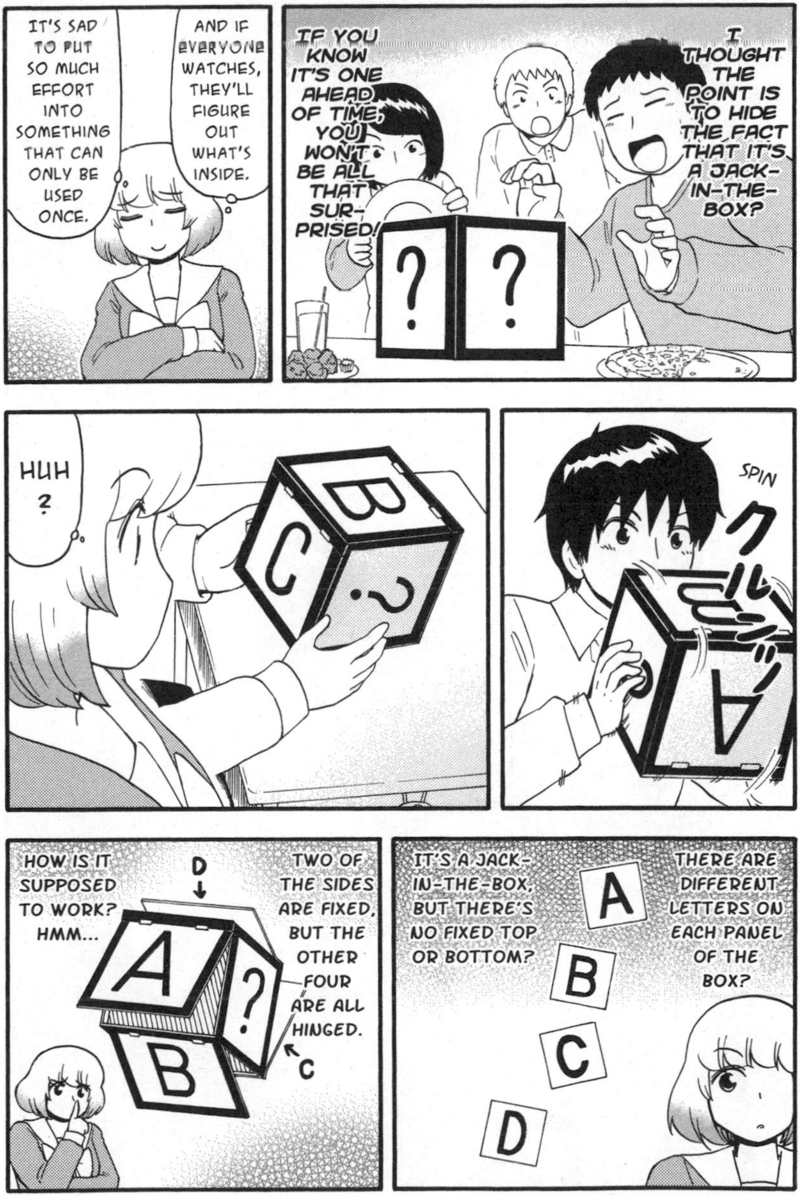
IT'S SAD TO PUT SO MUCH EFFORT INTO SOMETHING THAT CAN ONLY BE USED ONCE.
AND IF EVERYONE WATCHES, THEY'LL FIGURE OUT WHAT'S INSIDE.
IF YOU KNOW IT'S ONE AHEAD OF TIME, YOU WON'T BE ALL THAT SUR-PRISED!
I THOUGHT THE POINT IS TO HIDE THE FACT THAT IT'S A JACK-IN-THE-BOX?
HUH?
SPIN
HOW IS IT SUPPOSED TO WORK? HMM...
D
C
TWO OF THE SIDES ARE FIXED, BUT THE OTHER FOUR ARE ALL HINGED.
IT'S A JACK-IN-THE-BOX, BUT THERE'S NO FIXED TOP OR BOTTOM?
THERE ARE DIFFERENT LETTERS ON EACH PANEL OF THE BOX?

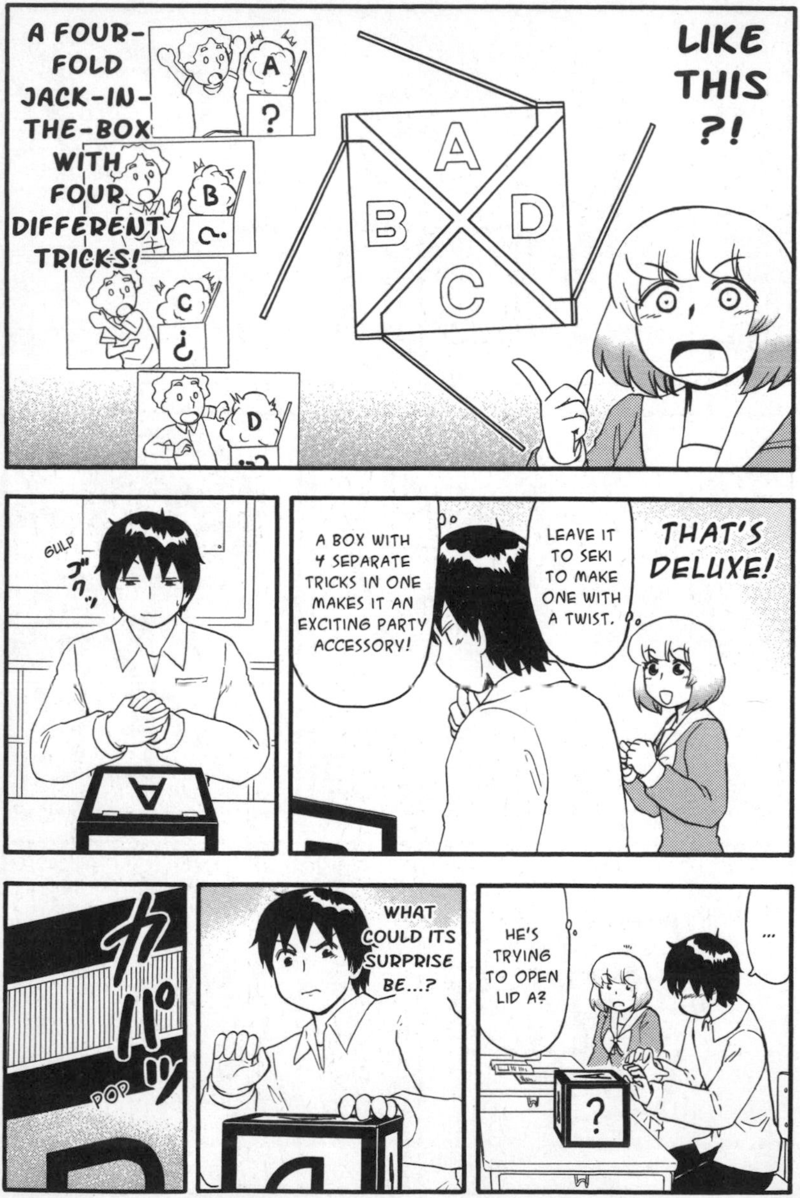
LIKE THIS ?!
A FOUR-FOLD JACK-IN-THE-BOX WITH FOUR DIFFERENT TRICKS!
A
B
C
D
THAT'S DELUXE!
LEAVE IT TO SEKI TO MAKE ONE WITH A TWIST.
A BOX WITH 4 SEPARATE TRICKS IN ONE MAKES IT AN EXCITING PARTY ACCESSORY!
ゴクッ
GULP
...
HE'S TRYING TO OPEN LID A?
WHAT COULD ITS SURPRISE BE...?
カパッ
POP

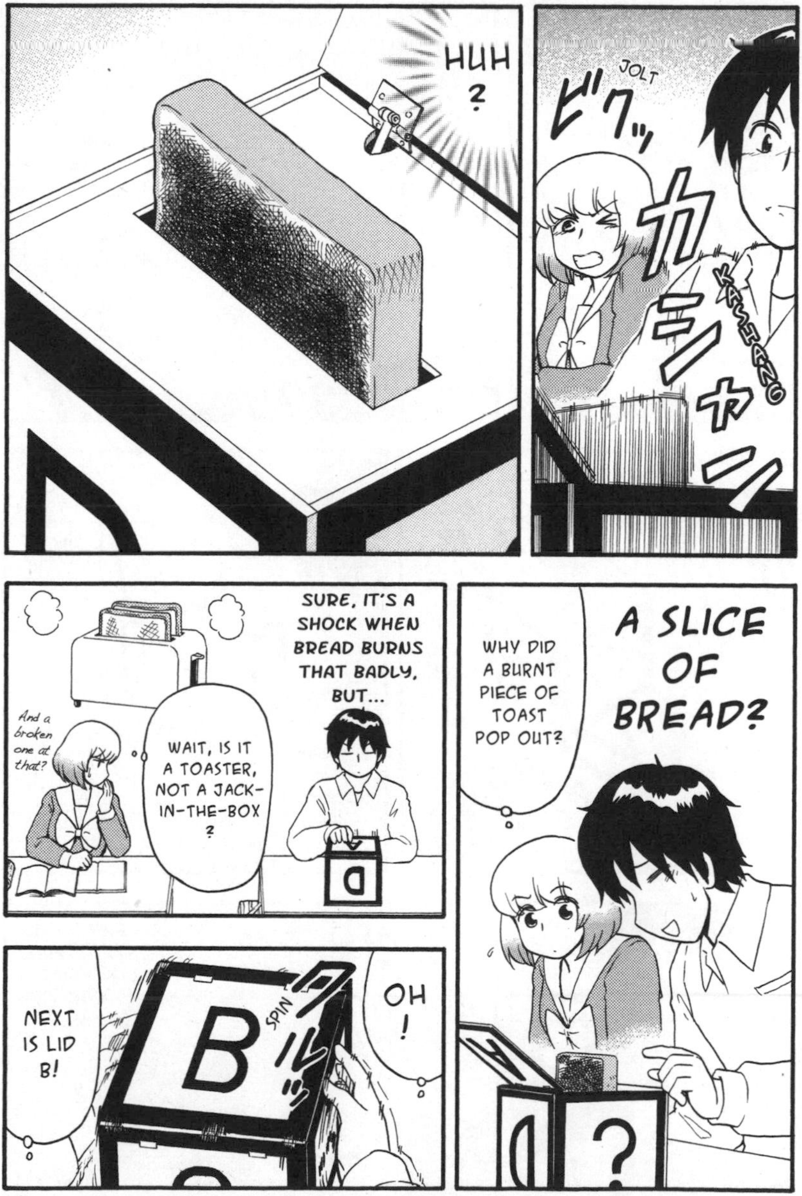
JOLT
ビクッ
カシャン
KASHANG
HUH ?
A SLICE OF BREAD?
WHY DID A BURNT PIECE OF TOAST POP OUT?
SURE, IT'S A SHOCK WHEN BREAD BURNS THAT BADLY, BUT...
WAIT, IS IT A TOASTER, NOT A JACK-IN-THE-BOX ?
And a broken one at that?
OH !
SPIN
クルッ
NEXT IS LID B!

A DEAD ONE?

NO, MAYBE IT'S FAKE.

A CICADA?!

HUH?!

ひょこっ

POP

BZZ BZZ BZZ BZZ

ビビビビッ

ビクッ

JUMP

NOT SOMETHING I WANNA SEE...

BUT NOT THAT SHOCKING, EITHER...

HE CHOSE THE CONTENTS FOR REALISM!

I'M STARTING TO SEE SEKI'S PLAN.

IT WAS JUST PLAYING DEAD?!

LIKE CICADAS OFTEN SEEN TOWARDS THE END OF SUMMER

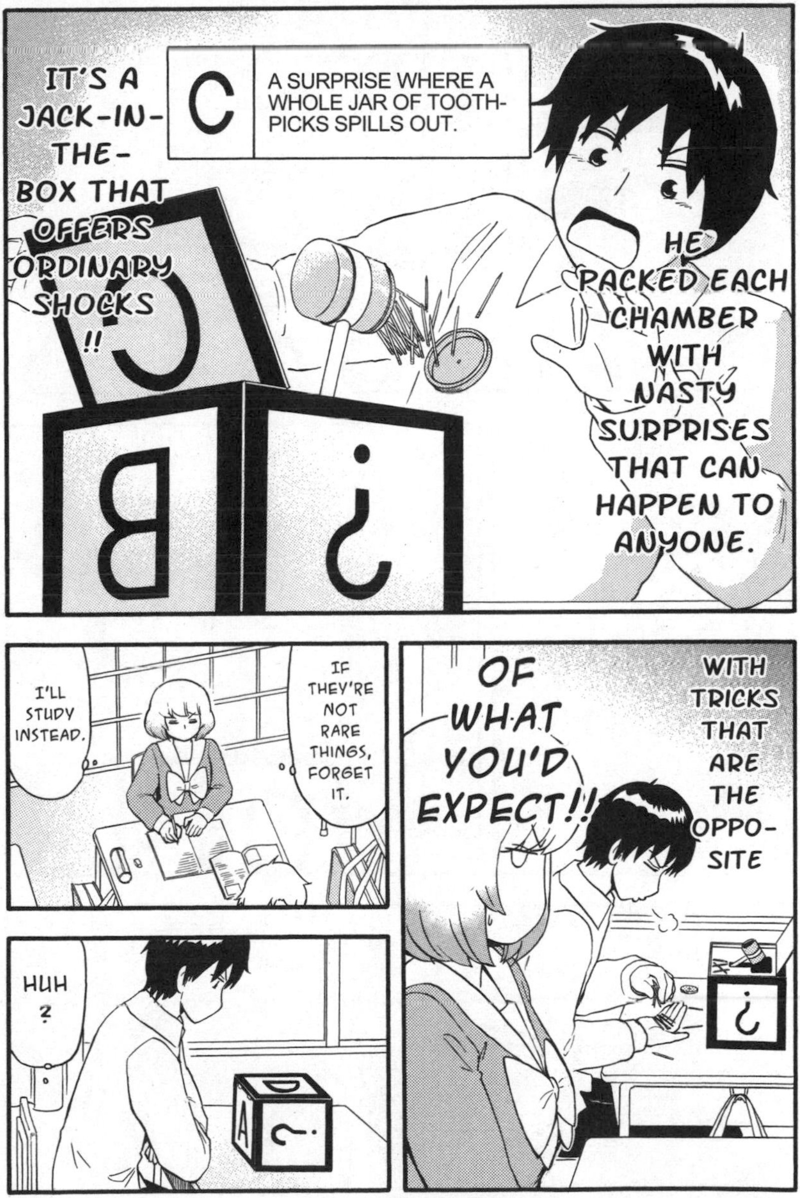
HE PACKED EACH CHAMBER WITH NASTY SURPRISES THAT CAN HAPPEN TO ANYONE.
C
A SURPRISE WHERE A WHOLE JAR OF TOOTH-PICKS SPILLS OUT.
IT'S A JACK-IN-THE-BOX THAT OFFERS ORDINARY SHOCKS!!
WITH TRICKS THAT ARE THE OPPO-SITE
OF WHAT YOU'D EXPECT!!
IF THEY'RE NOT RARE THINGS, FORGET IT.
I'LL STUDY INSTEAD.
HUH?

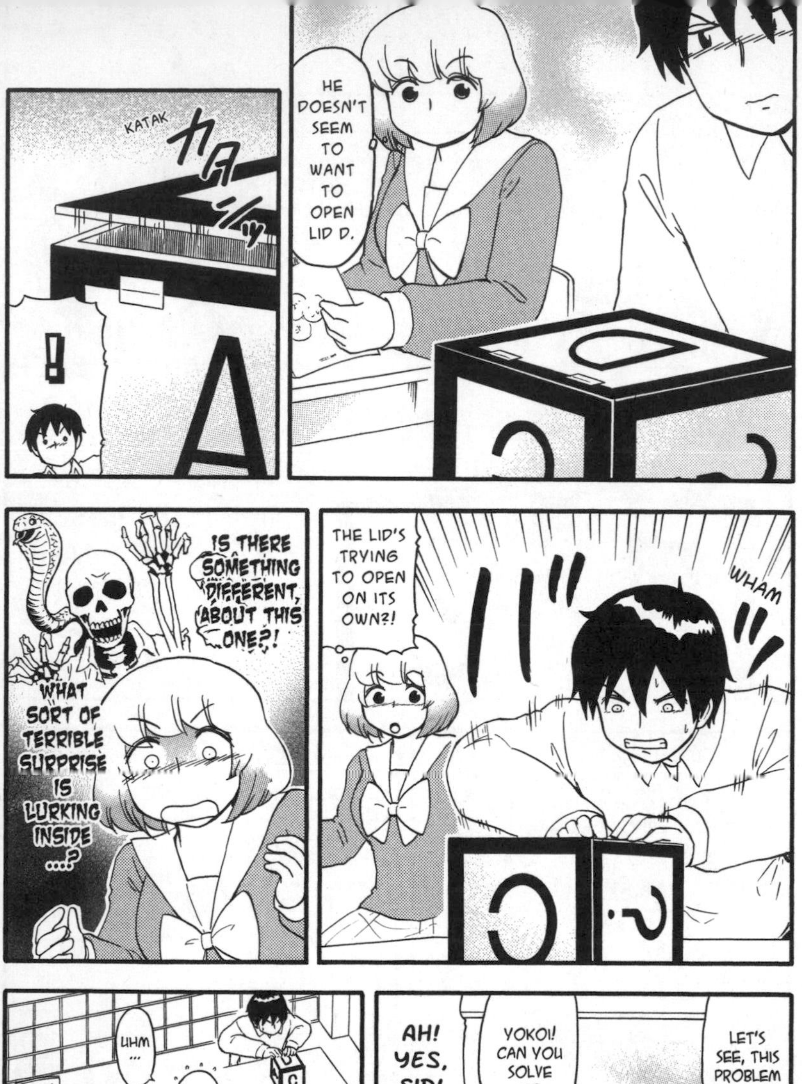
HE DOESN'T SEEM TO WANT TO OPEN LID D.
KATAK
!
THE LID'S TRYING TO OPEN ON ITS OWN?!
WHAM
IS THERE SOMETHING DIFFERENT ABOUT THIS ONE?!
WHAT SORT OF TERRIBLE SURPRISE IS LURKING INSIDE ...?
LET'S SEE, THIS PROBLEM ...
YOKOI! CAN YOU SOLVE IT?
AH! YES, SIR!
UHM ...

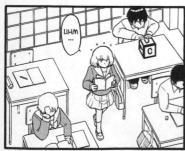

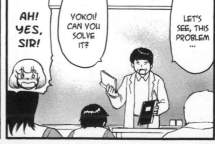

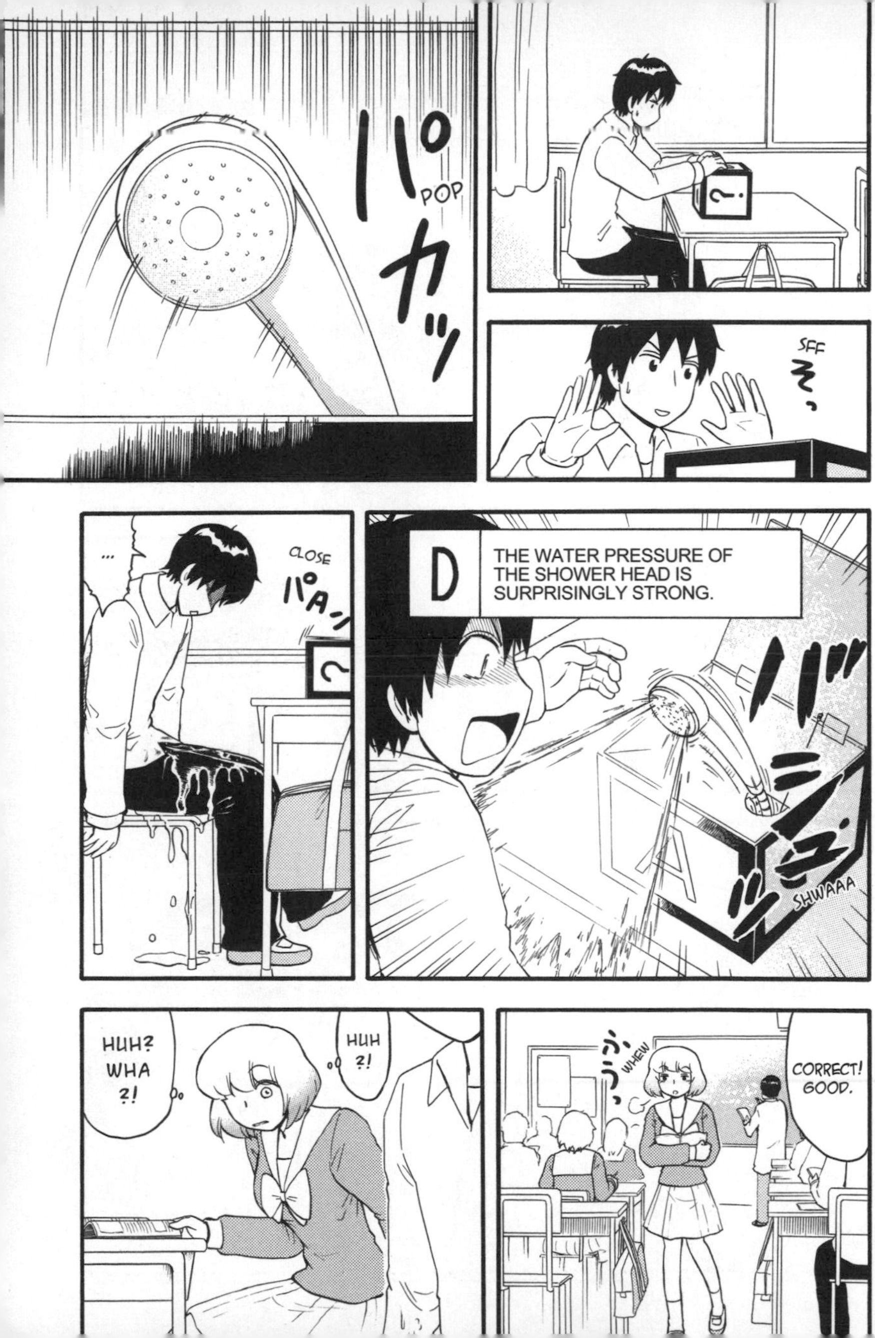
パカッ
POP
SFF
そっ
D
THE WATER PRESSURE OF THE SHOWER HEAD IS SURPRISINGLY STRONG.
SHWAAA
...
CLOSE
ふぅっ
WHEW
CORRECT! GOOD.
HUH? WHA ?!
HUH ?!

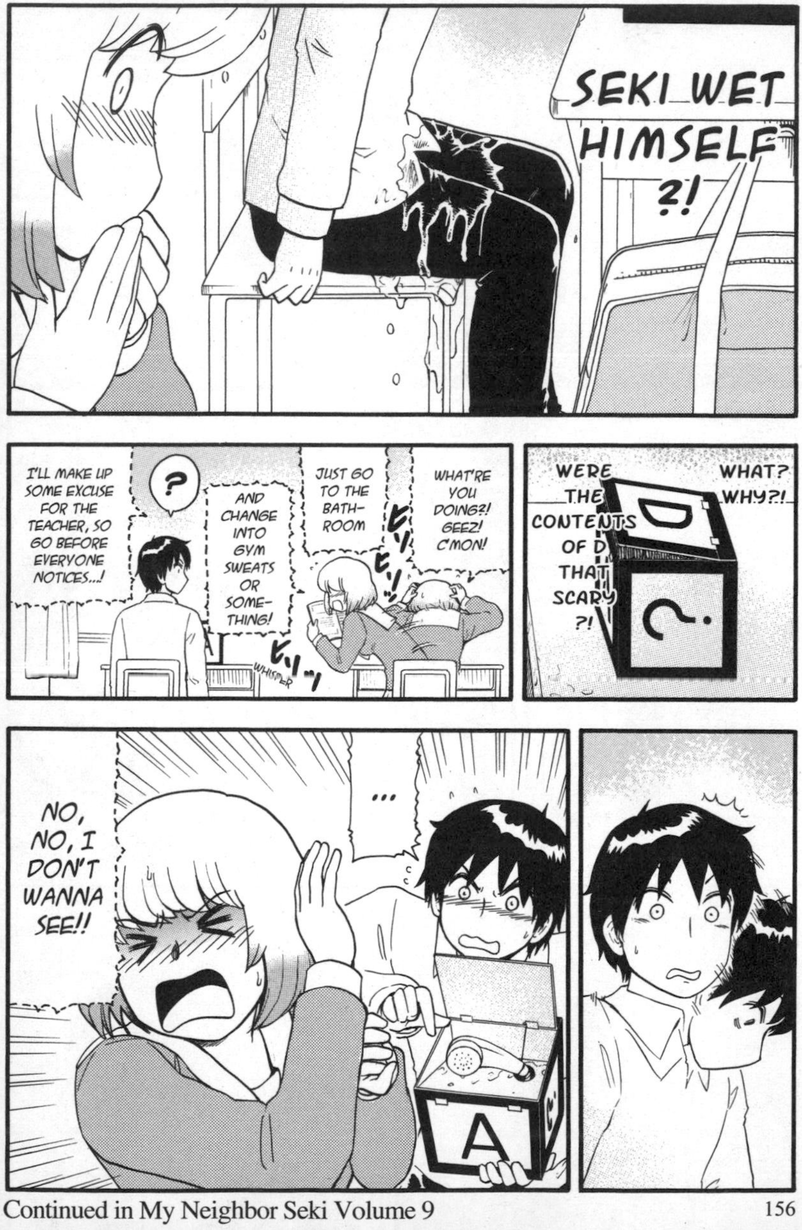
SEKI WET HIMSELF ?!
WHAT? WHY?!
WERE THE CONTENTS OF D THAT SCARY ?!
WHAT'RE YOU DOING?! GEEZ! C'MON!
JUST GO TO THE BATHROOM
AND CHANGE INTO GYM SWEATS OR SOMETHING!
I'LL MAKE UP SOME EXCUSE FOR THE TEACHER, SO GO BEFORE EVERYONE NOTICES...!
?
WHISPER
...
NO, NO, I DON'T WANNA SEE!!

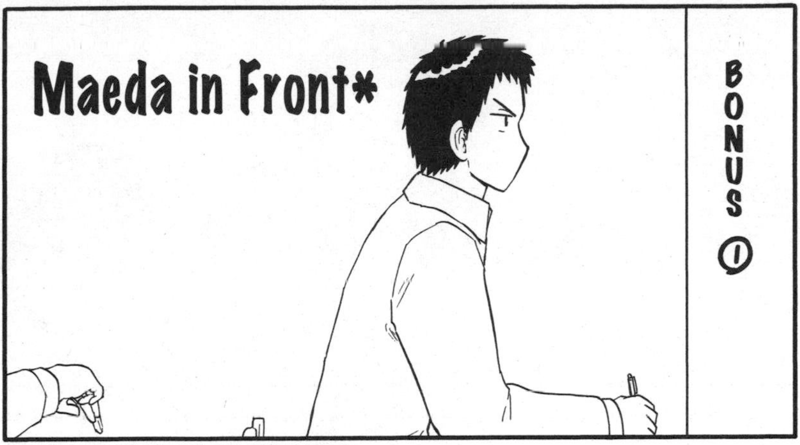
Maeda in Front*
BONUS 1

*THE "MAE" IN "MAEDA" MEANS "FRONT."

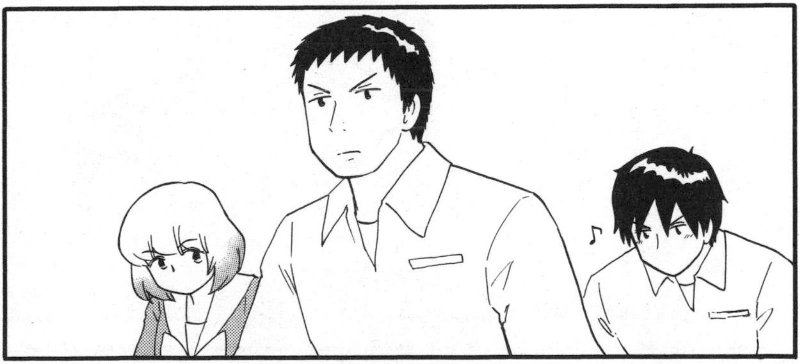
♪

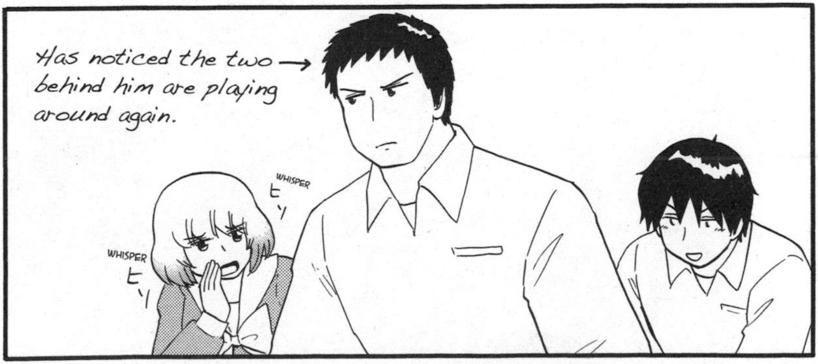
Has noticed the two → behind him are playing around again.
WHISPER
ヒソ
WHISPER
ヒソ

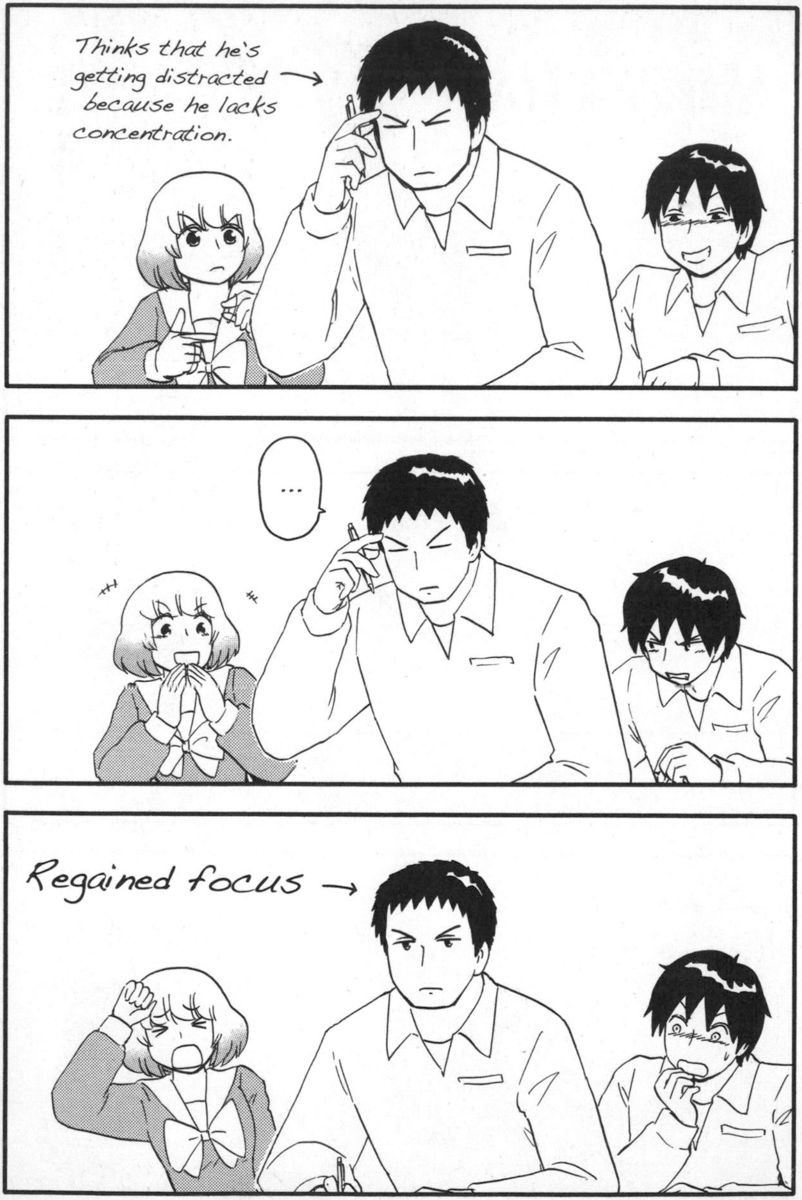
Thinks that he's getting distracted because he lacks concentration.
...
Regained focus

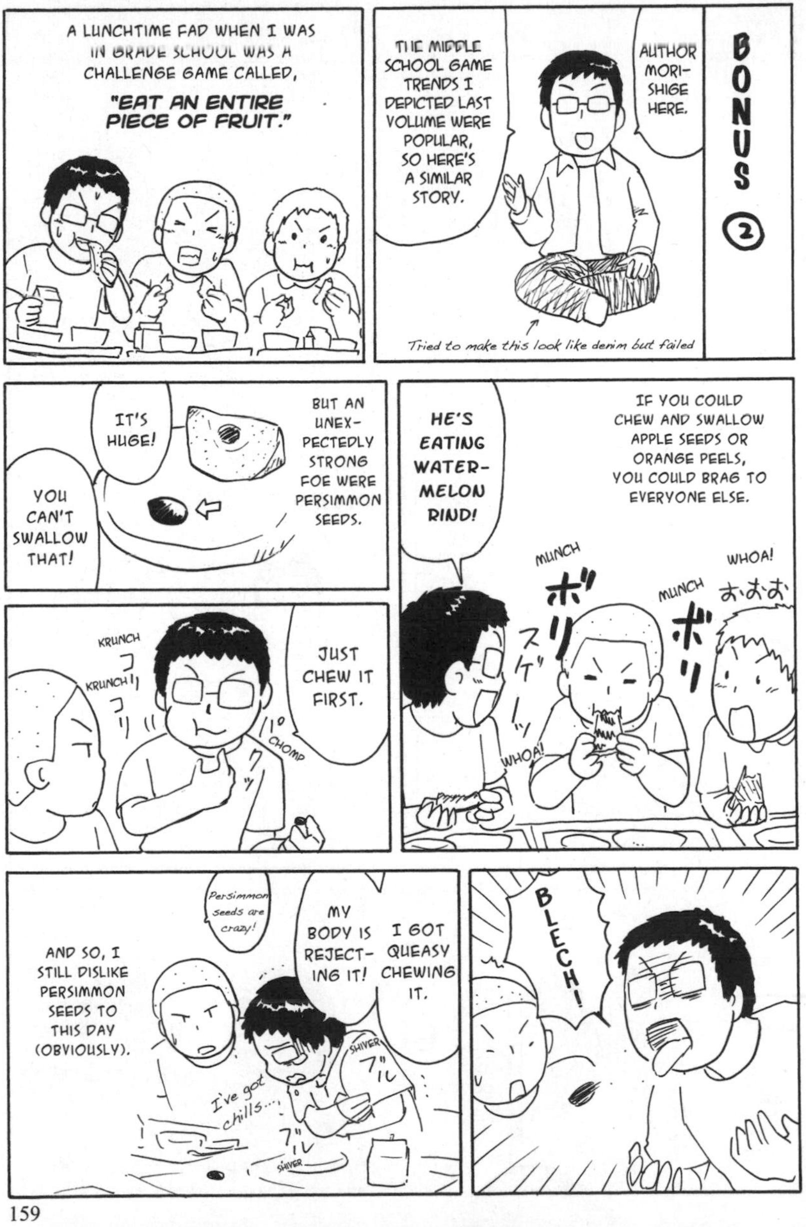
BONUS ②
AUTHOR MORI-SHIGE HERE.
THE MIDDLE SCHOOL GAME TRENDS I DEPICTED LAST VOLUME WERE POPULAR, SO HERE'S A SIMILAR STORY.
Tried to make this look like denim but failed
A LUNCHTIME FAD WHEN I WAS IN GRADE SCHOOL WAS A CHALLENGE GAME CALLED,
"EAT AN ENTIRE PIECE OF FRUIT."
IF YOU COULD CHEW AND SWALLOW APPLE SEEDS OR ORANGE PEELS, YOU COULD BRAG TO EVERYONE ELSE.
HE'S EATING WATER-MELON RIND!
WHOA!
おおお
MUNCH
ボリ
MUNCH
ボリ
WHOA!
スゲーッ
BUT AN UNEX-PECTEDLY STRONG FOE WERE PERSIMMON SEEDS.
IT'S HUGE!
YOU CAN'T SWALLOW THAT!
JUST CHEW IT FIRST.
CHOMP
パク
KRUNCH
コリ
KRUNCH
コリ
BLECH!
I GOT QUEASY CHEWING IT.
MY BODY IS REJECT-ING IT!
Persimmon seeds are crazy!
SHIVER
ブル
I've got chills....
ブル
SHIVER
AND SO, I STILL DISLIKE PERSIMMON SEEDS TO THIS DAY (OBVIOUSLY).

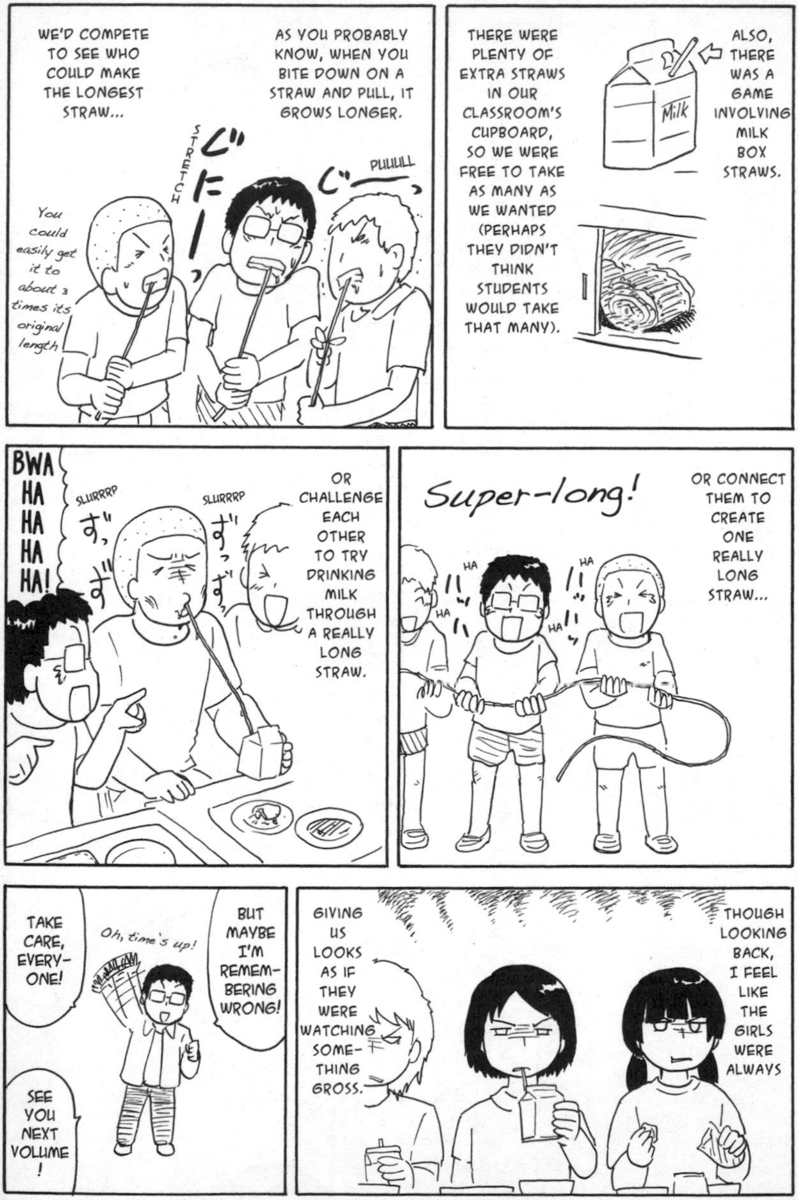
ALSO, THERE WAS A GAME INVOLVING MILK BOX STRAWS.
Milk
THERE WERE PLENTY OF EXTRA STRAWS IN OUR CLASSROOM'S CUPBOARD, SO WE WERE FREE TO TAKE AS MANY AS WE WANTED (PERHAPS THEY DIDN'T THINK STUDENTS WOULD TAKE THAT MANY).
AS YOU PROBABLY KNOW, WHEN YOU BITE DOWN ON A STRAW AND PULL, IT GROWS LONGER.
WE'D COMPETE TO SEE WHO COULD MAKE THE LONGEST STRAW...
STRETCH
PUUULL
You could easily get it to about 3 times its original length
OR CONNECT THEM TO CREATE ONE REALLY LONG STRAW...
Super-long!
HA
HA
HA
HA
OR CHALLENGE EACH OTHER TO TRY DRINKING MILK THROUGH A REALLY LONG STRAW.
SLURRRP
SLURRRP
BWA HA HA HA HA!
THOUGH LOOKING BACK, I FEEL LIKE THE GIRLS WERE ALWAYS
GIVING US LOOKS AS IF THEY WERE WATCHING SOME-THING GROSS.
BUT MAYBE I'M REMEM-BERING WRONG!
Oh, time's up!
TAKE CARE, EVERY-ONE!
SEE YOU NEXT VOLUME!